About Shelters and Encounters
An Array of Theological Voices

*Journal of the European Society of Women
in Theological Research*

*Revista de la asociación europea de mujeres
para la investigación teológica*

*Jahrbuch der Europäischen Gesellschaft
für theologische Forschung von Frauen*

Volume 30

**Bibliographical information and books for review
in the Journal should be sent to:**
*Prof.[in] Dr.[in] Agnethe Siquans,
Universität Wien, Schenkenstraße 8-10, 1010 Wien, Austria*

**Articles for consideration for the Journal
should be sent to:**
*Prof.[in] Dr.[in] Agnethe Siquans,
Universität Wien, Schenkenstraße 8-10, 1010 Wien, Austria*

About Shelters and Encounters

An Array of Theological Voices

Editors:
*Agnethe Siquans, Martina Bär, Anne-Claire Mulder,
Mireia Vidal i Quintero*

PEETERS
LEUVEN – PARIS – BRISTOL, CT
2022

Journal of the European Society of Women
in Theological Research, 30

A catalogue record for this book is available from the Library of Congress.

© 2022, Peeters Publishers, Leuven / Belgium
ISBN 978-90-429-4980-5
ISSN 1783-2454
eISSN 1783-2446
D/2022/0602/67
Cover design by Margret Omlin-Küchler

All rights reserved. No part to this publication may be reproduced, stored in a retrieval system, or transmitted, in any form of by any means, electronic, mechanical, photocopying, recording or otherwise, without the prior permission of the publisher.

CONTENTS – INHALT – ÍNDICE

Editorial 1

Inaugural Address
Mariecke van den Berg
Meanwhile, Back at the Shelter: A Queer Theology of Coming Home 15

Texts
Akke van der Kooi and Magda Misset-van de Weg
A *Rencontre* of Women and Disciplines in Relation to Luke 1:39-56 33

Julia Münch-Wirtz
Identifikationspotential biblischer Texte im Horizont eines genderbewussten Religionsunterrichts 61

Anna Alabd
Einblicke in die Forschung über die Herausforderungen der Autonomie von christlichen und muslimischen Frauen. Eine Analyse aus interreligiöser Perspektive 73

Anne-Claire Mulder
To Whom Do You Attribute Religious Authority? A Pilot Study ... 89

Round Table
African Female Theologians Telling Stories: 'Connected but Disconnected' 123

   Introduction 125

   Thandi Soko-de Jong
   Prologue 127

   Tabitha Poline Moyo
   The Returning Insider: Tensions and Challenges of an African Female Researcher Conducting Research in her Own Country ... 133

Heleen Joziasse
A *Muzungu* Woman Navigating Outsider-Insider Academic Research in Kenya 139

Shingirai Eunice Masunda
Running the Metaphor Blend with Jesus: How the Canaanite Woman Transformed Jesus' Metaphor 147

Anne-Claire Mulder
Intersectionality. In-Between Spaces. Authority. Some Concepts to Reflect on the Relations between Insider and Outsider 153

Reviews

Irmtraud Fischer, Angela Berlis, Christiana de Groot (Hg.),
Frauenbewegungen des 19. Jahrhunderts; und *Irmtraud Fischer, Edith Petschnigg, Nicole Navratil, Angela Berlis, Christiana de Groot (Hg.)*,
Die Bibel war für sie ein politisches Buch. Bibelinterpretationen der Frauenemanzipationsbewegungen im langen 19. Jahrhundert   161

Silvia Martínez Cano
Teología feminista para principiantes. Voces de mujeres en la teología actual 164

Andrea Günter
Philosophie und Geschlechterdifferenz. Auf dem Weg eines genealogischen Geschlechterdiskurses 167

Editorial

About Shelters and Encounters. An Array of Theological Voices

For the first time in the history of the Journal of the ESWTR, the editors publish an issue without a theme or topic. Until now, the theme of an issue was either that of the last conference or suggested at the general meeting. But Covid changed that rhythm as it changed so many other rhythms, though it offered the editors the opportunity to launch an open call for contributions. The result of this call is the current issue, which presents a colourful palette of texts and book reviews.

Inaugural Address

The text *Meanwhile, Back at the Shelter: A Queer Theology of Coming Home* is the first inaugural address published in the Journal. Mariecke van den Berg gave this address at the occasion of her acceptance of the endowed Chair for Feminism and Christianity – the Catharina Halkes Chair – at the Radboud University in Nijmegen, NL. In her contribution, Mariecke van den Berg picks up an off-hand remark comparing same-sex marriages with "a shelter in a broken life", discusses the hierarchies implied by (the context of) the metaphor, and then appropriates and develops this image further. In keeping with this, she highlights the transient character of the constructions that provide shelter and their position on the margin – in and out of the (Christian) tradition – while presenting it as a 'room of one's own' and as the home of the o/Other.

Texts

The four texts that follow this inaugural lecture are all peer-reviewed texts.

Together, Akke van der Kooi and Magda Misset-van de Weg wrote *A Rencontre of Women and Disciplines in Relation to Luke 1:39-56*. The text is "an experimental exercise in interdisciplinarity", staging multiple encounters: between the two women authors, between two disciplines (NT-exegesis and Systematic Theology), between the text of Luke and three works of art, which portray the rencontre of Mary and Elisabeth. The visual exegesis of the works of art of Pontormo, Viola and Albertinelli and of Luke 1:39-56 are combined with a reflection on revelation and the revelatory power of (these) works of art. The authors thereby highlight the theme of joy and of mutual care in Luke as well as "the double impulse in the movement of revelation: the gift of God's mystery *and* the creative potential in humanity to imagine God's presence".

In her text *Identifikationspotential biblischer Texte im Horizont eines genderbewussten Religionsunterrichts,* Julia Münch-Wirtz addresses the necessity as well as two points of special interest for a gender-conscious religious education: the necessity to ensure that in the choice of Biblical texts and themes sufficient attention is paid to a variety of identification figures for the pupils, instead of the – easy and dominant – practice to choose stories with male protagonists. Her other point of special interest is the development of a gender-conscious use of language, especially when referring to God and in translations of the Biblical texts. She argues that it is important for the pupils to learn to "think about God in the plural". Both these points of interest should open the space for an identification in which ambivalence and the different shades of grey can be perceived, and new insights into oneself and the relation to God can come up.

Anna Alabd presents in *Einblicke in die Forschung über die Herausforderungen der Autonomie von christlichen und muslimischen Frauen. Eine Analyse aus interreligiöser Perspektive* an analysis of a qualitative-empirical study into the ethical dilemmas Christian and Muslim women encounter with respect to their religious tradition on the one hand and their autonomy on the other. She approaches their dilemmas from the perspective of inter-religious ethics, which searches for shared (social-)ethical foundations and principles in the context of a secular society. She also highlights the similarities and differences between her interviewees in dealing with the tensions between religious traditions and women's search for autonomy.

To Whom Do You Attribute Religious Authority? A Pilot Study by Anne-Claire Mulder is the report of empirical research among the participants of the Seventh Synod-weekend of the Ecumenical Women's Synod in the Netherlands, asking them when and why they would attribute religious authority to someone else and whether it would make a difference if the "authority" would be female or male. The research showed that while the female respondents rejected hierarchical forms of authority relations, they valued being inspired by another and someone's wisdom as important criteria for granting someone authority. For many, the sex of this other did not matter for the attribution of authority, although the power of this principle of equality was contradicted by the outcome that the faith of the majority of the respondents was inspired by (books of) other women.

Round-Table Discussion
In the section called *Round-table*, the reader will find another text, or better, five texts with the title *African Female Theologians Telling Stories*. Under this title, the edited essays of the first symposium of the African Female Theologians in Europe collective are presented. This symposium, held in June 2021 and with the theme *Connected but Disconnected*, was devoted to critically exploring how African Female Theologians – as insiders-outsiders – in discussion with some Dutch sisters negotiate the (dis)connections they encounter as they participate in Dutch/Flemish theological discourse. Thandi Soko-de Jong, Tabitha Polina Moyo, Heleen Joziasse, Shingirai Masunda and Anne-Claire Mulder approach this theme of insider-outsider each in her own way, moving from personal experience to scholarly reflection and back.

Book Reviews
The editors of the Journal are very happy that we can present the reader with four book reviews.

Ruth Albrecht has written a review of two books which describe the women's movement in the 19th century, notably of *Frauenbewegungen des 19. Jahrhunderts* edited by Irmtraud Fischer, Angela Berlis and Christiana de Groot, and of *Die Bibel war für sie ein politisches Buch. Bibelinterpretationen der Frauenemanzipationsbewegungen im langen 19. Jahrhundert,* edited by Irmtraud Fischer, Edith Petschnigg, Nicole Navratil, Angela Berlis and Christiana de Groot. Albrecht presents both books as important additions to the already existing literature about the women's movement of that period because they present the activism, thoughts and theology of many unknown women, among others from India, Armenia and Iceland. Both books call for more research, especially into their (international) networks.

Silvia Martínez Cano's book, *Teología feminista para principiantes. Voces de mujeres en la teología actual* is reviewed by Mireia Vidal i Quintero. The book is an introduction to feminist theology, in which Martínez Cano draws from her experience as university reader in feminist theology and as artist, primarily aimed at a Spanish lay public. Vidal indicates, though, that the historical survey of the development in feminist theology from a Spanish perspective might be of interest to those who are not familiar with the Spanish developments. According to Vidal, this book is a welcome introduction to (the main tenets of) feminist theology and a benchmark in the Spanish context from a dissemination point of view.

The newest book by Andrea Günter, *Philosophie und Geschlechterdifferenz. Auf dem Weg eines genealogischen Geschlechterdiskurses* is reviewed by Silke Petersen. Petersen argues that this book is not about sexual difference, but about the entanglement of fundamental categories (of the history) of philosophy with the discourse on the sexes, thereby creating their own categorisation fields. Analysing this entanglement, Günter moves through the history of philosophy, paying special attention to Plato, Aristotle and Parmenides as well as to Arendt and Simone de Beauvoir. Although this book asks for some philosophical background, Petersen concludes that it is interesting for those willing to think (about) sexual difference beyond the usual binaries.

The editorial team / El equipo editorial / Die Herausgeberinnen.

Editorial

Sobre refugios y encuentros: un elenco de voces teológicas

Por primera vez en la historia de la Revista de la ESWTR, las editoras publican un volumen sin tema. Hasta ahora, el tema de un volumen era o bien el del último congreso de la Asociación o bien sugerido por su asamblea general. Pero la pandemia de la COVID-19 ha cambiado el ritmo habitual, como también ha cambiado muchos otros. A la vez, ha sido ocasión para que las editoras lanzaran una convocatoria abierta para la Revista. El resultado de esta convocatoria es el presente volumen, que ofrece una rica paleta de colores en forma de textos y recensiones.

Lección inaugural

El texto *Meanwhile, Back at the Shelter: A Queer Theology of Coming Home* ("Mientras tanto, volvamos al refugio: una teología *queer* de la vuelta al hogar") es la primera lección inaugural que se publica en la Revista. Se trata del discurso que Mariecke van den Berg ofreció con motivo de su instalción en la cátedra Catharina Halkes de Feminismo y Cristianismo en la Universidad Radboud en Nimega (Países Bajos). En su contribución, Mariecke van den Berg reflexiona sobre un comentario casual que asemeja el matrimonio entre personas del mismo sexo a "un refugio en medio de una vida rota", reflexiona sobre las jerarquías implícitas en el contexto de esta metáfora y se la apropia para desarrollarla aún más. A través de este recorrido, la autora destaca el carácter pasajero de las construcciones que ofrecen refugio, así como su posición en los márgenes, es decir, dentro y fuera de la tradición cristiana. Igualmente, las presenta como "una habitación propia" y hogar para el/la o/Otro/a.

Artículos

Los cuatro textos que siguen a la lección inaugural son todos artículos que han sido revisados por pares.

A Rencontre *of Women and Disciplines in Relation to Luke 1:39-56* ("Un *rencontre* entre mujeres y disciplinas a colación de Lucas 1,39-56") es fruto de la escritura conjunta de Akke van der Kooi y Magda Misset-van de Weg. El texto es "un ejercicio experimental en interdisciplinariedad" que aborda múltiples encuentros: entre las dos autoras, entre dos disciplinas (Nuevo Testamento y teología sistemática), entre el texto de Lucas y tres obras de arte que presentan el encuentro entre María e Isabel. La exégesis visual de las obras de Pontormo, Viola y Albertinelli y Lucas 1,39-56 se entrelaza con reflexiones sobre la revelación y su impronta en estas obras de arte. Las autoras enfatizan el tema de la alegría y el cuidado mutuo en Lucas así como "el doble impulso en el movimiento de revelación: el don del misterio de Dios y el potencial creativo presente en la humanidad para imaginar la presencia de Dios".

En *Identifikationspotential biblischer Texte im Horizont eines genderbewussten Religionsunterrichts* ("Potencial de identificación de los textos bíblicos en el horizonte de la educación religiosa con conciencia de género"), Julia Münch-Wirtz aborda la necesidad de una educación religiosa con conciencia de género. Lo hace destacando dos puntos. El primero es la importancia de asegurar que, cuando se escogen textos o temas bíblicos, se atienda a la variedad de figuras con las que los alumnos pueden identificarse, evitando así la práctica habitual y dominante de escoger historias con protagonistas masculinos. Su segundo foco de atención es el desarrollo de un lenguaje de género consciente, sobre todo en referencia a Dios y en las traducciones de los textos bíblicos. Münch-Wirtz argumenta que es importante que los alumnos "piensen en Dios en plural". Estas dos cuestiones deberían abrir espacios de identificación en los que la ambivalencia y los grises puedan captarse, suscitando así nuevos entendimientos sobre uno/a mismo/a y la relación con Dios.

Anna Alabd ofrece un análisis de un estudio cualitativo y empírico sobre los dilemas que las mujeres cristianas y musulmanas encuentran al navegar sus tradiciones religiosas y su autonomía personal. Su artículo, *Einblicke in die Forschung über die Herausforderungen der Autonomie von christlichen und muslimischen Frauen. Eine Analyse aus interreligiöser Perspektive* ("La investigación sobre los retos de la autonomía de las mujeres cristianas y musulmanas. Un análisis desde una perspectiva interreligiosa"), aborda estos dilemas desde una perspectiva ética interreligiosa que busca identificar fundamentos y principios socio-éticos compartidos en el contexto de una sociedad secular. La autora destaca también las similitudes y diferencias que las entrevistadas encuentran al abordar la tensión entre sus respectivas tradiciones religiosas y la búsqueda de autonomía como mujeres.

El artículo *To Whom Do You Attribute Religious Authority? A Pilot Study* ("¿A quién atribuyes autoridad religiosa? Un estudio piloto") de Anne-Claire Mulder es resultado de una investigación empírica llevada cabo entre las participantes del Séptimo Sínodo de Fin de Semana del Sínodo Ecuménico de Mujeres en los Países Bajos. La investigación preguntaba a las participantes cuándo y por qué conceden autoridad religiosa a alguien y si el hecho de que tal persona sea hombre o mujer tiene alguna relevancia. La investigación demuestra que, aunque las encuestadas rechazan las estructuras jerárquicas en las relaciones de autoridad, valoran como criterios importantes para reconocer autoridad a alguien sentirse inspiradas por esa persona o bien por su sabiduría. La mayoría respondió que el sexo de la persona no importa a la hora de atribuir autoridad religiosa, pero los resultados cuestionan este principio de igualdad porque la mayoría de las participantes identifican libros escritos por mujeres como fuentes de inspiración para su fe.

Mesa redonda
En la sección titulada mesa redonda, se ofrece otro texto o, más bien, cinco textos distintos bajo el título *African Female Theologians Telling Stories* ("Teólogas africanas que cuentan historias"). La mesa redonda agrupa así los ensayos editados del primer simposio del colectivo Mujeres Teólogas Africanas en Europa. Este simposio, que se celebró en junio de 2021 con el título *Conectadas. Desconectadas,* exploró críticamente cómo las integrantes de Mujeres Teólogas Africanas, junto con algunas compañeras holandesas, negocian las (des)conexiones que encuentran al participar en el diálogo teológico holandés/flamenco. Por un lado, se hallan ubicadas en el interior de este diálogo, pero por otro se les asigna una posición externa. Thandi Soko-de Jong, Tabitha Polina Moyo, Heleen Joziasse, Shingirai Masunda y Anne-Claire Mulder exploran esta cuestión cada una desde su propia sensibilidad, recorriendo el camino de la experiencia personal y académica en un movimiento de ida y vuelta.

Recensiones
Las editoras de la Revista se alegran de poder presentar a las lectoras cuatro recensiones de libros.

Ruth Albrecht recensiona dos libros que exploran los movimientos de mujeres en el siglo XIX. Se trata de *Frauenbewegungen des 19. Jahrhunderts* ("Movimientos de mujeres del siglo XIX"), editado por Irmtraud Fischer, Angela Berlis y Christiana de Groot, y de *Die Bibel war für sie ein politisches Buch. Bibelinterpretationen der Frauenemanzipationsbewegungen im langen 19. Jahrhundert* ("Para ella, la Biblia era un libro político. Interpretaciones bíblicas de los movimientos de emancipación de mujeres en el siglo XIX"), editado por Irmtraud Fischer, Edith Petschnigg, Nicole Navratil, Angela Berlis y Christiana de Groot. Albrecht considera que ambos libros son contribuciones importantes a la ya existente literatura sobre movimientos de mujeres del periodo porque presentan el activismo, pensamiento y teología de muchas

Editorial

mujeres hasta ahora desconocidas y procedentes de India, Armenia o Islandia, entre otros. Ambos volúmenes invitan a seguir profundizando en la investigación, en particular en sus redes y conexiones internacionales.

Mireia Vidal i Quintero recensiona el libro de Silvia Martínez Cano, *Teología feminista para principiantes. Voces de mujeres en la teología actual*. El libro es una introducción a la teología feminista pensado para un público general, para lo cual Martínez Cano recurre a su experiencia como profesora en teología feminista y artista. Vidal señala, sin embargo, que la panorámica histórica del desarrollo de la teología feminista en España puede ser de interés para quienes no están familiarizadas con ella. Según Vidal, el libro supone una adicción significativa a los fundamentos de la teología feminista y está llamado a ser un título de referencia para su divulgación.

Silke Petersen recensiona el nuevo libro de Andrea Günter, *Philosophie und Geschlechterdifferenz. Auf dem Weg eines genealogischen Geschlechterdiskurses* ("Filosofía y diferencia de género. Hacia un discurso genealógico del género"). Peterson afirma que este libro no trata tanto sobre la diferencia sexual como sobre la imbricación entre categorías fundamentales en la historia de la filosofía y el discurso sobre los sexos, creando así sus propias categorías. Para desenrredar este ovillo, Günter explora la historia de la filosofía, prestando especial atención a Platón, Aristóteles y Parménides, así como a Arendt y Simone de Beauvoir. Aunque el libro requiere cierto trasfondo filosófico, Petersen concluye que es interesante para quienes desean pensar la diferencia sexual más allá de los binarios habituales.

The editorial team / El equipo editorial / Die Herausgeberinnen.

Editorial

Über Zufluchtsorte und Begegnungen. Theologische Stimmen

Zum ersten Mal in der Geschichte der Zeitschrift der ESWTR veröffentlichen die Herausgeberinnen eine Ausgabe ohne ein Thema oder einen Gegenstand. Bislang war das Thema der Ausgabe entweder das der letzten Konferenz oder es war von der Mitgliederversammlung vorgeschlagen worden. Doch Covid veränderte diesen Rhythmus wie so viele andere Rhythmen auch. Dennoch bot diese Situation den Herausgeberinnen die Möglichkeit, einen offenen Call for Papers zu starten. Das Ergebnis dieses Aufrufs ist die vorliegende Ausgabe, die eine bunte Palette von Texten und Buchbesprechungen enthält.

Antrittsrede

Der Text *Meanwhile, Back at the Shelter: A Queer Theology of Coming Home* ist die erste Antrittsrede, die in diesem Journal veröffentlicht wird. Mariecke van den Berg hielt diese Rede anlässlich ihres Rufes auf den Stiftungslehrstuhl für Feminismus und Christentum – der Catharina-Halkes-Lehrstuhl – an der Radboud-Universität in Nijmegen (Niederlande). In ihrem Beitrag greift Mariecke van den Berg eine beiläufige Bemerkung auf, in der gleichgeschlechtliche Ehen mit einem „Zufluchtsort für zerbrochenen Leben" verglichen worden sind. Sie diskutiert die impliziten Hierarchien dieser Metapher (und ihren Kontext), und entwickelt dann dieses Sprachbild in folgende Richtung weiter: Sie hebt den vergänglichen Charakter der Bauten, die Zuflucht bieten und ihre marginalisierte Position – innerhalb und außerhalb der (christlichen) Tradition – hervor. Zugleich präsentiert sie diese Zufluchtsorte als „eigenen Raum" und als Heimat des Anderen und des Andersseins.

Texte

Bei den vier Texten, die auf diese Antrittsrede folgen, handelt es sich allesamt um Texte eines Peer-Review-Verfahrens.

Akke van der Kooi und Magda Misset-van de Weg haben den Text *A Rencontre of Women and Disciplines in Relation to Luke 1:39-56* gemeinsam geschrieben. Der Text ist „eine experimentelle Übung in Interdisziplinarität", die mehrere Begegnungen inszeniert: zwischen den beiden Autorinnen, zwischen zwei Disziplinen (neutestamentliche Exegese und Systematische Theologie), und schließlich zwischen dem Lukas-Text und drei Kunstwerken, die die Begegnung zwischen Maria und Elisabeth darstellen. Die visuelle Exegese der

Editorial

Kunstwerke von Pontormo, Viola und Albertinelli und die biblische Exegese von Lukas 1:39-56 werden mit einer Reflexion über die Offenbarung und die Offenbarungskraft der Kunst (und dieser Werke im Besonderen) verbunden. Die Autorinnen heben dabei das Thema der Freude und der gegenseitigen Fürsorge im Lukasevangelium hervor sowie „den doppelten Impuls in der Bewegung der Offenbarung: die Gabe des Geheimnisses Gottes *und* das kreative Potenzial der Menschheit, sich die Gegenwart Gottes vorstellen zu können".

In ihrem Text *Identifikationspotential biblischer Texte im Horizont eines geschlechterbewussten Religionsunterrichts* diskutiert Julia Münch-Wirtz die Notwendigkeit eines geschlechterbewussten Religionsunterrichts sowie zwei spezielle Punkte, die dabei von besonderem Interesse sind. Erstens muss bei der Auswahl biblischer Texte und Themen auf eine Vielfalt von Identifikationsfiguren für die Schülerinnen und Schüler geachtet werden, statt die – einfache und dominante – Praxis fortzusetzen, Geschichten mit männlichen Protagonisten auszuwählen. Zweitens legt sie Wert auf die Entwicklung eines geschlechterbewussten Sprachgebrauchs, insbesondere in Bezug auf Gott und bei der Übersetzung biblischer Texte. Sie argumentiert, es sei wichtig, dass die Schülerinnen und Schüler lernen, „über Gott im Plural zu denken". Diese beiden Interessensschwerpunkte sollen die Möglichkeit einer Identifikation eröffnen, in der Ambivalenzen und Grauschattierungen wahrgenommen werden können sowie neue Einsichten über sich selbst und die Beziehung zu Gott entstehen können.

Anna Alabd präsentiert in *Einblicke in die Forschung über die Herausforderungen der Autonomie von christlichen und muslimischen Frauen. Eine Analyse aus interreligiöser Perspektive* die Ergebnisse einer empirisch-qualitativen Studie über die ethischen Dilemmata, denen christliche und muslimische Frauen im Hinblick auf ihre religiöse Tradition einerseits und ihre Autonomie andererseits begegnen. Sie nähert sich diesen Dilemmata aus der Perspektive der interreligiösen Ethik, die die gemeinsamen ethisch-sozialen Grundlagen und Prinzipien von Religionen im Kontext der säkularisierten Gesellschaft untersucht. Sie zeigt auch die Gemeinsamkeiten und Unterschiede ihrer Interviewpartnerinnen im Umgang mit den Spannungen zwischen religiösen Traditionen und dem Selbstbestimmungsstreben von Frauen auf.

To Whom Do You Attribute Religious Authority? A Pilot Study von Anne-Claire Mulder ist ein Bericht einer empirischen Untersuchung, die unter den Teilnehmerinnen des siebten Synodenwochenendes, das von der Ökumenischen Frauensynode in den Niederlanden organisiert wurde, durchgeführt wurde. Die Teilnehmerinnen wurden gefragt, wann und warum sie jemandem religiöse

Autorität zuschreiben würden, und ob es einen Unterschied machen würde, wenn die „Autorität" weiblich oder männlich wäre. Die Untersuchung ergab, dass die befragten Frauen zwar hierarchische Formen von Autoritätsbeziehungen ablehnen, aber Inspiration und Weisheit als wichtige Kriterien der Zuerkennung von Autorität werten. Für viele spielt das Geschlecht der anderen Person keine Rolle, wenn es darum geht, ihr Autorität zuzuschreiben. Die Kraft dieses Gleichheitsgrundsatzes wurde jedoch dadurch widerlegt, dass der Glaube der meisten Befragten von (Büchern) anderer Frauen inspiriert wurde.

Gespräch am Runden Tisch
Im Abschnitt *Runder Tisch* findet die Leser*in einen weiteren Text, oder besser gesagt, fünf Texte mit dem Titel *African Female Theologians Telling Stories*. Unter diesem Titel werden die redigierten Essays des ersten Symposiums des Kollektivs *African Female Theologians in Europe* vorgestellt. Dieses Symposium, das im Juni 2021 unter dem Motto *Connected but Disconnected* stattfand, widmete sich der kritischen Untersuchung, wie afrikanische Theologinnen – als Insider-Außenseiterinnen – im Gespräch mit einigen niederländischen Schwestern die Verbundenheit oder Trennung aushandeln, die ihnen bei der Teilnahme am holländisch/flämischen theologischen Diskurs begegnen. Thandi Soko-de Jong, Tabitha Polina Moyo, Heleen Joziasse, Shingirai Masunda und Anne-Claire Mulder behandeln die Insider-Outsider-Frage jeweils auf ihre eigene Art und Weise, indem sie von der persönlichen Erfahrung zur wissenschaftlichen Reflexion und wieder zurückgehen.

Buchbesprechungen
Die Herausgeberinnen der Zeitschrift freuen sich, ihren Leserinnen vier Buchbesprechungen präsentieren zu können.

Ruth Albrecht bespricht zwei Bücher, die die Frauenbewegung im 19. Jahrhundert beschreiben, nämlich *Frauenbewegungen des 19. Jahrhunderts*, herausgegeben von Irmtraud Fischer, Angela Berlis und Christiana de Groot, und *Die Bibel war für sie ein politisches Buch. Bibelinterpretationen der Frauenemanzipationsbewegungen im langen 19. Jahrhundert* von Irmtraud Fischer, Edith Petschnigg, Nicole Navratil, Angela Berlis und Christiana de Groot. Albrecht hält beide Bücher für einen wichtigen Beitrag zur bestehenden Forschungsliteratur über die Frauenbewegung jener Zeit, da sie den Aktivismus, das Denken und die Theologie vieler unbekannter Frauen, unter anderem aus Indien, Armenien und Island, vorstellen. Beide Bücher verlangen nach weiterer Forschung, insbesondere über ihre (internationalen) Netzwerke.

Editorial

Das Buch von Silvia Martínez Cano, *Teología feminista para principiantes. Voces de mujeres en la teología actual* wird von Mireia Vidal i Quintero besprochen. Martínez Cano schöpft darin aus ihrer Erfahrung als Universitätsdozentin und Lektorin für feministische Theologie sowie als Künstlerin. Das Buch ist eine Einführung in die feministische Theologie, die sich in erster Linie an ein spanisches Laienpublikum richtet. Vidal weist jedoch darauf hin, dass der historische Rückblick auf die Entwicklung der feministischen Theologie aus spanischer Sicht auch für diejenigen von Interesse sein könnte, die mit den spanischen Entwicklungen nicht vertraut sind. Laut Vidal ist dieses Buch eine willkommene Einführung in die feministische Theologie und ihrer Schwerpunkte. Es ist ein Benchmark im spanischen Kontext unter dem Gesichtspunkt der Verbreitung.

Das neueste Buch von Andrea Günter, *Philosophie und Geschlechterdifferenz. Auf dem Weg eines genealogischen Geschlechterdiskurses* wird von Silke Petersen besprochen. Petersen argumentiert, dass es in diesem Buch nicht um die sexuelle Differenz geht, sondern um die Verflechtung der grundlegenden Kategorien der Philosophie(geschichte) mit dem Geschlechterdiskurs und damit um die Schaffung eigener Kategorisierungsfelder. Um diese Verflechtung zu analysieren, zeichnet Günter die Geschichte der Philosophie nach, mit besonderem Augenmerk auf Platon, Aristoteles und Parmenides, aber auch auf Arendt und Simone de Beauvoir. Obwohl dieses Buch einen gewissen philosophischen Hintergrund voraussetzt, kommt Petersen zu dem Schluss, dass es für all diejenigen interessant ist, die bereit sind, über sexuelle Differenz jenseits der üblichen Binaritäten nachzudenken.

Agnethe Siquans is Professor for Old Testament Studies at the Faculty of Catholic Theology of the University of Vienna (Austria). agnethe.siquans@univie.ac.at
Agnethe Siquans es catedrática de Antiguo Testamento en la Facultad de Teología Católica de la Universidad de Viena (Austria). agnethe.siquans@univie.ac.at
Agnethe Siquans ist Professorin für Alttestamentliche Bibelwissenschaft an der Katholisch-Theologischen Fakultät der Universität Wien (Österreich). agnethe.siquans@univie.ac.at

Martina Bär is Professor of Fundamental Theology at the Faculty of Catholic Theology of the University of Graz (Austria). martina.baer@unigraz.at

Editorial

Martina Bär es catedrática de Teología Fundamental en la Facultad de Teología Católica de la Universidad de Graz (Austria). martina.baer@unigraz.at
Martina Bär ist Professorin für Fundamentaltheologie an der Katholisch-Theologischen Fakultät der Universität Graz (Austria). martina.baer@unigraz.at

Anne-Claire Mulder is associate professor for Women's and Gender Studies in Theology and supervisor of the internships for the ministry at the Protestantse Theologische University (The Netherlands). acmulder@pthu.nl
Anne-Claire Mulder es profesora asociada de Teología de las Mujeres y Estudios de Género y supervisora de las becas interinas para el ministerio en la Universidad Teológica Protestante (Países Bajos). acmulder@pthu.nl
Anne-Claire Mulder ist assoziierte Professorin für Frauen- und Genderstudien in der Theologie und Betreuerin des Praktikums für angehende Pfarrer*innenan an der Protestantischen Theologischen Universität (Niederlande). acmulder@pthu.nl

Mireia Vidal i Quintero is a PhD candidate in New Testament and Christian Origins at the University of Edinburgh (Scotland). Her dissertation is devoted to the Empty Tomb tradition. M.Vidal-Quintero@sms.ed.ac.uk
Mireia Vidal i Quintero es doctoranda en Nuevo Testamento y Orígenes del Cristianismo en la Universidad de Edimburgo (Escocia). Su tesis está dedicada a la tradición de la tumba vacía. M.Vidal-Quintero@sms.ed.ac.uk
Mireia Vidal i Quintero ist Doktorandin im Fach für Neues Testament und Ursprünge des Christentums an der Universität von Edinburgh (Schottland). Sie promoviert über die Tradition des leeren Grabes.
M.Vidal-Quintero@sms.ed.ac.uk

Mariecke van den Berg

Meanwhile, Back at the Shelter:
A Queer Theology of Coming Home

Abstract
This article is a slightly revised version of the author's inaugural lecture, held on the 12th of November 2021 at Radboud University in Nijmegen, upon accepting the chair of Feminism and Christianity (Catharina Halkes Chair). It takes as its point of departure an off-hand remark in a church report on the position of LGBTIQ+ believers in a small Protestant denomination in the Netherlands. In the report it is stated that while heterosexual marriage is at home in God's creation, same-sex relationships are "a shelter in a broken life". The article argues for a queer approach where the shelter is reclaimed as a theological space and positionality. Generations of cabin dwellers in past and present times have taught us to nurse a certain amount of healthy house scepticism, which in this article is applied to the solid "house" of Christian traditions. Building on arguments from feminist and queer architecture, it is furthermore argued that shelters (or cabins, or huts) allow us to think in terms of "scrap theology". This is a theology that provides shelter by using the left-overs from tradition to build new dwellings that are positioned on the uncomfortable border between "in" and "out" of the tradition, thus confronting it with what it has deemed its expendable "surplus".

Resumen
Este artículo es una revisión ligeramente revisada del discurso inaugural que la autora ofreció el 12 de noviembre de 2021 en la Universidad de Radboud (Nimega) con motivo de su instalación en la cátedra Catharina Halkes de Feminismo y Cristianismo. Una observación casual sobre la situación de los creyentes LGBTIQ+ en un informe eclesial de una pequeña denominación protestante en los Países Bajos es su punto de partida. En el informe se afirma que, a pesar de que el matrimonio heterosexual responde al propósito original de Dios para su creación, las relaciones entre personas del mismo sexo son "un refugio en medio de una vida rota". Este artículo propone una lectura en la que se reivindica el refugio como espacio teológico a la vez que posicionalidad. Generaciones pasadas y presentes que han habitado en la cabaña nos han enseñado a tener un cierto grado de sano escepticismo al pensar en la casa, una actitud que en este artículo se aplica al "edificio" de las tradiciones cristianas. Recurriendo a argumentos procedentes de la arquitectura feminista y *queer*, se arguye que los refugios,

ya sean cabañas o cobertizos, nos permiten pensar en una "teología de las sobras". Se trata de una teología que construye nuevas moradas en las que refugiarse usando las sobras de la teología tradicional, por bien que ello nos posiciona en la incómoda frontera que existe entre el estar "dentro" y "fuera" de la tradición. La teología tradicional se ve así confrontada con aquello que considera un excedente desechable.

Zusammenfassung

Dieser Artikel ist eine leicht überarbeitete Fassung der Antrittsvorlesung der Autorin, die sie am 12. November 2021 an der Radboud Universität in Nijmegen anlässlich ihres Rufes auf den Lehrstuhl für Feminismus und Christentum (Catharina Halkes-Lehrstuhl) hielt. Der Ausgangspunkt ist die beiläufige Bemerkung in einem kirchlichen Bericht einer kleinen protestantischen Konfession in den Niederlanden über die Stellung von LGBTIQ+-Gläubigen. In dem Bericht heißt es, dass die heterosexuelle Ehe in Gottes Schöpfung zu Hause ist, während gleichgeschlechtliche Beziehungen „ein Zufluchtsort für zerbrochene Leben" sind. Der Artikel spricht für einen queeren Ansatz, bei dem der Zufluchtsort als locus theologicus und als theologische Position zurückgewonnen wird. Generationen von Hüttenbewohnern in der Vergangenheit und Gegenwart lehren uns, eine gewisse gesunde Skepsis gegenüber dem Haus zu pflegen, die in diesem Artikel auf das solide „Haus" christlicher Traditionen angewandt wird. Aufbauend auf Argumenten feministischer und queerer Architektur argumentiert die Autorin, dass Zufluchtsorte wie Unterstände (oder Kabinen oder Hütten) uns ermöglichen, in Begriffen der „Schrott-Theologie" zu denken. Es handelt sich um eine Theologie, die Schutz bietet, indem sie die Überbleibsel der Tradition nutzt, um neue Wohnhäuser zu bauen; eine Theologie, die sich an der unbequemen Grenze zwischen „In" und „Out" der Tradition positioniert und die Tradition mit dem konfrontiert, was sie als ihren entbehrlichen „Überschuss" ansieht.

Keywords: Queer theology, shelters, architecture, home, scavenger methodology.

Habitation

Marriage is not
a house or even a tent

it is before that, and colder:

the edge of the forest, the edge
of the desert
the unpainted stairs
at the back where we squat
outside, eating popcorn

the edge of the receding glacier

where painfully and with wonder
at having survived even
this far

we are learning to make fire

Margaret Atwood[1]

Introduction: A Shelter in a Broken Life[2]

In 2015, the Netherlands Reformed Churches (NRC), a 30,000-member Protestant community which I am part of, published a report on whether it was permissible for cohabiting gay and lesbian church members to hold a church office.[3] A majority viewpoint in the report recommended opening the way to such members holding the offices of elder and deacon; a recommendation which, incidentally, was not adopted. But what struck me in particular was one sentence in the report, a line which did not refer to church offices but appeared in a long appendix on marriage and relationships. The sentence read: "Marriage

---

[1] Margaret Atwood, *Selected Poems (1965-1975)* (Houghton Mifflin: Boston 1987), here 133.
[2] Inaugural lecture on the occasion of receiving the Professorship Feminism and Christianity (Catharina Halkes Chair) at the Faculty of Philosophy, Theology and Religious Studies at Radboud University in Nijmegen, the Netherlands, on 12th of November 2021.
[3] NRC Report *'Ambt en homoseksualiteit: een verantwoord perspectief?' Report by the Church Office and Homosexuality Committee, for the purpose of the 2013 National Assembly of the Netherlands Reformed Churches in Zeewolde.* LV2013 02.02.02, 2015.

of a man and a woman is at home [in the sense of belonging] in God's original creation, a homosexual relationship is a shelter in a broken life."[4]

If you parse this sentence carefully, you will see that it contains multitudes; enough to write a doctoral thesis about. Actually, it is a courageous statement, because the author – going against all past and current church frameworks – advises the church to bless same-sex relationships. But it took some time to start appreciating this courage; my initial reaction was not one of admiration, but irritation. That is because this sentence is also typical of the way some churches try to straddle the divide between the principle of equality and the difference between heterosexual and same-sex relationships. While the metaphor "a shelter in a broken life" strikes me as an accurate and poetic expression of what relationships and friendships can be, it applies just as well to heterosexual partnerships. But most of all, the term 'shelter' reeks of condescension. It lacks generosity. From the comfortable perspective of those who are secure in the knowledge that they are at home, that they belong, in God's original creation, LGBTIQ+ people[5] should be thankful for a lowly cabin, a "hut in a garden of cucumbers".[6] My first impulse was therefore to reject this offer of a shelter, be it a hut, a cabin or whatever. On deeper consideration, though, there are good reasons not to discard this metaphorical refuge – reasons both personal and academic, because the metaphor offers a glimpse of the very kind of theology I hope to develop and encourage from my new position. Let me start by expanding on my personal connection with huts or cabins.

When I was about eight years old, I had no ambition to become an Endowed Professor of Feminism and Christianity. My dream was to move to Canada, become a hunter-gatherer and live in a log cabin. This is why, when I was tempted to turn up my nose at the shelter invoked by the Netherlands Reformed Churches, my childhood self began to kick up a fuss. Memories came back of how I had imagined my life in the cabin: with a roaring wood fire in the winter and refreshing swims in the lake during the summer. It was these recollections of my strong hankering for solitude and silence that made me decide to give

---

[4] Jan Mudde, "Bijlage 4: Van Sjibbolet naar Sjalom. Ruimte voor homoseksuelen in de gemeente van Christus."*Appendix to the* NRC Report *'Ambt en homoseksualiteit: een verantwoord perspectief?' Report by the Church Office and Homosexuality Committee, for the purpose of the 2013 National Assembly of the Netherlands Reformed Churches in Zeewolde.* LV2013 02.02.02, 2015, here 200.

[5] LGBTIQ+ refers to lesbian women, gay men, and bi-sexual, transgender, intersex and queer people.

[6] Isaiah 1:8 (NKJV).

the cabin a chance. I would move into this "shelter in a broken life" for a while. I would give it a try, to see how I liked it, all nice and quiet.

But when I got to the cabin, I discovered not solitude but a buzz of activity. The shelter housed a motley crew including Henry David Thoreau, Dutch literary figures Betje Wolff and Aagje Deken, Harriet Beecher Stowe's Uncle Tom, Martin Heidegger, Ludwig Wittgenstein, a group of kids, Eastern European migrant workers, lots of refugees and God. The hut turned out to be a lively place, inhabited by not only Netherlands Reformed LGBTIQ+ churchgoers, but a large number of exiles, too, as well as by enslaved people, adventurers, workers, established philosophers and writing women; a highly diverse collection of those who either chose or were forced to take shelter, and who, taken together, formed quite a queer group of people. Shelters, huts and cabins go back a long way, and if you study the writing by their dwellers, you will see that they have always found ways to talk back to those who looked down on them from their sturdier edifices.

It is an excellent queer strategy to co-opt a term meant to reject you, and to wear it as an activist badge of honor. The word 'queer' is a prime example of this praxis; it evolved from a neutral word denoting 'odd' into an insult for gay men, until sexual and gender minorities started deliberately applying the term to themselves. The word queer gave them an identity, but most of all, a perspective on the world, a way to expose and denounce heteronormativity.[7] Today I would like to propose something similar. I suggest that instead of letting the shelter get hijacked, we claim it as our own. I have already begun doing so. That is why, over the past year, I have started compiling a collection of huts, cabins and shelters in literature, poetry, films and the Bible. Hovels I stumbled on in the woods, and huts I collected from others' stories. My hope is that this collection will inspire us to think about two things of great personal and professional interest to me, both of which I will discuss here. One thing is the relationship between mainstream Christian traditions and the people and perspectives marginalized by those traditions. And the other is how you can make those margins theologically productive. In short, I propose to explore the possibilities the shelter offers as a location to speak from, a positionality,

---

[7] For a genealogy and current use of the word queer, see Nikki Sullivan, *A Critical Introduction to Queer Theory* (New York University Press: New York 2003), here 43-50; Kath Browne, "Queer Spiritual Spaces: Conclusion", in: Kath Brown, Sally R. Munt and Andrew K.-T. Yip (eds.), *Queer Spiritual Spaces: Sexuality and Sacred Places* (Routledge: London and New York 2010), 231-244.

to be used by those for whom there has never been a place in the solid constructions of tradition, or only under unacceptable terms.[8]

This exploration ties in with the work that Susannah Cornwall, Lisa Isherwood and Marcella Althaus-Reid have already done, precisely in relation to these questions. Susannah Cornwall has pointed out that since it is obvious that queer Christians are a permanent part of the tradition, it is time not only to indict Christianity's excluding mechanisms, but also to start looking for what positives the tradition has to offer. One thing this entails is a permanent dialogue.[9] But here lurks the risk of assimilation; LGBTIQ+ people face the prospect of relinquishing their own voice, hermeneutics and critical position in the community in return for acceptance and equality. To quote Marcella Althaus-Reid and Lisa Isherwood: "Queer Theology [...] is a theology from the margins that wants to remain at the margins."[10] What I present here today is an attempt to deal constructively with that tension.

The Power of the Comma
Let us start by looking at how margins are created in the first place. If we grammatically parse our Sentence of the Day ("Marriage of a man and a woman is at home in God's original creation, a homosexual relationship is a shelter in a broken life"), we notice that it is divided by a comma. The comma is all we have to go on, because the author does not use a conjunction. But behind it lies a world of meaning. This small, seemingly insignificant punctuation mark causes, in its casual placement, a division between the people to its left and to its right. This comma raises many questions, for example: Which other commas does it echo? And: Who, historically, was included in God's original creation, and who only came into view when the word 'broken' needed a face? At another level: What conventions allow some people to appropriate the considerable power of the comma? Who is allowed to put the commas in our traditions? And, ultimately, what sort of theology is possible

---

[8] Donna Haraway, "Situated Knowledges: The Science Question in Feminism and the Privilege of Partial Perspective", in: *Feminist Studies*, 14 (Autumn/1988), 575-599; Adrienne Rich, "Notes Toward a Politics of Location", in: Myriam Díaz-Diocaretz and Iris M. Zavala (eds.), *Women, Feminist Identity and Society in the 1980's: Selected Papers* (John Benjamins Publishing Company: Amsterdam and Philadelphia 1984), 7-22.

[9] Susannah Cornwall, "'Something There is That Doesn't Love a Wall': Queer Theologies and Reparative Readings", in: *Theology & Sexuality* 21 (February/2015), 20-35.

[10] Marcella Althaus-Reid and Lisa Isherwood, "Thinking Theology and Queer Theory," in: *Feminist Theology* 15 (May/2007), 302-314, here 304.

on either side of the comma? What image of God do terms like 'original' and 'home' engender, and what image of God arises from 'shelter' and 'broken life'? Is the comma a curse that causes an irreparable separation between people? Or is it a blessing that creates a lee, a shelter, an isolation where new forms of theology can originate? I propose to take the latter as our point of departure and to see the comma as a productive punctuation mark.

Theology of Scraps
This calls for a methodology that feels at home in the shelter, that is based in experiences to the right of the comma. One of my goals is to continue to develop such a methodology over the next few years. I found a starting point in the work of queer scholar Jack Halberstam. In his book *Female Masculinities*, Halberstam coins the term "scavenger methodology".[11] Scavengers look for the leftovers, the cast-offs, the surplus, the scraps. They use it to build something new, a cobbled-together construction in which materials and objects are repurposed. Huts are usually built out of scraps. The materials are cast-offs from nature: dead tree limbs and blowdowns. Or waste from human construction sites: corrugated iron, tarps or pieces of house wrap and PVC pipes. If we imagine the hut as a theological space, the scavenger methodology helps us to see the hut as a space where we collect the waste of tradition, repurpose it and build something new. Scavenger methodology is a good description of my research method for the past few years and gives me a handle on more explicitly developing a methodology for a queer feminist "theology of scraps": a theology focused on people and ideas that have been deemed less important, subordinate clauses or extras; on what Foucault calls subjugated knowledge: knowledge seen as second-class or less authoritative.[12] In other words, I am focusing on knowledge produced by the 'surplus' to the right of the comma.

Another important characteristic of Halberstam's scavenger methodology is a willingness to transgress academic disciplines when necessary, in order to make new, surprising connections. I consider this interdisciplinary "grazing" an important element of scrap theology. Allow me to take you on a sample

---

[11] Jack Halberstam, *Female Masculinity* (Duke University Press: Durham and London 1998), here 13.
[12] Michel Foucault, "Two lectures," in Colin Gordon (ed.), *Power/Knowledge: Selected Interviews and Other Writings 1972-1977, Michel Foucault* (Pantheon Books: New York 1980), 87-108, here 81-82.

disciplinary outing, and I will show you some parallels between insights from theology and architecture. If we are talking about huts, we are talking about buildings, after all. This raises questions about how we design, lay out and furnish those huts. And how buildings are constructed to the left of the comma.

The Opposite of Huts: Houses

Let us start with the latter, constructions to the left of the comma. If LGBTIQ+ people are allocated a hut or some similarly primitive, temporary shelter, what type of construction is implicit in the main clause before the comma? What is the opposite of huts? In what type of structure does the author of this now infamous sentence live? In the literature in my hut collection, the opposite of the hut is the house. Uncle Tom's cabin sits in the shadow of Mister Shelby's house. Heidegger owned a log cabin in Germany, and Wittgenstein owned one in Norway, which they used as writer's retreats for a few weeks out of the year before returning to their houses in the city. Houses have a certain persistence. They tend to infiltrate our conversations, ensconce themselves there and usurp all our attention. Today I tried to talk mostly about huts, and I was struck by how difficult it was to get there and how overbearing everything house-related is. It is hard to think outside of the box we call the house.

The same is true of Christian tradition. The house is a phantom presence in our Sentence of the Day; it is the norm that the shelter deviates from. The statement that marriage is at home, in the sense of belonging, in God's original creation aligns with a considerable body of references in scripture and Christian tradition that invite us to think in terms of good designs underpinning sturdy buildings with solid, earthquake-proof foundations. I am talking about references to things like the Temple, and God's name as a strong tower, a stronghold, a mighty fortress.[13] To the house of David and the wise man who built his house on the rock.[14] The main clause to the left of the comma reflects the type of muscle-flexing architecture that accommodates words and phrases like "original" and "at home".

Although these references are the dominant narrative, they are not the only representations of building and dwelling. The Bible is also full of things collapsing: the walls of Jericho,[15] the tower of Babel[16] and the tower of Siloam.[17]

---

[13] Psalms 61:3; 62:3; 91:2.
[14] Matthew 7:24-27.
[15] Joshua 6.
[16] Genesis 11:1-9.
[17] Luke 13:4.

And there is also another, messy body of references to the vulnerability of dwelling. It employs the imagery of temporary and ramshackle constructions. It is represented in tents, huts,[18] and even homelessness.[19] These references invite scepticism of houses; they cast doubt on the dominance of houses in our representation of dwelling and being at home. Perhaps now there is enough momentum for this scepticism in the Netherlands, given the housing crisis and the recurring lockdowns that make us feel like the walls are closing in on us. At this time in our history, our houses have lost much of their luster.

But I think house scepticism also has a religious dimension. An early impetus for a more spiritual brand of house scepticism was proposed by Kahlil Gibran about a century ago. We find a juxtaposition between houses and huts in his work *The Prophet*. This novella is about a sage who, for a time, lived with a certain people, the people of Orphalese, but who in his old age wants to return to his country of origin. Before he boards the ship that will take him home, the people of Orphalese take the opportunity to ask him one last time for his wise counsel on several subjects. They ask him to speak of love, friendship, children and death. And of houses:

> Then a mason came forth and said, Speak to us of Houses. And he answered and said: Build of your imaginings a bower [hut] in the wilderness ere you build a house within the city walls. [...] Would that I could gather your houses into my hand, and like a sower scatter them in forest and meadow. [...] In their fear your forefathers gathered you too near together. And that fear shall endure a little longer. A little longer shall your city walls separate your hearths from your fields. And tell me, people of Orphalese, what have you in these houses? And what is it you guard with fastened doors?[20]

In a way, Kahlil Gibran hands us the motto to explore that second line of thinking, the one about huts, and asks us to consider what these houses offer

---

[18] There is not enough room to explore the difference between tents and huts, but there is an important distinction. They differ at least in the following respects: tents have a pre-defined structure and are set up with certain materials that are reused time and again. Huts do not necessarily have a pre-defined form, particularly not when they are constructed with whatever materials happen to be around. Tents enable a mobile or nomadic lifestyle, while huts are in principle static buildings, which – although temporary and unfinished – always remain in the same spot.
[19] For instance Matthew 8:20.
[20] Kahlil Gibran, *The Prophet* (Project Gutenberg 2021) (https://www.gutenberg.org/files/58585/58585-h/58585-h.htm#link37, 5 April 2022).

us, in spiritual or sense-making terms, too. What is stored there, what does this house stand for? And why does this have to be protected at all costs?

Interventions from Feminist and Queer Architecture
Insights from feminist and queer architecture can help us to more fully articulate house scepticism, but also to explore an alternative perspective on construction. Feminist architecture argues that a human-constructed space is never neutral, but necessarily reiterates and reimposes society's normative gender, class and race relations.[21] Feminist architects like Katarina Bonnevier have pointed out that the whole process of design and construction is subject to gendered norms. In architecture, it used to be the norm that men built the homes that women lived in. Men design the structures, women do the interior decoration.[22] Interior decoration as a phenomenon was therefore seen as quintessentially female, and also as non-Western, an expression of bad taste by the lower classes, as gay and amateur.[23] This gave it a lower status than the core business of architecture: the big bold lines of design and construction.

An interesting voice who builds on these feminist insights is Colin Ripley, specialist in queer architecture from Ryerson University in Toronto. I would like to discuss Ripley's arguments here because his work helps us to explore the relationship between mainstream and margin. First of all, Ripley wonders whether queers are able to live in houses at all, since these buildings are so clearly not designed for them. What he is thinking of here is a standard suburban house or townhouse – like kids usually draw – with a master bedroom to conceive the kids that can later populate the smaller bedrooms. It has a workshop, a craft room and a walk-in closet to lock up any homosexual family members. According to Ripley, the normative house is so entangled with the architectonic expression of heteronormativity, that a queer house is actually impossible.[24] To him, 'queer house' is a contradiction in terms.

Ripley suggests several ways queers can position themselves vis à vis houses. We can also apply these stances to mainstream Christianity and its

---

[21] Leslie Kanes Weisman, "Architecture", in: Cheris Kramarae and Dale Spender (eds.), *Encyclopedia of Women. Global Women's Issues and Knowledge* (Routledge: New York and London 2000), 86-109, here 86.
[22] Katarina Bonnevier, *Behind Straight Curtains: Towards a Queer Feminist Theory of Architecture* (Axl Books: Stockholm 2007), here 17-18.
[23] Bonnevier, *Behind Straight Curtains*, 19.
[24] Colin Ripley, "Strategies for Living in Houses", in: *FOOTPRINT* (December/2017), 95-108, here 98.

margins. He details four strategies: occupation, intervention, transformation and avoidance. I will briefly discuss all four:

1. *Occupation* describes how we queers can live in houses, but do so like squatters. In other words, we appear from the outside to have adapted, but in fact we are merely temporary denizens. We paint graffiti on the walls and leave behind empty champagne bottles and used condoms.[25]
2. *Intervention* means queering the material reality of the house itself. Rather than adapting yourself to the house, you adapt the house to yourself and fly the rainbow flag. Ripley argues that while this is a more visible strategy, it leaves the concept of the house as such unchallenged.[26]
3. A strategy that Ripley himself tries to develop, giving examples of this in his own work, is *trans-forming* or "transing" the house. Rather than adapting to the house, or vice versa, you go back to the drawing board, back to the level of *design*. The issue is not whether houses transed in this way are actually built, but whether we can imagine them; whether we can come up with designs that raise questions about what it takes to be a house, to come home, to live somewhere, to engage in relations with others.[27] His *Dreams* design is an example of this (Figure 1). The house was designed to accommodate a dream, which we see here in the shape of a large, Totoro-like substance that will not be restricted by the structures of the house but instead breaks right through the rafters and into the basement.
4. A fourth strategy, finally, is *avoidance*. While in practice, Ripley opts for transformative architecture, he actually prefers the avoidance strategy in all its extremism and resulting impracticability. Here – and if you are a homeowner, hold on to your seat – I quote Ripley:

> [I]n the end we all know, deep down, that there is only one acceptable strategy. We need to demand an end to houses and to all existing housing. We need to burn it all down and start again. We need to produce means of shelter that are not simply expressions of the hetero norm, structures that allow all of us to be who we are in whatever social and material systems we choose. We live in tents and huts of our own making. We sleep wherever and with whoever we want. We build a new world in our own image.[28]

---

[25] Ripley, *Strategies*, 98.
[26] Ripley, *Strategies*, 99-100.
[27] Ripley, *Strategies*, 100.
[28] Ripley, *Strategies*, 99.

Mariecke van den Berg
Meanwhile, Back at the Shelter: A Queer Theology of Coming Home

Figure 1: *Dreams*, by Colin Ripley. Published with permission of the author.

Ripley's argument reminds me of how I look at Christian tradition in my more cynical moods. That tradition is as solid as a brick house, and it is doubtful that it offers room for queers because they did not have a place at the drawing board when it was designed. Just like there were neither women present, nor enslaved or illiterate people. The past century and a half have brought the emancipation of all these people in various waves and ways. For Christianity, this means that we have to explore whether the house that was built suits the needs, desires and bodies of the people who live in it.

Ripley's strategies, as I said, can be translated into the options people on the wrong side of the comma have at their disposal to position themselves in relation to the Christian tradition. You can choose to occupy, in other words, to stay, but act disruptively. You can intervene by suggesting new decorations: a rainbow candle, a rainbow flag. You can try to trans(form), that is to say, you can attempt to get others to go back to the drawing board and collectively create a new design. Or you can avoid the tradition, leave and start something new.

In Ripley's view, huts fall into the last category. In what follows, however, I would like to explore the concept of the hut not as a new construct that replaces the house and parts ways, but as part of the category of scrap that by definition belongs to the house, because my point is that the two are condemned to each other. What I am saying is that the hut reminds the house of its own surplus and as such possesses critical and subversive potential. I am doing this in the knowledge that the house is not an innocent metaphor or material reality, and that the hut likewise, is not an unambiguous or romantic alternative to the house.

A Taxonomy of the Shelter

That huts, cabins and tents are no straightforward alternative to houses is evident from the motley collection of shelter inhabitants I described earlier, who I would now like to allow to speak so that we can arrive at a provisional taxonomy of the shelter. Through the centuries, people have taken refuge in huts or cabins for many different reasons and not every shelter lends itself to the critical theology of scraps that I wish to construct. Therefore, I will dwell only briefly on what is probably the most famous literary shelter: the 19th-century hut described by Henry Thoreau in *Walden*.[29] Thoreau built this hut and lived in it for two years in a quest to become one with nature – though so close to the town of Concord that he could do his shopping there every day. In his book, we find a lovely rant about how people get tied down by their homes and mortgages, stuck in their typical lifestyles and ways of looking at life. The tirade would fit seamlessly into our current housing crisis. But I would venture to say that his critique is only skin deep. Thoreau symbolizes a broad movement of Western adventurers who seek refuge in a primitive dwelling to escape everything they perceive as suffocating about modern life. But for them, this shelter is only a temporary stop, perhaps for a summer or a few seasons. Their house always remains as a safety net. The hut

---

[29] Henry David Thoreau, *Walden; or, Life in the Woods* (Dover Publications, Inc.: Mineola 1995 [1854]).

in their narrative fits in the wider trope about returning to nature and to the original, simple but adventurous place where humans (usually men) are from.[30] Above all, it is a place to be inhabited by the individual. The statement it makes is that of the man and his hut. The ascetic lifestyle that goes with this is, paradoxically, an expression of privilege. The happy few who can afford this lifestyle seldom reflect on the life of people who have no other choice but to permanently live in huts, or hovels, without a comfortable house to resort to. When the privileged do consider the permanent hut dweller, they tend to romanticize the image, as Thoreau did with the native Americans' wigwam.[31] So, these huts do, in my view, qualify as a form of social commentary because they critique overconsumption and complacency. However, they do not question the exclusionary mechanisms employed by those to the left of the comma, namely their thinking in terms of origin and belonging. To name just one example, Thoreau's hut contrasts starkly with the shelters used by current-day Easter European migrant workers who have lost their jobs due to COVID and now live in our woods. Hence, shelters can be places of privilege, but also places of bare-bones survival.

A Place for Play and Imagination: Children
Children learn that huts are also places where they can play and use their fantasy. At least, that is what Ann Cline argued. This architect, who sadly died at a relatively young age, penned the book *A Hut of One's Own* (1997).[32] Cline was an admirable person who conducted her research in an extraordinary way. Like Thoreau, she lived alone, in a self-built hut, for years. However, she kept her living circumstances a secret until she was awarded tenure by the university for fear of being cast as a looney. Her work focuses on the cultural meaning of the hut in China and Japan as compared to the Western context. She pioneered the architectural and sociohistorical formulations of the hut. Like me, Ann Cline took as her point of departure the wish to evaluate a childhood memory and to treat the knowledge of young girls as legitimate knowledge. She recollected the importance of the hut as a place for play, and especially the intense happiness that she once felt when she was holed up in her hut.[33]

---

[30] Thoreau was for instance idolized by Christopher McCandless, who ventured into the Alaskan wilderness and lived there in an abandoned bus for months until he died of food poisoning. His life was the inspiration for Jon Krakauer's book *Into the Wild* (1996), which was filmed by Sean Penn in 2008.
[31] Thoreau, *Walden*, 19.
[32] Ann Cline, *A Hut of One's Own: Life Outside the Circle of Architecture* (MIT Press: Cambridge and London 1997).
[33] Cline, *A Hut of One's Own*, xi.

It is no accident that the hut figures prominently in a great many children's books. For children, Cline argues, the hut is also a liminal place, a location on the border between childhood and adulthood. The hut offers you a space to withdraw from the boring adult existence that has been laid out for you.[34]

The huts in children's books also taught me that huts are vulnerable. Huts are often threatened with destruction. They are frequently built in public spaces, in small areas of no man's land. Rarely do they belong to anyone. You cannot take out a mortgage on a hut, but you also cannot lay claim to one. The biggest threat to huts comes from bullies. I do not have enough time or desire to explain how to deal with bullies. Besides, that is why we have that substantial body of knowledge called feminist theology.

Women and Queers

Children are not the only ones that need the hut as a place where they can let their imagination roam. Women, too, historically have used the hut for this purpose. When the house and its expectations became too restrictive, women sometimes found another location. Ann Cline's hankering for the hut had precedents. The Dutch 18th-century writing duo Betje Wolff and Aagje Deken had a shed in the garden of their villa in Beverwijk, where they wrote *De Historie van Mejuffrouw Sara Burgerhart* (1782), the book recognized as the first 'real' Dutch novel.[35] A writer's cabin or 'retreat' was a well-known phenomenon. Poet and writer Elisabeth Maria Post[36] had one, too. It is questionable, of course, whether the garden shed should be included in my collection of shelters and whether that muddles the category. To include it would require a fairly lengthy apology for the garden shed, which I will surely return to one day. For now, let it suffice to say that a garden shed is a construction that struggles with its identity: am I a hut? A house? A shed? But it is precisely this uncertain and fluid identity that we welcome in a queer approach.

---

[34] Cline, *A Hut of One's Own*, xii.
[35] Many details about Wolff and Deken's garden shed can be found in: Meta Bison, Lieve van Ollefen et al. (eds.), *Ô Laage Hut! Meer Grootsch dan Vorstelyke Hoven. Het kluisje van Betje Wolff en Aagje Deken in Beverwijk* (De stichting tot behoud van het tuinhuisje van de dames Betje Wolff en Aagje Deken te Beverwijk: Beverwijk 1993).
[36] Elisabeth Maria Post (1755-1812) was a self-taught poet and novelist who spent most of her life in the countryside and became famous for her epistolary novel *Het Land* (The Land). In the novel, as well as her poetry, nature plays an important role. She was also one of the first Dutch authors to openly challenge the institution of slavery.

This garden shed where Wolff and Deken wrote shows us that huts are transitory. The shed is particularly hutlike in terms of the materials it is made of: mainly wood and thatch. It is one of the few historical constructions of its kind that has remained standing. It can still be visited in Beverwijk. Experts agree, however, that after the many restorations it has been through, it is unlikely that any of the original material has survived. An important question is whether these two writers, in addition to being feminist role models, are also two of our queer predecessors? What did these two ladies get up to in that garden shed? It is known that Betje Wolff had female lovers. Whether Aagje Deken was one of them, cannot be proven. As we concluded earlier, though, huts are spaces that invite us to use our imagination. Regardless, what is clear from Betje Wolff and Aagje Deken's dikey hideaway, is how important it is for women and queers to have a place, a room or a hut of one's own.

The Other's Hut: The Enslaved

Finally, I would like to invite you into a last shelter, the one we come across in Harriet Beecher Stowe's 1852 classic *Uncle Tom's Cabin*, which she wrote as a denunciation of slavery based on the tragic life of the enslaved Tom. Toni Morrison explores the meaning of the cabin in her collection of essays *The Origin of Others*.[37] What strikes her is the warmly inviting, friendly and even ebullient manner in which the cabin is introduced in the novel. I quote Beecher Stowe:

> The cabin of Uncle Tom was a small log building, close adjoining to 'the house', as the negro par excellence designates his master's dwelling. In front, it had a neat garden-patch, where, every summer, strawberries, raspberries, and a variety of fruits and vegetables flourished under careful tending. The whole front of it was covered by a large scarlet bignonia and a native multiflora rose, which, entwisting and interlacing, left scarce a vestige of rough logs to be seen.[38]

From the outside, Uncle Tom's cabin looks a bit like a cosey summer cottage. It is nice on the inside, too. We see the cabin through the eyes of Young Master George, the master's son, who comes by for a friendly visit. Through his perspective, the reader learns that there is no need to fear the cabin. It is a place of hospitality and warmth, where laughter can be heard and good food is served all the time, the way only Aunt Chloe can make it. Morrison argues that this

---

[37] Toni Morrison, *The Origin of Others* (Harvard University Press: Cambridge and London 2017).
[38] Harriet Beecher Stowe, *Uncle Tom's Cabin or, Negro Life in the Slave States of America* (Wordsworth Editions: Hertfordshire 2002 [1852]), here 20.

romanticized image of slavery belies actual fear. The black man's cabin, she concludes, can only be entered by the white man when this space has been rendered completely harmless, decorated with so many flowers, frills and humour that it is unquestionably clear the black man poses no danger whatsoever.[39]

The cabin is the Other's space and, in that sense, an unpredictable, potentially perilous place. When you expel people from the house, whenever you put a comma between yourself and the Other, you lose sight of that other. Who knows what mutiny might be plotted in that cabin? If the house can feel so threatened by a ramshackle cabin, maybe it is not as strong as we think.

A Theology of the Shelter

An inaugural lecture is a time to outline your plans for research and teaching. I hope to do what I was always planning to do, that is: build shelters. If not in Canada, then here at Heyendael.[40] That is adventurous, too. I hope to be able to do that together with you. I will conclude, therefore, with a small manifesto of the shelter, a first sketch of what a theology of hut-building could look like. Take it as an invitation to join me.

Manifesto of the Shelter

We are building a shelter.

We are building a shelter because we do not want to choose between staying and leaving. We do not accept the logic of either-or. Our shelters are a new kind of space which is neither part of, nor outside of, tradition. Instead, it constantly pushes against that uncomfortable border because we are building the shelter in your front yard. Our improvised, messy constructions are ruining the view of your lovely houses. There goes the neighbourhood.

We are building a shelter because we need a theology of the tomboy. A theology for girls with scraped knees and dirty fingernails. Girls that we cannot find anywhere in the Bible and that, to be honest, are also rare in feminist and queer theology.

We are building a shelter because we need a clubhouse. We are starting a club for people who want to show solidarity with the scraps of our tradition in their exegesis. We read the texts that do not make it into the lectionaries. We are a club for misunderstood eldest sons, daughters that went unmentioned, women that bore only their husbands' names, people from strange

---

[39] Morrison, *The Origin of Others*, 13.
[40] Heyendael is the estate in the city of Nijmegen where Radboud University is located.

cultures with strange gods. Stepping-stone characters that only serve the purpose of introducing the real heroes. Any character that does not even make it into my lectures on feminist theology because she is not a 'strong woman' is hereby declared an honorary club member.

We are building a shelter because we need spaces of solidarity with hut dwellers of the past and present. Hut dwellers on the edges of Europe, hut dwellers in our own woods.

We are building a shelter that is not meant to last into eternity. It need only be for now, need only offer immediate protection. Tomorrow is another day. Our shelter is rickety and vulnerable and easy to blow down. But you can also choose not to do that.

We are building a shelter because instead of *being at* home, we want to *come* home. Being at home is an entitlement based on conformism. It is the language of those who have arrived, the language of being built according to a blueprint. Coming home is a process, it is always in progress, and it is never entirely finished, but that is the beauty of it. Coming home is, by definition, temporary, unfinished, surprising, based on shared imagination and the pleasure of play. It is not based on templates, categorizations or blood ties.

Shelters move you. It is hard to walk by a hut and not feel something, if only nostalgia. But I hope that it makes you feel more than that. I hope that you get a tingling feeling, that you feel like joining in the fun of playing, imagining, building. I hope that you have felt this way while listening to this inaugural lecture: as an invitation to you to come out and play.

Translated from Dutch by Mischa Hoyinck and Robert Chesal

Mariecke van den Berg is endowed Professor of Feminism and Christianity at Radboud University in Nijmegen (Catharina Halkes Chair) and Assistant Professor of Interreligious Studies at VU Amsterdam. She studied Theology (BA) and Gender Studies (RMA) at Utrecht University and holds a PhD from the University of Twente, where she researched connections between ethnic background and informal care. She held post-doc positions at VU Amsterdam and Utrecht University, researching public debates on religion and homosexuality, and discourses on gender and religious conversion. At Atria, the Amsterdam based institute for emancipation and women's history, she conducted research on the representation of transgender people in the media. Mariecke is an editor of the international peer reviewed journal *Religion and Gender* and board member of the Dutch Society of Queer Theologians.

Akke van der Kooi and Magda Misset-van de Weg

A *Rencontre* of Women and Disciplines in Relation to Luke 1:39-56

Abstract
The birth narrative in the Gospel of Luke, and especially the so-called Visitation – the *rencontre* between Elisabeth and Mary – has found its way into the doctrines and life of the churches, into diverse cultures, in art, and into the hearts of many Christians. Through time, many aspects of the narrative received ample scholarly attention, eliciting different responses, but the scene also captivated the imagination of a multitude of artists. In our contribution, we "listen" to a number of these different voices. To a certain extent, however, we distance ourselves from traditional modes of reading, listening and analysing in order to make room for a *rencontre* between theology and art that facilitates other experiences and perceptions of the meeting in the hill country. *Rencontre* captures not only the meeting of the women in the text but also the dynamics, the dialogue, the meeting of contrasting positions and, moreover, the encounter of a Systematic theologian and a Biblical scholar. This *rencontre*, that is, our interdisciplinary approach, enlarged and deepened our observations and perceptions of the "texts", which appeared to be instrumental in unlocking other potentials and dynamics. An example of this is, on the one hand, a sharpened sensibility for the everyday life and the social situation of the women in the hill country and, on the other hand, a rethinking of the concept of revelation that honours the double impulse in the movement of revelation: the gift of God's mystery and also the creative potential in humanity to imagine God's presence.

Resumen
La narrativa del nacimiento en el Evangelio de Lucas, especialmente la así llamada visitación (el encuentro entre Isabel y María), se ha hecho un lugar en las doctrinas y la vida de las iglesias, en diversas culturas, en el arte y en el corazón de muchos cristianos y cristianas. Con el correr de los siglos, muchos aspectos de esta narrativa han recibido la atención de los estudiosos, suscitando distintas respuestas. Pero la escena también ha cautivado la imaginación de multitud de artistas. En esta contribución, queremos "escuchar" a varias de estas voces. Sin embargo, también queremos distanciarnos hasta cierto punto de la manera tradicional de leer, escuchar y analizar a fin de hacer espacio para un encuentro entre la teología y el arte que facilite otras experiencias

y percepciones del encuentro entre Isabel y María en las montañas. *Rencontre* se refiere, pues, no solo a la reunión de las mujeres en el texto bíblico, sino también a las dinámicas, el diálogo y el encuentro de posiciones opuestas; en particular, se refiere al encuentro de una teóloga sistemática y una biblista. Este *rencontre*, es decir, nuestro tratamiento interdisciplinar, ha profundizado y ensanchado nuestras observaciones y percepciones de los "textos", lo cual ha sido esencial para liberar otros potenciales y dinámicas. Un ejemplo de ello es, por un lado, una mayor sensibilidad y perspicacia hacia las condiciones cotidianas y situación social de las mujeres que se encuentran en la montaña. Por otro, un volver a pensar el concepto de revelación de tal forma que dé cuenta del doble impulso que lo anima: el don del misterio de Dios y el potencial creativo en la humanidad para imaginar la presencia de Dios.

Zusammenfassung

Die Geburtserzählung im Lukasevangelium und insbesondere die sogenannte Heimsuchung – das *rencontre* zwischen Elisabeth und Maria – beeinflusste die Lehre und das Leben der Kirchen, verschiedene Kulturen, die Kunst und die Herzen vieler Christ*innen. Im Laufe der Zeit haben viele Aspekte der Erzählung die Aufmerksamkeit der Wissenschaft erregt und unterschiedliche Reaktionen hervorgerufen; die Szene hat auch die Phantasie einer Vielzahl von Künstler*innen beflügelt. In unserem Beitrag „hören" wir eine Reihe dieser verschiedenen Stimmen. In gewissem Maße entfernen wir uns jedoch von den traditionellen Formen des Lesens, Zuhörens und Analysierens, um Raum für ein *rencontre* zwischen Theologie und Kunst zu schaffen, das andere Erfahrungen und Wahrnehmungen der Begegnung im Bergland ermöglicht. *Rencontre* umfasst nicht nur die Begegnung der Frauen im Text, sondern auch die Dynamik, den Dialog, das Aufeinandertreffen gegensätzlicher Positionen und darüber hinaus die Begegnung einer Systematischen Theologin und einer Bibelwissenschaftlerin. Dieses *rencontre*, d.h. unser interdisziplinärer Ansatz, hat unsere Beobachtungen und Wahrnehmungen der „Texte" erweitert und vertieft, was sich als nützlich erwiesen hat, um weitere Potenziale und Dynamiken freizusetzen. Einerseits zum Beispiel eine geschärfte Sensibilität für den Alltag und die soziale Situation der Frauen im Bergland, andererseits ein Überdenken des Offenbarungsbegriffs, der den doppelten Impuls in der Bewegung der Offenbarung würdigt: die Gabe des Geheimnisses Gottes und das kreative Potential der Menschheit, sich Gottes Gegenwart vorzustellen.

Keywords: The Gospel according to Luke, Mary, Elisabeth, (visual) art, revelation, *rencontre*.

Introduction

In this contribution, resulting from a *rencontre* of a Biblical Scholar and a Systematic Theologian, our focus is the birth narrative in the New Testament gospel of Luke, more specifically the so-called Visitation (Lk 1:39-56) – the *rencontre* between Elisabeth and Mary. Through time, many aspects of the narrative did, of course, receive scholarly attention, eliciting different responses. The Visitation scene did however not only find its way into Christian doctrines and life of the churches, but also into a plethora of secondary literature, into diverse cultures and captivated the imagination of a multitude of artists. In their artistic expressions, we saw different ways of re-tellings of biblical texts but also totally new interpretations. We are, of course, very much aware of the fact that artists have their own conventions, traditions and may even disconnect themselves from the text.[1] Through its openness, the text engages all human senses, and each encounter with the text can therefore be significant. The artist and the theologian read the same text, but their approach differs; they look differently, and may thus emphasise different aspects, new dimensions. In that sense, we see art as a commentary on the text. This *rencontre* between theology, biblical texts and art became the incentive for our *rencontre*, our joint approach of the narrative. This contribution also reflects the outcome of our experimental exercise in interdisciplinarity.

We were very much taken by two paintings and a video presentation of the Visitation scene and immediately saw how we might link or combine these specific perspectives with those connected with our disciplines and how that could open up new perspectives that might enrich the interpretation of the meeting of the women in the hill country.

As regards our theological orientation and/or our disciplines, we just want to position ourselves briefly. Up and until the last century, art often functioned as theology's *ancilla*, that is, art served theological argumentation. Sometimes, not always, art can however lead theology instead of the other way around. Art has something to offer that the conceptual language of theology cannot entirely incorporate: a surplus. As David Brown once stated: "Art is participation in an ongoing process of revelation", and: "Art can correct key

---

[1] On the subject, see: Barbara Baert, "The Pact between Space and Gaze: The Narrative and the Iconic in *Noli me tangere*," in: Reimund Bieringer et al. (eds.), Noli me tangere *in interdisciplinary perspective: Textual, iconographic and contemporary interpretations* (Peeters: Leuven etc. 2016), Bibliotheca Ephemeridum Theologicarum Lovaniensium 283, 191-216, here 211.

integrators of explanation of Christian tradition."[2] In our contribution, these statements will function as important guidelines. But before we start our exercise, we wish to position ourselves in line with theologians like Amos Wilder, Stanley Romaine Hopper, Catherine Keller, Roland Faber, John Caputo and Richard Kearney, who propagate in their new style of "doing theology"[3] a renewed engagement with the "little things" of everyday life, which they, consequently, consider to be an essential part of the divine. They are in pursuit of a theology beyond the bloodless abstractions of frozen doctrines, a theology well-founded on biblical literature, a theology offering perspectives to act, a theology that recognises that the truth of the Christian religion can only be grasped when reason and imagination are both operative.[4]

In part 1, New Testament Scholar Magda Misset-van de Weg revisits the Lukan text by focussing on the 16th-century Florentine painter Jacopo da Pontormo's presentation of the Greeting and Bill Viola's refiguring of this painting, with the objective to see, hear and experience their take on the narrative. Following from this, she highlights the aspects of time and space, hope and joy in the narrative.

---

[2] Brown made these statements during the yearly conference of the American Academy of Religion in 2011. Cf. also: David Brown, *Tradition and Imagination: Revelation and Change* (Oxford University Press: Oxford 1999) and David Brown, *Discipleship and Imagination: Christian Tradition and Truth* (Oxford University Press: Oxford 2000). See also the contributions of "The Society of the Arts in Religious and Theological Studies" [SARTS] and the projects of "The Centre for Arts and the Sacred," King's College, as well as the activities of the "Institute for Theology, Imagination and the Arts in the University of St Andrews".

[3] See for example: Amos N. Wilder, *Theopoetic: Theology and the Religious Imagination* (Fortress Press: Minneapolis 1976), The Amos Wilder Library; David L. Miller, "Introduction" to Stanley R. Hopper, *Why Persimmons? And Other Poems: Transformations of Theology in Poetry* (Scholars Press: Atlanta 1987), Scholars Press Studies in the Humanities Series; Richard Kearney, *Poetics of Imagining: Modern to Postmodern* (Fordham University Press: New York 1998); John D. Caputo and Catherine Keller, "Theopoetic/Theopolitic", in: *Cross Currents* 56/4 (2006-2007), 105-111; L.B.C. Keefe-Perry, "Theopoetics: Process and Perspective", in: *Christianity and Literature* 58/4 (summer 2009), 579-601; Malcolm Guite, *Faith, Hope and Poetry: Theology and the Poetic Imagination* (Ashgate Publishing: Farnham 2010), Ashgate Studies in Theology, Imagination and the Arts; Trevor Hart, *Between the Image and the Word: Theological Engagements with Imagination, Language and Literature* (Ashgate Publishing: Farnham 2013), Ashgate Studies in Theology, Imagination and the Arts.

[4] Cf. Erik Borgman, "Openbaring als poëzie", in: *Tijdschrift voor Theologie. Themanummer Kunst, Theologie en Openbaring* 54/1 (2014), 59-63. Cf. Hart, *Between the Image and the Word*, 142-143.

In part 2, Systematic Theologian Akke van der Kooi dwells on an example of medieval ecclesial art: an image of the Visitation by the Florentine painter Mariotto Albertinelli (1503). Through her reflection on the painting and in connection with the Lukan narrative, she attempts to deepen the traditional understanding of *revelation*, one of the key concepts of Christian doctrine. In what sense can we benefit from religious perceptions represented in art forms for our understanding of "revelation"? What is their "revelatory" aspect?

Part I
Successive Contexts of Reading and Visual Exegesis

Reading is, apart from pure pleasure, an act of interpreting that is per se a subjective and partial act. But read we must, because the biblical text cannot read itself, we have to read it. Nowadays, in our increasingly interconnected world, we can also profit from a great variety of reading perspectives. Subsequently, we, as readers, through various kinds of discursive strategies, will add our interpretations. Among the "we" as readers, I count artists who, in their own specific way, inspired by their historical contexts – including the history of interpretation of Scripture –, "read" texts, translate, actualise and concretise their reading into a poem, a painting, a statue, a film, a video, et cetera. Their expressions constitute a specific form of *Nachleben* of the biblical texts that often triggers, for example, the poetical side thereof, which, in turn, may inspire theologically modulated exegesis. In my view, such a trajectory of visualisation, or visualising the effect of the text through image, can indeed be an important and inspiring form of exegesis.[5] Visual exegesis may open up different, new, sometimes surprising or inspiring, provocative or extra-ordinary horizons and dynamics in the texts.[6] It can enrich one's understanding of

---

[5] Cf. Heidi J. Hornik and Mikeal C. Parsons, *Illuminating Luke: The Passion and Resurrection Narratives in Italian Renaissance and Baroque Painting* (T&T Clark: New York and London 2008), 8. Hornik and Parsons add that discursive strategies are, of course, intertwined with the social, political, and religious contexts as well as with the sources and precedents at the disposal of interpreters of every kind. Iconography in their work is therefore understood as part of the actualization process of visual exegesis.

[6] Recently, Christopher J. Nygren introduced the term "Graphic Exegesis" as an alternative to visual exegesis. See his article "Graphic Exegesis: Reflections on the Difficulty of Talking about Biblical Images, Pictures, and Texts", in: Vernon K. Robbins et al. (eds.), *The Art of*

biblical texts, feed one's interpretation[7] or shape one's contemporary reading, actualisation and even implementation of Scripture.[8]

Making the choice to use visual narrative as a source of (religious) interpretation and therefore to observe, listen, and work with visual interactions between art and biblical texts, sharpened my focus, sometimes set my mind wandering in different directions and thus opened my eyes for different textual elements. In the end, this approach resulted in a sharpened sensibility for the everyday life of the women in the hill country.[9] I shall now present the specific readings, or the visual exegesis of the Visitation scene in Luke by two artists.

Going "Beyond the Surface": Pontormo's and Viola's Re-presentation of the Visitation

An inspiring representation of Lk 1:39-56 is the beautiful painting created by Jacopo da Pontormo, the 16th-century Florentine painter and pupil of Mariotto Albertinelli, who will be extensively introduced in Part II of this article. Pontormo's re-presentation of the Greeting has been designated as one of the most formidable paintings of that time, and Pontormo's work as an outstanding symbol of everything the style called Mannerism stood for.[10] Mannerism can, in a nutshell, be described as "mannered" in that it emphasised complexity and virtuosity over naturalistic representation. The adherents generally favoured compositional tension and instability rather than the balance and clarity of earlier Renaissance painting.[11]

Visual Exegesis: Rhetoric, Texts, Images (Society of Biblical Literature: Atlanta 2017), Emory Studies in Early Christianity, 271-302.

[7] Or, as Anthony Thistleton concludes: "Wrestling with *Wirkungsgeschichte* or reception history opens the door to exegesis as explication: an explication that permits us to see dimensions of meaning that successive contexts of reading bring into sharper focus for our attention." Thus quoted in Hornik and Parsons, *Illuminating Luke*, 9.

[8] See, e.g., Wim Weren and Caroline Vander Stichele, "Dood in de Bijbel en de moderne kunsten", in: *Tijdschrift voor Theologie* 52/2 (2012), 105-106.

[9] For visual narrative as an entrance to everyday religious practices, I have been inspired by and made use of: Maaike de Haardt, "Visual Narratives: Entrance to Everyday Religious Practices", in: R. Ganzevoort et al. (eds.), *Religious Stories We Live By: Narrative Approaches in Theology and Religious Studies* (Brill: Leiden 2013) Studies in Religion and Theology 19, 209-217.

[10] The painting has recently been restored and can be admired in the church S. Michele at Carmignano.

[11] The term "Mannerism" is derived from the Italian *maniera*, used by 16th-century artist and biographer Giorgio Vasari. "Mannerism refers to the movement in the visual arts that spread through much of Europe between the High Renaissance and Baroque periods. It originated in Italy, where it lasted from about 1520 to 1600 [...] By the mid-sixteenth century, the influence

Pontormo used perspective in a completely innovative way, and some of his trademarks are: the entwining of figures, gestures and movement, and violent contrasts of colour. The women in the foreground, who form a diamond shape, stand out, which tells us that we are to focus on them, not on the figures in the background: they are just watching, like I do. The viewer is guided towards focussing on the serenity and beauty of the faces of the two women in the front, but also on their colourful clothing, or better drapery, which speaks a "floating language" of its own and makes the women almost defying gravity. Pontormo thus *re*-presents this special event in the Lukan story, interprets, shapes, contextualises, dramatises et cetera, and, in fact, presents his own narrative. I leave this beautiful painting to speak for itself because the main reason for drawing attention to it here is that Pontormo's re-presentation of the Greeting has functioned as an intermediate step, an interpretative filter between the Lukan narrative and the 20th-century visualisation thereof in the video-installation made by the American artist Bill Viola (Flushing, New York 1951).

Viola, as an artist, makes use of contemporary technology for his fascinating video installations. When he was six years old, he fell into a lake all the way to the bottom, to a place that seemed to him like paradise. This event never left his mind. It shimmers under the surface of his works and re-emerges in his dictum "There is more than just the surface of life. The real thing is under the surface."[12] He discovered video in 1969 and is said to be the inventor of video art. Whether or not that is the case, he creates visual poems that deal with questions of the human condition in an entirely new way – especially by steering the visitors to submerge and be drawn into his "poem", or into a sense-making dimension.

Initially, *The Greeting* was part of Viola's contribution at the Venetian Biennale in 1995. It can now be experienced in the museum De Pont in Tilburg in the Netherlands, where a totally dark room is reserved for the video.[13]

---

of Mannerism had spread far beyond Florence." Important representatives of the movement were Parmigianino (1503-1540), the Venetian artist Jacopo Tintoretto (1519-1594), Jacopo da Pontormo, some of the works by El Greco and the sculptor B. Cellini, et cetera. This information was found in and quoted from: Ross Finocchio, "Mannerism: Bronzino (1503-1572) and his Contemporaries", in: *Heilbrunn Timeline of Art History* (The Metropolitan Museum of Art: New York 2000). (http://www.metmuseum.org/toah/hd/zino/hd_zino.htm, November 2015)

[12] Cf. the interview "Bill Viola: Cameras are Soulkeepers", *Louisiana Channel*, Published 18 April 2013.

[13] More information can be found on the website of the Museum: http://www.depont.nl/collectie/kunstenaar/viola/the-greetin/.

Bill Viola, *The Greeting*, 1995, foto/photo Kira Perov,
Collection De Pont Museum, Tilburg.

The projection is dramatised in a masterly way, precisely through the isolation from the outside, the size – an entire wall – and also through the extreme slow motion: Viola did slow down the original take of 45 seconds to 10 minutes. All of that is intensified by an initially rustling sound of the wind that gradually swells into a kind of roar.

Such elements as the diamond shape of the three figures, the fluttering drapery of the women, the bright colours, the shadowy/vague figures as well as the renaissance architecture of the gate in the background show that Viola was not only inspired by, but almost incorporated Pontormo's work. Nevertheless,

Jacopo Pontormo, *Visitazione* (1528-1529).
Courtesy of the parish of San Michele Arcangelo, Carmignano.

Viola's contextualised version of Pontormo's interpretation of the Lukan text does become Viola's story, with an evident narrative structure of its own, in which in particular space, time and action are actuated.[14]

One aspect that caught my eye is the contextualisation of the women. Just as the people in Pontormo's time may have recognised the women as contemporary to them, so do I see women I know and want to know more about. I am attracted

---
[14] Cf. Michael Rush, *New Media in Late 20th Century Art* (Thames and Hudson: London 1999), 107-111.

by the vivid colours and the movement of their dresses, but most of all by the joy the two women in the front radiate. This is, in a way, accentuated by the third woman, who when "Mary" arrives, moves to the background.[15] The colours of her dress are grey and blue, which fits her mostly non-descript rather pale face. With a view to Lk 1, one might consider whether she embodies the Spirit. I do, however, rather hear the Spirit (*ruach*) in the sound of the wind that increases at the moment of the *rencontre* of the other two women. The third woman might also embody all those who are excluded in the Lukan story, where the meeting takes place in an exclusive time and space. The outsiders have to stand back and can only try to imagine and envision the invisible which is, as has been pointed out by Martin Buber, present when two persons meet. A real *rencontre* "is 'pregnant' with new life and of another order than can be observed."[16]

This made me realise that the installation or any art form does indeed sharpen my senses and understanding, but at the same time conceals, as do texts for that matter. Viewers and/or readers are challenged to be open to conflicting realities in language and images, or to realities under the surface of text and image, and to discover overlooked meanings or meanings that resist traditional interpretations! For example: The harmony between the two women, supported by the colours and the sound, is beautifully and graphically shown in the video, but may also be said to cover up social reality that should also be seen and voices that should also be heard in the Lukan texts. I shall expand on this after having stepped back to Luke's narrative. For, in order to be able to account for identifying either a surplus, or resistance, I need to at least provide an impression of Lk 1:39-56 and its immediate literary context.

Lk 1:39-56 Revisited

Luke, as a responsible writer, situates himself (1:1-4) and introduces in his first chapter the main characters, important others and themes that are constitutive for his narrative. As J. Drury writes: "Every episode in his prologue is planted with the seeds of episodes to come and rings with the poetry of prophets and psalms."[17] Some of those "seeds" that, in my view, are important for

---

[15] Viola replaces the two accompanying women in Pontormo's painting by this one woman.
[16] Cf. "Annunciatie en visitatie: Lucas 1", in: Marcel Barnard and Gerda van de Haar (eds.), *De Bijbel cultureel: De Bijbel in de kunsten van de twintigste eeuw* (Meinema/Pelckmans: Zoetermeer/Kapellen 2009), 338-340, here 340.
[17] Cf. John Drury, "Luke", in: Robert Alter and Frank Kermode (eds.), *The Literary Guide to the Bible* (The Belknap Press: Cambridge, MA 2002), 418-439, esp. 419.

understanding Luke's story because they structure his narrative are time, space, images of the Divine and joy.

First, I want to highlight the importance of the aspect *time* in Lk 1 and 2. Time resounds in the verb πληροφορέω ("fulfil") in Lk 1:1 and a little later in the theme "waiting" and "expecting." Throughout his Gospel, Luke expands on πληροφορέω, emphasising that fulfilment of the promises voiced by the prophets determines time and history.[18] For Luke, Jesus is the last one in the line of the prophets and, as such, he is the centre of time: he not only fulfils the time of the prophets but also heralds a new era or messianic times (1:13-20 and especially 32-33). Luke seems to be acutely aware of the given that history did neither begin nor ends with his Gospel. History flows from the Jewish past towards the Christian future, so that this centre of time creates room for hope, even if only for a little while. Apart from the prophetic and messianic times, at least three other intertwined timelines can be discerned in Lk 1 and 2:

– Political/historical time – it all happens "in the days of King Herod of Judea" (1:5), the Governor Quirinius and the Emperor Augustus (2:1.2).[19]
– Biological/individual time, connected with a ticking biological clock (Elisabeth and Zechariah, cf.1:7.18: "For I am an old man and my wife is getting on in years"), fatherhood and male descendants.
– Religious/cultic time – for example, the rhythm of male priesthood (1:8.11.21.23).

There is yet another timeline – and now I go into the submerging mode – that comes to the fore when, all of a sudden, the prophetic/messianic sphere and space are interrupted and a new phase is inserted, distinguished by a gynocentric time rhythm that unfolds within a gynocentric space.[20] It comes to the foreground when Luke starts to relate how in the sixth month of Elisabeth's pregnancy, Mary rushes through the hills to the city in Judea to see her cousin Elisabeth who has isolated herself.[21] Joseph and Zechariah then disappear from

---

[18] Cf. Drury, "Luke", 419.
[19] Whether or not this concerns what we would classify as historically accurate data is a discussion that is known to me, but not of importance here. That this aspect of time is to be classified as "gendered time" seems obvious as time is measured by the actions of political rulers.
[20] Interruption also comes to the fore in several related instances, such as: infertility and priestly service.
[21] It is strange and unheard of that a young woman would rush of into the mountains without an escort, but apparently a side lane the audience is not supposed to go into. The same applies to

the stage – their time and space are suspended (maybe "taken over"), and they remain outside the picture until the sons are born. The divine mystery of the pregnancy thus happens in a time and space reserved for the mothers. Priests and men are excluded, which is a mystery in itself![22]

Refiguring Time and Space and the Dawning of Hope

But there is more that comes to the surface in Luke's remarkable change of narrative space. Through addressing his "account" to the most excellent Theophilus, he initially situates his story in the sphere of elite men. However, almost immediately, Luke interrupts that sphere by staging two women in a rather rebellious, revolutionary sphere, who proclaim that God shall bring down the powerful from their thrones;[23] social and political relations are turned upside down, to the point that a new world order without dominion and submission, without shortage, is dawning. Within that space, occupied by two pregnant (!) women only, hope seems to take possession of time and space, prophecies are fulfilled, the messianic time has come.[24]

---

the question why Elisabeth chose her isolation. Solutions have been suggested, varying from a literary ploy because Elisabeth's pregnancy needed to be revealed to Mary, to an example of the honour/shame pattern, "shame avoids sight", and references to Jewish mysticism. See Luzia Sutter Rehman, "Der Glanz der Schekhinah und die Verhüllung Elisabets (Lukas 1,24)", in: *Lectio Difficilior* 1 (2005) (http://www.lectio.unibe.ch). As far as I am concerned, the matter remains unsolved.

[22] Even though I do not work with films in this contribution, I would like to mention that films like *Je vous salue Marie*, *Nostalghia*, *l'Annonce faite à Marie* dramatise that the divine mystery of the pregnancy happens in a time and space reserved for mothers. Priests and other men are excluded. Cf. Barnard and Van der Haar (eds.), *De Bijbel cultureel*, 344-346. Luke does indeed provide ample space for it by isolating the meeting between Mary and Elisabeth.

[23] Cf. Brigitte Kahl, "Reading Luke Against Luke: Non-Uniformity of Text, Hermeneutics of Conspiracy and the 'Scriptural Principle' in Luke 1", in: Amy-Jill Levine with Marianne Blickenstaff (eds.), *A Feminist Companion to Luke* (Bloomsbury T&T Clark: London and New York 2002), Feminist Companion to the New Testament and Early Christian Writings 3, 70-88, esp. 75.

[24] Cf. Kahl, "Reading Luke against Luke", 79-80 and Drury, "Luke", 421. In the way Luke interweaves space, and the diverse moments in time, interrupts time, hints at a critical moment of a radically different time that interrupts human/chronological/cultic time, all of which rather fits the category of poetic time and space, that is, a time that is not concerned with verification but with manifestation, a time within a discourse that offers a frame of linguistic reference other than the normal descriptive/referential function. Cf. Rowan Williams, *On Christian Theology: Challenges in Contemporary Theology* (Blackwell Publishers Ltd.: Oxford and Malden 2000), Challenges in Contemporary Theology, 133-134. The amazing fact that "only" two women share the powerful hymn could thus be understood and placed in the same poetic frame.

Hopeful words are beautiful, but alas, sometimes too good to be "true." Entering a textual world with different eyes also results in seeing that the extraordinary unfolds within the ordinary. Aspects of reality, patriarchal structures, gender patterns are not overturned; social and moral codes are not interrupted or disrupted but affirmed. This concerns such conventional ideas as, for example, bearing children as the cause of a woman's life, or that it is, of course, not Zechariah but Elisabeth who is not fertile and therefore needs God's mercy (1:57), and that it is nevertheless Zechariah's prayer that is heard and that *he* will have a son. Apart from the fact that, historically speaking, all of this is not so amazing, it is obvious that Luke in his Gospel rather emphasises that women in the Jesus movement behave themselves in conformity with predominant, Hellenistic moral visions and standards.[25] Besides, Luke simply did not write a story about or for women. Which is good, notes Loveday Alexander, because defining a narrative as a woman's story is "to risk confining it to the ghetto: 'women's stories', notoriously, are felt to have nothing to teach men."[26] This does not mean that Luke should thus be released from androcentrism or that there is no room for other perspectives. On the contrary, under the surface of Luke's polyphone text, contrapuntal voices can be heard that a feminist-critical "counter-reading" might bring to the surface.[27] So what then could such a reading yield?

A Feminist-Critical "Counter-Reading"

I shall try and illustrate this by distancing myself for a moment from the idealised images and, instead, looking with realistic eyes at this meeting of two women in her time and circumstances. I then see a meeting between an older

---

[25] See Mary Rose D'Angelo, "The ANHP Question in Luke-Acts: Imperial Masculinity and the Deployment of Women in the Early Second Century", in: Levine with Blickenstaff (eds.), *A Feminist Companion to Luke*, 44-69.

[26] Loveday C. Alexander, "Sisters in Adversity: Retelling Martha's Story", in: Levine and Blickenstaff (eds.), *A Feminist Companion to Luke*, 197-213, esp. 213. According to Adele Reinhartz, Luke is in his narratives not addressing women only but deepening the theological insights of all of his hearers and readers. That especially women may have identified with the narratives featuring women is another matter. See Adele Reinhartz, "From Narrative to History", in: Amy-Jill Levine (ed.), *Women Like This: New Perspectives on Jewish Women in the Greco-Roman World* (Society of Biblical Literature: Atlanta 1991), Society of Biblical Literature Early Judaism and its Literature, 1, 161-184, esp. 171 and 184.

[27] A contrapuntal voice is a voice that does not seem to fit with the genre/image. For a further explanation, see Kahl, "Reading Luke Against Luke", 70-88, and Turid Karlsen Seim, "The Gospel of Luke", in: E. Schüssler Fiorenza (ed.), *Searching the Scriptures* (SCM Press, New York 1993), II: *A Feminist Commentary*, 728-762, esp. 727.

woman and a girl: παρθένος as a social category, in combination with betrothal, indicates a girl of 13/14 years of age. From a narrative and symbolical angle, this yields an interesting contrast between Elisabeth and Mary: the contrast between infertility and virginity. A "reality check", however, reveals that there is also a decisive difference between the infertility of a married woman who is supposed to be capable of bearing children and the virginal status of a young betrothed girl whose purity ought to be untouched. Being childless means sorrow and shame for the married woman, which can only be taken away by pregnancy. The opposite is true for a virgin.[28] Mary's position implies a situation in which pregnancy means neither happiness nor safety because an extramarital pregnancy was considered to be a disgrace and an infringement of the law. Hence Mary's story is a confrontation with the conventional patriarchal values that Elisabeth's story affirms. Elisabeth's praises when she meets her cousin reflect the values of her story and Mary's words in the *Magnificat* that God has looked with favour on her, reflects her story.[29]

Yet, the meeting between these two women is, after all, a special event. A beautiful hymn is sung that has always drawn attention, and rightfully so. But, from another perspective, we might also stop at and catch a glimpse of the social-cultural practice in which women stand by women, for instance through pregnancy and birth. Seen from this viewpoint, there is much more to Mary's visit to Elisabeth than the prenatal meeting of John with Jesus. These women may have needed each other badly. The unwed mother and the woman of age may have needed and exchanged understanding, acceptance, moral support, comfort, relatedness, and also physical help.

Interestingly enough, there is one moment in Viola's video where this is, as it were, hinted at. When the women embrace, the silence is broken in the sense that Mary whispers: "Can you help me, I need to talk to you right away."

---

[28] See also Turid Karlsen Seim, "The Virgin Mother: Mary and Ascetic Discipleship in Luke", in: Levine and Blickenstaff (eds.), *A Feminist Companion to Luke*, 89-105, here 100.

[29] God's concern for the degraded and humiliated is a Lukan theme. That Mary is presented as a "servant" could however place her in the sphere of submission and acceptance of female inferiority, dependency and helplessness. On the other hand, "servant of God" was used as a honorary title and applied to outstanding men in the history of Israel (Moses, Joshua, Abraham, Jacob, Isaac, David, the prophets). Cf. Jane Schaberg, "Luke", in: Carol A. Newsom and Sharon H. Ringe (eds.), *The Women's Bible Commentary* (SPCK: London 1992), 284. Schaberg also points out that the *Magnificat* "was probably written in the circles of the Jewish Christian '*anawim*' ('poor' in a spiritual and often literal sense)." Mary represents their hope.

Sharing Joy

I now return to the important and structural aspect of joy in Luke's Gospel, which Viola's interpretation accentuates. In her most interesting study *Die Freude im Lukasevangelium*, Anke Inselmann puts flesh on the bones of "text-psychological exegesis" and applies it to the theme of "joy" in Luke.[30] She argues that precisely the affect of joy is a supporting theme in the Third Gospel. It is an ideal implying that it cannot be experienced in isolation because an important characteristic of joy is precisely that it is an emotion that needs to be shared.[31] Refusal to do so paves the way to hell: witness the refusal of the rich man to share his joy with the poor Lazarus (Lk 16:19-31),[32] which could illustrate that and how joy is tied up with ethics.

Mary's motivation to go and see Elisabeth could thus be connected with the wish to share the joy and hope that is also voiced in the Magnificat. In any case, the scene of the greeting connects the meeting with joy. Interestingly, the child in Elisabeth hears and reacts to the greeting by leaping [ἐσκίρτησεν τὸ βρέφος ἐν τῇ κοιλίᾳ – the child in the womb leapt], but it is Elisabeth who later interprets this as leaping for joy [ἐσκίρτησεν ἐν ἀγαλλιάσει τὸ βρέφος ἐν τῇ κοιλίᾳ μου – the child in my womb leapt for joy] (1:44). According to Inselmann, σκιρτάω ("leap, spring about as a sign of joy") demonstrates descriptively the dynamic aspect of the joy, while ἐν ἀγαλλιάσει expresses the joy explicitly.[33]

The theme of joy so attractively visualised by Bill Viola and developed by Inselmann is one of the structural elements of the Gospel of Luke. Joy surfaces especially in the first two chapters, but also in other "joyous passages", which, by the way, often belong to the so-called Lukan *Sondergut*, like the parables about what seems to be lost (Lk 15). It is a thematic aspect of the Beatitudes (Lk 6:20-23) and features at the end of this Gospel (Lk 24:52),[34] so that one can safely conclude that joy does indeed play a role from beginning to end.

As mentioned earlier, joy has a predominantly communal character that implies social orientation and focus – at least for those who let themselves be convinced by the message this Gospel proclaims. The affect-side, experiencing

---

[30] Anke Inselmann, *Die Freude im Lukasevangelium: Ein Beitrag zur psychologischen Exegese* (Mohr Siebeck: Tübingen 2012), Wissenschaftliche Untersuchungen zum Neuen Testament 2. Reihe, 322.
[31] Συγχαίρω ("feel joy with") in Lk 1:58 and 15:6,9 seems to highlight this.
[32] Inselmann, *Die Freude*, 175, n. 89.
[33] Inselmann, *Die Freude*, 176-177.
[34] "And they worshiped him, and returned to Jerusalem with great joy."

joy, and the effect-side, sharing joy, belong together – as is highlighted by Mary in the *Magnificat*. Inselmann concludes by emphasising that joy in Luke constitutes a carefully thought through theological and missionary program. It reflects the Lukan inner motivation to accept, live and pass on the Christian faith. Moreover, joy, both as an inner attitude and an expression of faith is in this Gospel not only a desideratum, but also emphatically demanded.[35]

To Conclude
How and in what sense then did the painting and the video installation sharpen my focus, which textual elements were opened up, surfaced, and thus led to observations in the sphere of real lives.

The art forms made me see two women almost escaping me because they seem to float, to defy gravity, to belong to another world. That which they seem to share, and the invisible presence they share, makes them intangible. Ironically, in a way, this confirms the mental picture of Luke's narrative I used to have. But, the artistic interpretations, together with re-reading the text of Lk 1, opened up another vista. The bright colours of the women's dresses, the intense expectant expression on their faces, the joy they radiate, the way they hold each other in both representations, and all of this against a vague background, made me see strong, targeted women, happy to see and support each other. It was precisely this that made me wonder about their real lives, about the dynamics behind the actual support they may have needed, about the social-cultural situation of an unwed mother and the aged woman, relegating them to the margins of their society. In the end, I imagined how they managed because they cared, respected and supported each other. I believe this to be the main message that surfaced and that I retain from my experiment with art and biblical texts.

Part II
Systematic Theology and Religious Art

What does a perspective activated by visual exegesis imply when it becomes the point of departure in the conversation of a Systematic theologian with a Biblical scholar about the narrative of the Visitation? Actually, the visual

---

[35] Inselmann, *Die Freude*, 425-426.

exegesis of the narrative stimulated the Biblical scholar to re-think the structural elements in the Gospel of Luke so that, consequently, the Systematic theologian does feel invited to re-think key concepts in Christian doctrine. In order to highlight this, I shall in the course of my reflection involve my readers in my experience vis-à-vis the image of the Visitation made by the Florentine painter Mariotto Albertinelli (1503), a teacher of the above mentioned Pontormo. Albertinelli's masterpiece, an example of traditional ecclesial art, is on display in the Uffizi in Florence, where I stood before it, overwhelmed by its beauty.

The nature of the relation between theology and arts is for me, precisely because I am a Systematic theologian, an essential point of interest. I want to dwell on this for a moment and wonder how art can affect theology when she sheds her *ancilla* function. And, challenged by David Brown's statement mentioned above that "art is participation in an ongoing revelation" and that art is "revelatory", makes me question what, in that case, the scope of the term "revelatory" might be.

As regards the latter, we all know that "revelation" is a traditional theological concept of Christian doctrine and that a great many books have been written on the subject.[36] In the past century it became a key concept in both catholic and protestant theology. The Roman Catholic theologian Karl Rahner (1904-1984) developed an anthropologically based theory of revelation in which this concept is not only understood in a propositional but rather in a personal and relational sense. In Rahner's view, "revelation" does not mean receiving particular information about God, captured in propositions, but he sees it as an invitation to be open to God as the living mystery turned towards and gratuitously sharing the divine with humanity.[37] This sharing in turn evokes in humanity the creative potential to imagine God's presence. Connecting

---

[36] For a study on, in particular, the meaning of "revelation" in modern theology, see Peter Eicher, *Offenbarung: Prinzip neuzeitlicher Theologie* (Kösel-Verlag: München 1977). See also Avery Dulles, *Models of Revelation* (Orbis Books: Maryknoll, NY ²1992). On the keyword "Revelation", see Alan Richardson and John Bowden (eds.), *A New Dictionary of Christian Theology* (SCM Press: London 1983), 503-506.

[37] See Chapter 3, "Divine Revelation and Human Perception", in: Richard Viladesau, *Theological Aesthetics: God in Imagination, Beauty, and Art* (Oxford University Press: New York and Oxford 1999), 73-101, esp. 91-96. On Rahner see also: Birgitta Kleinschwärzer-Meister, "Karl Rahner: Gnade als Mitte menschlicher Existenz", in: Peter Neuner and Gunther Wenz (eds.), *Theologen des 20. Jahrhunderts. Eine Einführung* (Wissenschaftliche Buchgesellschaft: Darmstadt 2002), 157-173.

Systematic theology and religious art may then lead to theological aesthetics that formulates anthropological prerequisites for the reception of revelation through sensory perception.[38]

Thus, "revelation" is a term that does not only tell us something about the divine mystery but also about human perception and interpretation. "Revelation", in the broadest sense, contains more than the gift of God's mystery: it encompasses the interpretation thereof in the faith community, acknowledgement of its meaning in a wide variety of circumstances, and the expression thereof in the arts and in certain ways of living.[39] In this regard, revelation is endless. The mystery remains.[40] And so does the touch of that mystery in humans' lives.

In line with Rahner and other thinkers – as, for example, Paul Tillich – about revelation as an encounter,[41] one does find in recent theological discourse initiatives to a re-thinking of this concept which respects the event-character of revelation of God's mystery in its lasting hiddenness. Unlike a theology that understands revelation as an instruction about a state of affairs,[42] we find in a relational understanding of revelation the awareness that when rational thinking about the divine mystery reaches a limit, we have to "attend to what is revealed." That is what, for instance, Karmen MacKendrick is underlining in her book *Divine Enticement*: the openness of listening belongs to epistemology.[43] "We make," MacKendrick writes, "we even are, here in our flesh, the space of revelation – endless revelation, not

---

[38] Cf. Viladesau, *Theological Aesthetics*, 97.
[39] Cf. Viladesau, *Theological Aesthetics*, 172-173. See also Trevor Hart who, with reference to Paul Fiddes, makes mention of a double impulse in the movement of revelation: "*from* Mystery to us" and "from the side of human reflection *towards* Mystery." This movement takes place "in numerous forms" and "all necessarily highly imaginative." Hart, *Between the Image and the Word*, 143 (italics Hart).
[40] This point is developed further in relation to feminist theological reflection by Elizabeth Johnson in her book *She Who Is*. With Rahner, Johnson states: "Revelation is [...] the history of the deepening perception of God *as* the mystery." Elizabeth A. Johnson, *She Who Is: The Mystery of God in Feminist Theological Discourse* (Crossroad Publishing: New York 1993), 105 (italics Johnson).
[41] Paul Tillich speaks in his *Systematic Theology* about revelation as "always a subjective and an objective event in strict interdependence." Paul Tillich, *Systematic Theology* (University of Chicago Press: Chicago 1951) 1, 111.
[42] Cf. Klaus von Stosch, *Einführung in die Systematische Theologie* (Verlag Ferdinand Schöningh: Paderborn 2006), 80.
[43] Cf. Karmen MacKendrick, *Divine Enticement: Theological Seductions* (Fordham University Press: New York 2013), 60.

some final truth to be found by tearing away the mysterious."[44] Is this not that which precisely became clear in the above visual exegesis of the Lukan text about the Visitation? The "space of revelation" of divine mystery is already there, in that narrative, before the birth of Jesus and in everything this birth will disclose about the divine. Therefore, one should not overlook what is happening here in this narrative of the Visitation, that is, finding oneself in a space of revelation.

A deepening of the understanding of this "space of revelation" I found in Magdalene Frettlöh's book *Theologie des Segens*. With reference to Lk 1:42, Frettlöh points out that Elisabeth is greeting the pregnant Maria with an explicit blessing: "Blessed are you among women, and blessed is the fruit of your womb." Pointing to the Old Testament connection of this text, Frettlöh says: "Hier deutet sich bereits an, dass der – schon prenatal – Gesegnete zum Segen für andere werden wird."[45] However, that the very meeting of the two women can be understood as revelatory, because in their approaching and listening to each other the divine mystery is illuminated, is not discussed. It is precisely the work of art that can point out here something that thinking does not reach. Below I come back to this in my encounter with the painting of the Visitation by Mariotto Albertinelli.

In her discussion of the theme of revelation and women's experience, Elizabeth Johnson asks for an emancipatory speech that values the experience of women as a central and compelling motif of revelation: "the story of salvation is told from a male point of view, while the creative reflection and participation of women is neglected or marginalised, most often restricted to the one important function of bringing forth sons for the men who are the bearers of promise."[46] In her critical conversation with classical theology, she reminds her readers that we are participating in God and, therefore, there are clues of the divine in our situation. Revelation is a given in women's experiences. That means that the divine mystery can be articulated in the light of women's dignity. The French philosopher Paul Ricoeur once argued in a profound essay on "The hermeneutic of the Idea of Revelation" that texts or images are revelatory, not in a descriptive sense but because they offer a "display" of a

---

[44] MacKendrick, *Divine Enticement*, 61.
[45] Magdalene L. Frettlöh, *Theologie des Segens: Biblische und dogmatische Wahrnehmungen* (Gütersloher Verlagshaus: Gütersloh ⁵1998), 322.
[46] Johnson, *She Who Is*, 76.

"possible world."⁴⁷ In the words of Rowan Williams: a text or an image is "revelatory" if they open up a reality, "a reality in which my human reality can also find itself; and in inviting me to its world, the text breaks open and extends my own possibilities."⁴⁸ And, "It manifests an initiative that is not ours inviting us to a world we did not make."⁴⁹ The revelatory moments in texts and images, such as those in Lk 1, tell us that we are rooted in the world into which God is inviting us. In such an approach, revelation, instead of being understood as propositional truth, underlines what is *generative* in our experiences and life events, breaking down existing frames of reference or opening up other possible ways of being human.⁵⁰ Thus, following Ricoeur and Williams, I understand a biblical statement like "God reveals himself" as a reference to the advent of newness in human life.⁵¹ Could this then be the way to look at Albertinelli's painting?

A few years ago, a Dutch theological journal published a special issue in which theologians and philosophers discussed the coherence between art, theology and revelation. They observed, among other things, that works of art that do not explicitly count as religious art nonetheless can and do feature typical elements, such as style, colour or forms, which allow the onlooker to experience that work of art as religious. The religious characteristics make the spirituality of the work tangible, and this spirituality symbolically makes sense of everyday reality. Besides, sometimes and whether or not in a concealed manner, artists draw on well-known works from the history of Christian art. An example of this is Andy Warhol's "Last Supper", which is connected with Da Vinci's "Last Supper."

The question that concerned the authors of the journal the most regards the place of revelation mediated by the arts and how this might be understood. By "revelation", they mean "a transcending movement",⁵² finding openings,

---

[47] Paul Ricoeur, "Toward a Hermeneutic of the Idea of Revelation," in: Paul Ricoeur, *Essays on Biblical Interpretation*, edited with an introduction by Lewis S. Mudge (Fortress Press: Philadelphia 1980), 73-118; Cf. Williams, *On Christian Theology*, 133.
[48] Ricoeur, "Toward a Hermeneutic of the Idea of Revelation", 1-37.
[49] Ricoeur, "Toward a Hermeneutic of the Idea of Revelation", 109.
[50] Cf. Williams, *On Christian Theology*, 134.
[51] Williams, *On Christian Theology*, 145.
[52] Martien E. Brinkman, *Jezus incognito: De verborgen Christus in de westerse kunst vanaf 1960* (Boekencentrum: Zoetermeer 2012), 215, cited by Wessel Stoker, *Tijdschrift voor Theologie* 54 (2014), 81.

"promises of meaning in a world of displacement."[53] Erik Borgman, for instance, refers to John Henry Newman, who considered religion in general and Christianity in particular to be both revelatory and poetical. Borgman sees here a possibility to re-form theology and to take the discipline beyond the fixation on intellectual values, in search of the revelatory light of the Christian religion: "It is necessary" – he says – "to re-invent Dogmatic or Systematic theology, in such a manner that the reality in which we live and the history we share open up as places of revelation."[54] Borgman also states, referring again to Newman, that Christian religion as revelatory takes us to a new world – a world of overwhelming importance. Treasures are hidden in the world we share. And, he argues, "The revelatory meaning of the lives of the faithful might be that the world as she is, does not reflect what they in their faith are."[55] Texts and religious forms of art can help us to let ourselves be re-imagined as image of God – *imago Dei*.

About Mariotto Albertinelli (1474-1515)

I now return to the room in the Uffizi with Albertinelli's painting of the Visitation. I put my luggage down so that I can clear my mind and be as receptive as possible.

First of all, I want to identify the painter, an artist of the Florentine School, founded by Giotto (and others), who introduced attention for three-dimensionality in painting and for emotion in portraying people. Mariotto Albertinelli is one of the painters described by the already mentioned artist and scholar Giorgio Vasari (1511-1574) in his *Vita* of great painters, sculptors and architects. Albertinelli is active in the transitional period between the early and high Renaissance. In his workshop in Florence, he worked closely together with Fra Bartolommeo until the latter, around 1500, entered a convent, much to Albertinelli's regret. The influence of illustrious masters like Raphael and Leonardo da Vinci is easily recognisable in Albertinelli's work, and his style has a great deal in common with Bartolommeo's. This concerns, as will be illustrated later, visualising the dignity of the human figures and the monumentality of the composition, wherein the implementation of the ideals of Renaissance Humanism becomes visible. Looking at

---

[53] Erik Borgman, "Redactioneel", *Tijdschrift voor Theologie* 54 (2014), 5.
[54] Borgman, "Openbaring als poëzie", 57.
[55] Borgman, "Openbaring als poëzie", 76-77.

Mariotto Albertinelli, *La Visitazione* (1503).
Courtesy of the Galleria degli Uffizi, Firenze.

these paintings, one also becomes touched by the stark contrast between light and dark.

The Visitation by Mariotto Albertinelli

Finding myself face to face with the painting, I would like to share with you the experience of being drawn and lifted into the world of the image. What I see is a very still image, as if, for a moment, the film comes to a standstill, creating a solidified movement of Elisabeth nearing Mary. The scene is captured and fixated at the moment their faces almost touch each other. I sense the rapprochement and the touch. I catch myself wanting to be a part of this intimacy. This in turn makes me focus on and turn to details in which much of interest is to be found.

Albertinelli, in line with his teachers, combined the physicality of the figures with the expression of an intense spirituality. The head coverings tell me about the age difference, while the colours make me suspect the opposite: the blue shade of Mary's robe makes a striking opposite of the almost golden cloak Elisabeth is wearing. The clothes make them more massive, which might mean that Albertinelli wants to highlight the importance of both the women and this specific meeting.

Equally eye-catching is the archway in the background. This edifice marks that we find ourselves in a new period of visual art, past the Gothic two-dimensionality. The arch supports the spiritual "pregnancy" of the scene and lends it an air of expectancy or anticipation of something this encounter will create or generate.

The scene is so vividly painted and so human at the same time that I expect the figures to start moving any moment now. I also notice a difference in the figures: a shadow is cast over Elisabeth's face, and she leans forward towards Mary. This could refer to a form of ranking that we find confirmed in the text: "he will make ready a people prepared for the Lord" (Lk 1:17) – Elisabeth's child shall prepare the way for Mary's child.

The image is so astonishingly powerful that the meeting as such can be experienced as revelatory – as a *rencontre* – apart from what is narrated in the texts. Within traditional theology, little thought is given to the passage on the Visitation. Instead, great interest is shown in the meaning of the "birth of the hero." The painting slows us down, prevents us from passing by and resists an immediate crossing over to a dogmatic discussion about either theological constructions regarding incarnation or the necessity of Jesus's coming into the world and the way in which the doctrine of the hypostatic union has tried to catch his significance.

Drawn to the Unseen

I would like to stress once again that this painting wants to affirm something that cannot be absorbed by what follows in the Lukan narrative, where all the attention is focused on Jesus's birth. Following Paul Fiddes, I specify it as the affirmation of divine grace and revelation at work in a human encounter.[56] The painting affirms a new reality that comes to light in the Visitation. In this sense, one can say that art has the potential to draw us to the divine, the unseen. The image has much more to tell us than a meeting of two pregnant women. It is telling us something about a *rencontre*. The serenity of the figures, in combination with the composition, evokes the thought that the entire image receives life from a source that remains invisible. That which has not been painted, or better, that which indirectly – through colour, form, composition, light and shadow – is referred to: the presence of a divine mystery. It is as if Albertinelli, in his sketch of the encounter and in the reverence it radiates, wants to show that this encounter is also a response: a response to an elusive mystery. Mary and Elisabeth are absorbed by the new reality they express in their songs of praise. They both detached themselves and set out on a journey; they were both brought out of their original situation (cf. Exodus 20:1). Could one therefore say that the encounter as such is "theomorphic"?[57] Can the encounter and everything it shows and tells us: the welcome, the blessing, the support, be called an expression of the divine? In short: is this encounter thus "revelatory", in the sense that it brings God's transforming reality to light?

The deepest level of what I encounter in this revealing image brings me close to the conclusions of Magda Misset in her analysis. That is to say: what is shown here is a new "sociality", a perspective on being human that we long for, grounded in *participation* in the divine mystery. Maybe Jesus came to this earth for precisely this new sociality?

The Visitation is εὐαγγέλιον, good news even before this εὐαγγέλιον was embodied in the life, death and resurrection of Jesus of Nazareth and finally found its way into the world. To phrase it in the words of Rowan Williams: "Christianity is a contact before it is a message."[58]

---

[56] Cf. Paul S. Fiddes, *The Promised End: Eschatology in Theology and Literature* (Blackwell Publishing: Oxford 2000), Challenges in Contemporary Theology, 75.
[57] Cf. Viladesau, *Theological Aesthetics*, 172.
[58] Rowan Williams, *Tokens of Trust: An Introduction to Christian Belief* (Canterbury Press: London 2007), 92.

Part III

We should now like to evaluate where our joint effort to do theology from a theopoetic perspective has brought us.

A point of departure was that the biblical text cannot read itself; we must read it, and this is precisely what we did. We tried to do that by looking through different lenses: theological, philosophical, exegetical ones, and especially those of a few artists. We shall summarise how and why we experienced this as enriching our understanding of the texts in the following evaluative notes.

It was in particular the visual exegesis of the two painters and the video artist, Albertinelli, Pontormo and Viola, that did not only trigger our imagination, but also stimulated our thinking and re-thinking and made us explore new layers of meaning and possibilities. Focussing on the scene of the encounter between Elisabeth and Mary, and absorbing the power of the images, took us past abstractions and frozen doctrines. This created a kind of freedom to look under the surface. In the process, we sharpened our (aesthetic) sensibility for the everyday life of the women in the hill country, for gynocentric time and space, for the counter-reading that can indeed bring overlooked meanings to the surface.

We discovered how works of art can radiate a strength that resists passing such interpretations by. Inspired by the narrative itself and the re-presentations thereof, we moved past the theological voices and images we are so familiar with, and instead let ourselves be inspired by the creative and evocative re-presentations. We subscribe that the theopoetic perspective that visual exegesis activates invites a theology beyond fixation on intellectual and/or doctrinal truths. Or, in the words of David Ford: "The stories are the heart of the matter, and the most important meanings are conveyed through characters and their interactions, not through general statements."[59]

We thus set ourselves free to submerge into the texts, to listen, to look closely and let the characters speak (or not), to see how they interact and what that might mean on a deeper level and also what the re-interpretations added to this or simply highlighted. It put us, for example, on the track of the deeper meaning of joy. We experienced the poetical/aesthetical side of our project. But because of that and through that, the ethical as it were presented itself. We saw – and

---

[59] David F. Ford (in step with Hans Frei), *The Drama of Living: Becoming Wise in the Spirit* (Canterbury Press Norwich: London 2014), 54.

this is an important case in point – how joy is a participatory emotion. Joy must be shared, or better, an intrinsic part of joy is the imperative to share which generates social orientation and is an important incentive for ethical reflection and action on a personal, social or may be even political level.

Another rather decisive moment regarding social normativity is the interruption in Viola's video where Mary is given a voice. She says: "can you help me, I need to talk to you right away." A totally new dimension is inserted here that interrupts indeed the often and much-praised serenity and silence of the women. As the answer is left open, this can be a creative moment or stimulate reflection that can travel in a myriad of directions.

Because biblical texts have been serving as our source and point of reference, we want to add that, in our opinion, joy is interwoven with faith, in the sense that it is *au fond*, and in the words of Rowan Williams, a creative response to a creative initiation,[60] which we see anchored in the biblical texts. Such a re-thinking of the concept of revelation honours the double impulse in the movement of revelation: the gift of God's mystery and also the creative potential in humanity to imagine God's presence.

Theologically speaking, the encounter between Elisabeth and Mary features the good news that they are what we should be: participants in a divine mystery that is reshaping sociality – as states Frances Young.[61] Women's openness to God's inbreathing is part of the encounter that is already showing something of the new creation amidst conflicting realities.

The Title "Rencontre"

We have experienced the making of this article as an experimental, but especially inspiring exercise in interdisciplinarity. Gradually we brought ideas and insights from our two disciplines to a *rencontre* that enabled us to unlock potentials and dynamics in the text, which, in turn, led us to semantic innovation and a sharpened sensibility for the everyday life and the social situation of the women in the hill country. The title *Rencontre* thus most certainly does capture the meeting of the women in the text, but also the dynamics, the dialogue, the meeting of contrasting positions and, last but not least, the *rencontre* of a Systematic theologian and a Biblical scholar. If the reader sometimes wonders "who speaks", the answer might very well be: both of us.

---

[60] Cf. Williams, *On Christian Theology*, 147.
[61] Cf. Frances Young, *God's Presence: A Contemporary Recapitulation of Early Christianity* (Cambridge University Press: Cambridge 2013), Current Issues in Theology 12, 341-342.

Akke van der Kooi was Senior Lecturer for Systematic Theology at the Protestant Theological University in Kampen and Groningen until her retirement in 2014. Her main area of research is Twentieth-Century Theology. Besides publications in the field of pneumatology and ecclesiology, she writes about topics relating to urban ministry and gender studies.

Magda Misset-van de Weg used to be Lecturer in New Testament and Biblical Theology at the Radboud University, Nijmegen and the Protestant Theological University, Kampen. She is now retired. She published on texts from the New Testament and Early Christian Literature.

Julia Münch-Wirtz

Identifikationspotential biblischer Texte im Horizont eines genderbewussten Religionsunterrichts

Zusammenfassung
Moses, Amos, Petrus! Mirjam, Debora, Maria?
Dass der Fokus im Religionsunterricht auf Protagonisten der Bibel liegt, scheint weit verbreitet. Frauengestalten hingegen gelten eher als Randerscheinung in Bildungsplänen und Unterrichtsmaterialien. Da die Charaktere der Bibel Schüler:innen Identifikationspotential bieten können, zeigt der Beitrag die Relevanz des genderbewussten Umgangs mit biblischen Texten für das religiöse Lernen – insbesondere für Identifikationsprozesse – auf. Zugleich wird der Blick hinsichtlich des Aspekts der gendergerechten Sprache geweitet und bibeldidaktische Konsequenzen gezogen.

Abstract
Moses, Amos, Peter! Miriam, Deborah, Maria?
It seems that the focus in religious education on male protagonists of the Bible is a widespread phenomenon. Female figures, on the other hand, are more of a marginal phenomenon in educational plans and teaching materials. Since the characters of the Bible can offer students potential for identification, the article shows the relevance of gender-conscious handling of biblical texts for religious learning – especially for identification processes. At the same time, the view is broadened with regard to the aspect of gender-appropriate language and biblical didactic consequences are drawn.

Resumen
¡Moisés, Amós, Pedro! ¿Mirian, Débora, María?
Es muy habitual que la educación religiosa se centre en los protagonistas varones de la Biblia. Por el contrario, las mujeres son consideradas más bien figuras marginales en los planes de estudio y en los materiales didácticos. Dado que los personajes de la Biblia pueden ofrecer un potencial de identificación a los alumnos y las alumnas, el artículo muestra la relevancia de emplear los textos bíblicos con conciencia de género en la enseñanza religiosa, de especial importancia para los procesos de identificación.

Al mismo tiempo, se amplía la perspectiva sobre aspectos del lenguaje con enfoque de género y se extraen consecuencias para la didáctica de la Biblia.

Keywords: Identification potential, biblical texts, gender sensitive, religious instruction.

„Ach, es gab auch Prophetinnen in der Bibel?!" Diese und ähnliche typische Ausrufe von verblüfften Schüler:innen über weibliche Charaktere in biblischen Erzählungen – fern ab von der alttestamentlichen Eva und der neutestamentlichen Maria – lassen die Frage aufkommen, ob Schüler:innen aufgrund der fehlenden bzw. wenigen biblischen Frauenfiguren Identifikationsmöglichkeiten im Rahmen des biblischen Lernens verschlossen bleiben.

Desiderate – Ein Blick in Bildungspläne und schulische Materialien

Ein Blick in Schulbücher und Materialien bestätigt den Eindruck, dass die Repräsentanz von weiblichen Charakteren aus der Bibel überschaubar ist. Exemplarisch kann dies an den Prophet:innen, die ein gängiges Thema in der Sekundarstufe 1 darstellen, verdeutlicht werden: Zwar sind zum Teil Kapitel in Schulbüchern mit „Propheten und Prophetinnen" überschrieben, allerdings werden in diesem Kontext meist keine alttestamentlichen Frauenfiguren – in wenigen Ausnahmen erfolgt ein Verweis auf Mirjam – sichtbar. Lediglich bei der Aktualisierung werden Vertreterinnen angeführt (u.a. das Wirken von Rigoberta Menchu oder Mutter Theresa).[1] Auch zeigt der Blick in den Bildungsplan 2016 von Baden-Württemberg, dass als zu behandelnde Beispiele mit Amos und Micha ausschließlich männliche Propheten genannt werden. Auffällig ist ebenfalls die maskuline Formulierung der inhaltlichen Kompetenz: „Die Schülerinnen und Schüler können (3) die Botschaft eines Propheten (zum Beispiel Amos, Micha) unter Berücksichtigung des Dekalogs sachgemäß und aktualisierend erläutern."[2]

---

[1] Zwischen der alttestamentlichen Forschung und der Bibeldidaktik gäbe es grundsätzlich bei der Vermittlung des Themas Prophet:innen Klärungsbedarf: Häufig werden diese verkürzt unter dem Fokus „Lernen am Vorbild" (role models) vermittelt. Vgl. Ruth Scoralick, „Priester als ‚Boten' Gottes (Mal 2,7)? Zum Priester- und Prophetenbild des Zwölfprophetenbuches", in: Rüdiger Lux und Ernst-Joachim Waschke (eds.), *Die unwiderstehliche Wahrheit. Studien zur alttestamentlichen Prophetie* (Evangelische Verlagsanstalt: Leipzig 2006), 415-430.

[2] Ministerium für Kultus, Jugend und Sport Baden-Württemberg, *Bildungsplan des Gymnasiums: Katholische Religionslehre* (http://www.bildungsplaene-bw.de/,Lde/LS/BP2016BW/ALLG/GYM/RRK/IK/7-8/02, 17. März 2022). Ein gelungenes Gegenbeispiel stellt der Bildungsplan

Die Bildungspläne von Hamburg, Rheinland-Pfalz, Sachsen und Niedersachsen tun es den baden-württembergischen Ausführungen gleich.[3]

Werden Prophetinnen seltener in Bildungsplänen und Schulbüchern explizit angeführt, ist davon auszugehen, dass Lehrpersonen eher auf die genannten Beispiele zurückgreifen als eigeninitiativ und bewusst Prophetinnen in ihrem Unterricht zu Wort kommen zu lassen. Die Möglichkeit der Identifikation von Schüler:innen mit weiblichen bzw. gleichgeschlechtlichen Figuren bleibt dadurch meist verschlossen. Aber gerade für die Entwicklung der Lernenden birgt die Identifikation, die in der Literaturwissenschaft als „Vorgang der ästhetischen Erfahrung, bei dem sich der Rezipient in ein bestimmtes, durch emotional aufgeladene Nähe charakterisiertes Verhältnis zu Figuren (…) oder anderen Textelementen setzt"[4] verstanden wird, ein enormes Potential im Kontext des biblischen Lernens.

Genderbewusste[5] Textauswahl – Identifikationspotential biblischer Charaktere

Die obigen Beobachtungen aus den Bildungsplänen und Unterrichtsmaterialien sind besonders bemerkenswert, wenn der Ansatz der Rezeptionsästhetik,[6] der

---

Bayerns dar: „Prophetisches Wirken im Dienste der Bewahrung der von Gott geschenkten Freiheit (Exoduserfahrung, Dekalog): prophetische Männer (z.B. Amos, Jeremia, Jesaja) und Frauen (z.B. Debora, Hulda) als „gerufene Rufer/innen im Auftrag Gottes" (vgl. https://www.lehrplanplus.bayern.de/fachlehrplan/gymnasium/8/katholische-religionslehre, 11. März 2022).

[3] Hamburg: biblische Propheten, M. L. King, Gandhi (vgl. https://www.hamburg.de/contentblob/2372656/167c590f8f51cfa53a238a25f19dce1b/data/religion-sts.pdf, 11. März 2022); Rheinland-Pfalz: Elia, Jeremia, M. L. King (https://religion.bildung-rp.de/fileadmin/_migrated/content_uploads/Rahmenlehrplan_katholische_Religion_01.pdf, 11.3.2022); Sachsen: Jesaja, Daniel (http://lpdb.schule-sachsen.de/lpdb/web/downloads/2346_lp_gy_katholische_religion_2019.pdf, 11. März 2022).

[4] Manfred Scholz, Dieter Burgdorf, „Identifikation", in: *Metzler Lexikon Literatur* (J.B. Metzler: Stuttgart 2007), 3, 338-339, 339.

[5] Im Folgenden wird häufig der allgemeinere Begriff genderbewusst verwendet. Daneben wird z.T. auf die Begriffe gendergerecht (um auszudrücken, dass Personen unabhängig von ihrer Geschlechtszugehörigkeit gleichermaßen angesprochen und repräsentiert sind) und gendersensibel (Bemühung, Menschen – vor allem sprachlich – unabhängig ihres Geschlechts und ihrer sexuellen Orientierung respektvoll und wertschätzend darzustellen) zurückgegriffen.

[6] Verweis zur Rezeptionsästhetik in religionspädagogischem Sinn: vgl. Thomas Weiß, „Neutestamentliche Streitgespräche. Religionspädagogische Überlegungen zur biblischen Gattung Streitgespräch in der markinischen Überlieferung", in: *ÖRF* 25 (2/2017), 40-46. Kritisch reflektiert wird die Rezeptionsästhetik in Bezug auf biblische Texte u.a. von Michael Fricke, der biblische Texte nicht als „literarische bzw. fiktionale Texte" (Michael Fricke, *„Schwierige" Bibeltexte im*

das Identifikationspotential für Leser:innen / Schüler:innen literarischer und biblischer Texte betont, ernst genommen wird. Denn dieser Ansatz, der (literarische) Texte als offene Kunstwerke betrachtet,[7] fragt „nach der Begegnung zwischen Text und Leser [sic!]"[8] und geht davon aus, dass „die Bedeutung eines (literarischen) Textes überhaupt erst im Lesevorgang generiert"[9] werde. Auch für biblische Erzählungen kann von dieser Polyvalenz ausgegangen werden,[10] da Texte als „kühle Medien"[11] die Rezipient:innen in hohem Maße zur „Beteiligung und Vervollständigung" auffordern. Dieser konstruktive und interpretierende Prozess, dem Text und seinen Protagonist:innen zu begegnen, hängt von vielfältigen Verstehensfaktoren ab (u.a. Alter, Erfahrungen, kulturell-soziale Prägungen) ab. Besonders die Leerräume in (biblischen) Texten, die nach Roman Ingardens als „schematische Gebilde"[12] zu verstehen sind, halten die Texte und alttestamentliche Protagonist:innen als Identifikationsangebote für heutige Leser:innen offen „für die anhaltende Aneignung in unterschiedlichen Kontexten."[13] Die Identifikationspotenziale von alttestamentlichen Texten und Protagonist:innen können sich somit nur durch den wechselseitigen Austausch entfalten. Vor dem allgemeingültigen religionspädagogischen

---

Religionsunterricht. Theoretische und empirische Elemente einer alttestamentlichen Bibeldidaktik für die Primarstufe (Vandehoeck & Ruprecht: Göttingen 2005), 229) sieht.

[7] Vgl. Umberto Eco, *Das offene Kunstwerk* (Suhrkamp: Frankfurt a.M. 1973); Georg Langenhorst, *Theologie und Literatur. Ein Handbuch* (wbg Academic: Darmstadt 2005). Im englischsprachigen Raum vgl. auch Stanley Fish, „Literature in the Reader. Affective Stylistics", in: *New Literary History*, Vol 2. No. 1, Autumn 1970, 123-162.

[8] Michael Fricke, „„Rezeptionsästhetisch orientierte Bibeldidaktik – mit Kindern und Jugendlichen die Bibel auslegen", in: Bernhard Grümme, et al. (eds.), *Religionsunterricht neu denken. Innovative Ansätze und Perspektiven der Religionsdidaktik* (Kohlhammer: Stuttgart 2012), 210-222, hier 210. Zu ergänzen sei an dieser Stelle, dass Verstehensprozesse sich in einem Dreieck von Autor:innen-Leser:innen-Text ereignen, vgl. Ilse Müllner, „Wie sind wir gemeint? Überlegungen zu einer identifikatorischen Lektüre biblischer Texte", in: *Bibel und Kirche* (1/2016), 17-23, hier 18.

[9] Alexandra Renner, „Bibellesen hat ein Geschlecht: Eine genderspezifische Lektüre des Juditbuchs", in: *Blickpunkt Gender* (2013), 185-196, hier 186. Vgl. auch: Alexandra Renner, „Identifikation und Geschlecht: die Rezeption des Buches Judit als Gegenstand empirischer Bibeldidaktik" (Lit-Verlag: Berlin 2013).

[10] Detlef Dieckmann-von Bünau, „Rezeptionsästhetik (AT)", in: *Das Wissenschaftliche Bibellexikon im Internet*, 2007 (www.wibilex.de, 30. April 2022).

[11] Marshall McLuhan, *Understanding Media. The Extensions of Man* (Mc Graw-Hill: New York 1965), 13.

[12] Roman Ingarden, *Das literarische Kunstwerk* (Niemeyer: Tübingen 1960), 266.

[13] Dorothea Erbele-Küster, „Narrativität," in: *Das Wissenschaftliche Bibellexikon im Internet*, 2009 (www.wibilex.de, 11. März 2022).

Postulat der Subjektorientierung kann der Prozess der Identifikation somit kein deduktiver sein, vielmehr muss die menschliche Freiheit der lernenden Subjekte und deren Vielfalt ernst genommen werden.

Ausgehend von diesem Verständnis, biblische Texte fungierten als „metaphorischer Möglichkeitsraum"[14] und biblische Charaktere laden zur Perspektivübernahme bzw. Identifikation ein, schlummert ein großes Potential im identifikatorischen Lernen. Besonders ein genderbewusster Umgang im Religionsunterricht scheint für Schüler:innen notwendig;[15] zumal Schüler:innen vielfältige Lebensentwürfe und Personen brauchen, mit denen sie sich identifizieren, aber von denen sie sich auch bewusst abgrenzen können.

Empirisch untermauern lassen sich diese Gedanken durch eine Studie von 2020, in der Carsten Gennerich und Mirjam Zimmermann betonen, dass „Mädchen grundsätzlich eher biblische Geschichten auswählen, die weibliche Identifikationsfiguren enthielten."[16] Während Schülerinnen mit 59% weibliche Identifikationsfiguren wählten, entschieden sich 65% der Jungen für männliche Identifikationsfiguren.[17] Insbesondere die Studien von Hans Klein (2000) und Michael Fricke (2005) zeigen, dass Mädchen und Jungen religiöse Texte durch die Brille des Geschlechts wahrnehmen und Mädchen biblische Texte eher identifikatorisch lesen.[18]

---

[14] Martina Kumlehn, „Von den Möglichkeitsräumen des Lebens erzählen. Narrativität als Dimension einer ästhetisch sensiblen Religionspädagogik", in: *Loccumer Pelikan* (2/2013) 2, 53-56, hier 54.

[15] Dorothea Erbele-Küster weist in ihren Forschungen u.a. darauf hin, dass die Rezeptionsästhetik häufig maskulin durchbuchstabiert wird. Hierzu: Dorothea Erbele-Küster, *Lesen als Akt des Betens. Eine Rezeptionsästhetik der Psalmen* (Neukirchener Verlag: Neukirchen-Vluyn 2001).

[16] Carsten Gennerich und Mirjam Zimmermann (eds.), *Bibelwissen und Bibelverständnis bei Jugendlichen. Grundlegende Befunde – Theoriegeleitete Analysen – Bibeldidaktische Konsequenzen* (Verlag W. Kohlhammer: Stuttgart 2020), 157-158.

[17] Erwähnenswert ist hier auch das Detail, dass Mädchen in Lernkontrollen über biblische Texte mit Protagonistinnen besser abschneiden als Jungen. Zwar schneiden Mädchen auch bei Erzählungen mit Protagonisten besser ab als Jungen, aber der Effekt ist hierbei geringer (vgl. Gennerich und Zimmermann (eds.), *Bibelwissen*, 158).

[18] Auch die Untersuchung von Friederike Pronold-Günthner weist auf dieselben Beobachtungen hin: Während Jungen häufiger Schwierigkeiten haben, sich mit Frauenfiguren zu identifizieren, sind Mädchen es häufiger gewöhnt, sich mit beiden Geschlechtern in Texten zu identifizieren (Friederike Pronold-Günthner, *Geschlecht und Identifikation. Eine empirische Untersuchung zur geschlechtsspezifischen Rezeption von Jugendbüchern* (Kovač: Hamburg 2010)).

Auch empirische Untersuchungen u.a. von Stuart Z. Charmé, Silvia Arzt[19] und Alexandra Renner zur Frage nach einer geschlechtsspezifischen Rezeption biblischer Texte haben gezeigt, dass Schüler:innen dazu tendieren, sich in biblischen Erzählungen mit gleichgeschlechtlichen Charakteren zu identifizieren;[20] es sei denn, die gegengeschlechtlichen Charakteren erscheinen im Vergleich zu gleichgeschlechtlichen attraktiver (vgl. Sündenfallerzählung). Dass biblische Texte allerdings nicht die gegenwärtige Leser:innenschaft im Blick haben, vielmehr an das antike Publikum gerichtet sind, liegt auf der Hand. Trotz der historischen Differenzen und der damit häufig einhergehenden Fremdheit können „viele Anknüpfungspunkte für eigene Erfahrungen"[21] in biblischen Texten gefunden werden. Denn gerade das Spannungsfeld zwischen Fremdheit und Vertrautheit beschreibt Ilse Müllner als „Wechselspiel von positiver Resonanz und Widerstand."[22] Dabei komme es darauf an, dass der Text nicht so fremd sein dürfe, dass kein Anhaltspunkt für unsere heutigen Erfahrungen bestünde. An diesen Gedankengang kann mit Werner Wolf angeschlossen werden, der von einer narrativen ästhetischen Illusion ausgeht, die zum einen ein Eintreten in die Textwelt und zum anderen eine Distanz zu dieser charakterisiert.[23]

Dass sich Mädchen eher mit biblischen Protagonist:innen identifizieren und sich wiedererkennen, ist nur ein Teil der Identifikation. So weist die empirische Literaturwissenschaftlerin Els Andringa[24] darauf hin, dass Identifikation auch bei Unähnlichkeiten zwischen dem Gelesenen und sich selbst auftreten

---

[19] Silvia Arzt, *Frauenwiderstand macht Mädchen Mut: die geschlechtsspezifische Rezeption einer biblischen Erzählung* (Tyrolia Verlagsanstalt: Innsbruck / Wien 1999).
[20] Gerade die Identifikation wird von der Lerntheorie von Albert Bandura als Lernen durch Nachahmung des Verhaltens eines Vorbilds verstanden. Vgl. Albert Bandura, *Lernen am Modell. Ansätze zu einer sozial-kognitiven Lerntheorie* (Klett Verlag: Stuttgart 1976).
[21] Ilse Müllner, „Wie sind wir gemeint? Überlegungen zu einer identifikatorischen Lektüre biblischer Texte", in: *Bibel und Kirche* (1/2016), 17-23, 17.
[22] Müllner, „Identifikatorische Lektüre", 21.
[23] Vgl. Werner Wolf, *Ästhetische Illusion und Illusionsdurchbrechung in der Erzählkunst. Theorie und Geschichte mit Schwerpunkt auf englischem illusionsstörenden Erzählen* (Tübingen: Niemeyer 1993).
[24] Els Andringa, "The Interface between Fiction and Life: Patterns of Identification in Reading Autobiographies", in: Poetics Today, 25_2 (2004), 205-240, hier 209-210.
Vgl. auch zur Identifikation mit „same-sex"-Personen bzw. „cross-sex"-Vorbildern: Renate Hofmann, „Geschlechtergerechter Religionsunterricht – Impulse für die Praxis", in: *theoweb* (2/2003), 53-60 (https://www.theo-web.de/zeitschrift/ausgabe-2003-02/hofmann-renate_geschlechtergerechter-RU.pdf, 30. April 2022), hier 56.

kann. Diese Differenzen können mitunter verstörend, irritierend, bzw. vom Bekannten abgrenzend empfunden werden. Gerade für das religiöse Lernen, das als Lernen in Beziehung[25] verstanden wird, ist das sich-in-Beziehung-setzen bzw. sich in biblische Texte / Menschen hineinversetzen von hoher Relevanz. Denn gerade die Identifikation mit dem Text bzw. Menschen kann Resonanzen[26] auslösen.

Angelehnt an die Religionspädagogik der Vielfalt[27] kann die Forderung formuliert werden, dass biblisches Lernen der Vielfalt bzw. Multiperspektivität angestrebt wird,[28] damit durch fixierte Geschlechterkonzeptionen Schüler:innen sich nicht eingeengt fühlen. Eine gendersensible Auswahl bei biblischen Texten sollte daher von besonderem Interesse sein; zumal allen Kindern und Jugendlichen gleiche Identifikationsmöglichkeiten eröffnet werden sollten. Der Mehrwert der Identifikationsmöglichkeit mit biblischen und literarischen Texten besteht vor allem auch darin, dass die Leser:innen einerseits sie selbst bleiben und gleichzeitig die Möglichkeit haben, sich in andere Personen hineinzuversetzen bzw. einfühlen.

Dass die Auseinandersetzung mit der Gender-Perspektive zur Identitätsbildung hinzugehört und bei der Auswahl der biblischen Protagonist:innen auf Vielfältigkeit zu achten ist, konnte deutlich gemacht werden. Zugleich greift die Frage nach Identifikation tiefer: Es geht nicht nur um vielfältige Identifikationsangebote für Schüler:innen, die durch entsprechende Beispiele in Bildungsplänen und Materialien angebahnt werden können, sondern auch um eine angemessene Sprache, die darauf abzielen sollte, sich z.B. von eindimensionalen Gottesvorstellungen zu befreien. So spielen – neben der inhaltlichen Vielfalt von biblischen Charakteren – ebenso sprachsensible Elemente eine wichtige Rolle für einen genderbewussten Religionsunterricht bzw. ein genderbewusstes biblisches Lernen.

---

[25] Vgl. u.a. den Ansatz von Reinhold Boschki, *'Beziehung' als Leitbegriff der Religionspädagogik: Grundlegung einer dialogisch-kreativen Religionsdidaktik* (Schwabenverlag: Ostfildern 2003).
[26] Vgl. Hartmut Rosa, *Resonanz. Eine Soziologie der Weltbeziehung* (Suhrkamp Verlag: Berlin 2021).
[27] Der Genderbegriff unterscheidet das biologische Geschlecht (engl. „sex") von dem „sozialen" oder „soziokulturellen" Geschlecht (engl. „gender"). Das „Geschlecht" ist somit das Ergebnis eines kulturellen Prozesses und grundsätzlich veränderbar. Zum Ansatz der Religionspädagogik der Vielfalt u.a. Thorsten Knauth und Rainer Möller und Annebelle Pithan (eds.), *Inklusive Religionspädagogik der Vielfalt: konzeptionelle Grundlagen und didaktische Konkretionen* (Waxmann: Münster 2020).
[28] Gerade in den unterschiedlichen Ansätzen der Bibeldidaktik spiegelt sich die Vielfalt der Dimensionen heutiger Lebenswirklichkeit von Schüler:innen wider.

Genderbewusste Sprache

Die Existenz des Christentums ist ohne Weitergabe durch Sprache undenkbar und das „Kommunizieren und Reflektieren über Gott, Jesus Christus oder Grundfragen der Lebensorientierung"[29] sind auf Sprachformen wie Metaphern und Erzählungen angewiesen. Obgleich die Gottbildlichkeit von Mann und Frau (Gen 1,27) und die davon abgeleitete Gleichwürdigkeit Kernbestand der biblischen Anthropologie ist, ist die biblische Tradition häufig patriarchal geprägt. Eine gendersensible Auslegung und damit weibliche Erfahrungen in biblischen Texten wiederzuentdecken – im Sinne einer Hermeneutik des Erinnerns – scheint notwendig. Gendersensible Übersetzungen wie zum Beispiel die Bibel in gerechter Sprache[30] sind eine Möglichkeit, vielfältige Identifikationen zu ermöglichen und für Genderbelange zu sensibilisieren.

Dass darüber hinaus beispielsweise die Übersetzung von „Adonai" oder „Hashem" Bestandteil des wissenschaftlichen Diskurses ist, scheint nachvollziehbar, zugleich verspielt z.B. die Neue Einheitsübersetzung, die den hebräischen Gottesnamen mit HERR wiedergibt, nach Ottmar Fuchs die Chance, „Solidarität mit den Frauen" und „Solidarität mit Gottes unendlicher Weite"[31] zu zeigen. Denn gerade die grundsätzliche Unverfügbarkeit Gottes, der jenseits aller Geschlechterbilder steht, ist zentral. In dieser Konsequenz schlägt Elisabeth Schüssler Fiorenza die englische Schreibweise G*d vor (G*tt). Damit sollen nicht die Augen vor der Tatsache verschlossen werden, dass menschliches Reden von Gott vor allem innerhalb eines männlich geprägten Erfahrungsraumes stattfand. Primär entwickelten sich überwiegend männlich konnotierte Gottesbilder, deren Verengung es bei der Übersetzung entgegenzutreten gilt. Auch die reiche Palette der Gottesbilder auszuschöpfen und damit die sprachliche Bandbreite zu erweitern (u.a. Gott als Hebamme, Henne, Geisteskraft), birgt Potential. Es geht dabei nicht um eine Gegenüberstellung und Ab- bzw. Umwertung von männlichen und weiblichen Gottesbildern. Vielmehr gehe es mit Renate Wieser darum, „stereotype Vorstellungen" zu vermeiden und Gott „in aller Vielfalt zu denken."[32] Denn die Bilder von Gott

---

[29] Christian Münch, „Sprachsensibler Fachunterricht und Bibeldidaktik, Lernwege in der ‚Fremdsprache Religion'", in: *Notizblock* 66 (2019), 15-18, hier 15.

[30] Ulrike Bail, *Bibel in gerechter Sprache* (Gütersloher Verlagshaus: Gütersloh 2011).

[31] Ottmar Fuchs, „Denn Gott bin ich und nicht ein Mann (Hos 11,9), in: *Feinschwarz.net*. Theologisches Feuilleton (https://www.feinschwarz.net/denn-gott-bin-ich-und-nicht-mann-hosea-119/, 30. April 2022).

[32] Renate Wieser, Art. Gender, in: *Wissenschaftlich Religionspädagogisches Lexikon im Internet* (www.wirelex.de), 2005, 1-20, hier 11.

sind reichhaltig und nicht binär und so sollten unsere Herangehensweise und unser Menschbild auch nicht binär sein. Gerade einem genderbewussten Religionsunterricht stünde es gut an, bei Übersetzungen genauer hinzuschauen und auf eine sprachliche Vielfalt zu achten, zumal Sprache für das Handeln und Denken der Schüler:innen prägend ist. Gerade die Verbindung zwischen fachlichem und sprachlichem Lernen hilft Schüler:innen „religiöse Mündigkeit auszubilden."[33] In diesem Zusammenhang ist es für Monika Jakobs „eine Selbstverständlichkeit geschlechtergerechte Sprache zu verwenden."[34] Denn diese spiele „eine entscheidende Rolle im beständigen Suchprozess nach der Wahrheit und der eigenen Identität."[35]

Auch der Ansatz des sprachsensiblen Religionsunterrichts,[36] der den hermeneutischen, performativen, kommunikationsorientierten und diskursorientierten Ansatz miteinander verbindet, kann im Sinne eines genderbewussten Religionsunterrichts verstanden werden.

Es gehe bei einer genderbewussten Rede von Gott mit Gabriele Theuer also darum, „Erfahrungen mit neuen, befreienden und lebensfördernden Gottesbildern" zu machen, Gottesbilder zu finden, die Schüler:innen „berühren und in ihrer Identitätsentwicklung ermutigen und bestärken."[37]

Bibeldidaktische Konsequenzen eines genderbewussten Lernens

Der getane Blick auf das Identifikationspotential biblischer Personen zeigt die Notwendigkeit eines sprach- und genderbewussten Einsatzes im Religionsunterricht. Zwei Herangehensweisen, die hinsichtlich der Identifikation besondere Aufmerksamkeit verdienen, seien in aller Kürze umrissen:

- Pädagogisch-didaktisch könnten subjektorientierte Ansätze – wie z.B. das Dialogische Lernen – die Identifikation der Schüler:innen mit den biblischen Texten fördern und dabei auch gendersensiblen Religionsunterricht

---

[33] Annegret Reese-Schnitker, „Sprache", in: Ulrich Kropač und Ulrich Riegel (eds.), *Handbuch Religionsdidaktik* (Kohlhammer: Stuttgart 2021), 406-412, hier 408.
[34] Monika Jakobs, „Geschlechtergerechte Sprache im Religionsunterricht", in: *Jahrbuch der Religionspädagogik, Sprachsensibler Religionsunterricht* (Vandenhoeck & Ruprecht: Göttingen 2021), 53-64, hier 61.
[35] Jakobs, „Geschlechtergerechte Sprache", 64.
[36] Stefan Altmeyer und Bernhard Grümme, et al. (eds.), „Sprachsensibler Religionsunterricht", *Jahrbuch der Religionspädagogik* (Vandenhoeck & Ruprecht: Göttingen 2021).
[37] Gabriele Theuer, „Weibliche Gottesbilder im Alten Testament: Impulse für eine gendergerechte Rede von Gott", in: Sabine Pemsel-Maier (ed.), *Blickpunkt Gender: Anstöß(ig)e(s) aus Theologie und Religionspädagogik* (Peter-Lang-Ed.: Frankfurt a.M. 2013), 31-58, hier 32.

unterstützen. Das Konzept des Dialogischen Lernens, das auf die Didaktiker Urs Ruf und Peter Gallin zurückgeht, stellt das Lernen auf eigenen Wegen in den Fokus. Auf diese Weise können Schüler:innen sich z.B. individuell mit einem biblischen Text auseinandersetzen und über Zusammenhänge in einen Dialog treten.[38]
– Ebenso bietet sich ein Vorgehen aus der empirischen Forschung, die Reminding-Methode von Steen F. Larsen und Uffe Seilman, für einen gendersensiblen Umgang mit biblischen Texten an: Mit dieser Methode werden Rezeptionsprozesse beim Lesen literarischer Texte erfasst, indem die Schüler:innen während des Lesens Textpassagen markieren, bei denen sie etwas denken, fühlen oder sich erinnern. Diese markierten Stellen werden im Anschluss durch die Schüler:innen schriftlich kommentiert und erläutert.

Das Identifikationspotential biblischer Texte im Horizont eines genderbewussten Religionsunterrichts wahr- und ernst zu nehmen erfordert grundsätzlich keine neuen Methoden und ist auch nicht gleichbedeutend mit dem Herunterbrechen der feministischen Exegese für das Lernen im Kontext Schule. Weit zentraler ist die Vielfalt der Protagonist:innenauswahl, die Bandbreite der Gottesbilder und die genderbewussten Übersetzungen. Diese Eckpunkte eröffnen Raum für die Identifikation, in dem Ambivalenzen und Zwischentöne wahrgenommen werden können, neue Einsichten über die eigene Person und die Beziehung zu Gott Platz haben.

Als promovierte Alttestamentlerin (Prof. Dr. Walter Groß) und Oberstudienrätin für die Fächer katholische Religion, Deutsch und Gemeinschaftskunde / Wirtschaft ist **Dr. Julia Münch-Wirtz** als Lehrerin an einem baden-württembergischen Gymnasium

---

[38] Christian Dern widmet seine Doktorarbeit dem Themenbereich der Dialogischen Bibeldidaktik: Christian Dern, *Dialogische Bibeldidaktik. Biblische Ganzschriften des Alten und Neuen Testaments in den Sekundarstufen des Gymnasiums. Ein unterrichtspraktischer Entwurf* (Kassel university press: Kassel 2013), Christine Lehmann und Martin Schmidt-Kortenbusch (eds.), *Handbuch Dialogorientierter Religionsunterricht. Grundlagen, Materialien und Methoden für integrierte Schulsysteme* (Vandenhoeck&Ruprecht: Göttingen 2016). Neben der Polyphonie von biblischen Deutungsmöglichkeiten muss auch der Fragmentarität Raum gegeben werden (vgl. Gerd Theißen, *Polyphones Verstehen. Entwürfe zur Bibelhermeneutik* (Lit: Berlin 2014); Markus Schiefer Ferrari, „Bibel – LeserInnen – Perspektiven: polyphon und fragmentarisch", in: *ÖRF* 25 (2/2017), 47-57) und das Kriterium der Plausibilität (vgl. Friedrich Schweitzer, „Wie Kinder und Jugendliche biblische Geschichten konstruierten. Rezeptionsforschung und Konstruktivismus als Herausforderung des Bibelunterrichts", in: *Jahrbuch für Religionspädagogik* 23 (2007), 199-208.

und als Schuldekanin tätig. Des Weiteren vertritt sie als wissenschaftliche Mitarbeiterin am Lehrstuhl für Religionspädagogik den Bereich Fachdidaktik an der Universität Tübingen in Forschung und Lehre. Ihre Arbeits- und Forschungsinteressen gelten den Bereichen Fachdidaktik des Religionsunterrichts in Theorie und Praxis (insbesondere Bibeldidaktik), Theodizee und aktuelle Krisen im religionspädagogischen Kontext, Religionsunterricht in konfessionell-kooperativer, ökumenischer und interreligiöser Perspektive, beziehungsorientierte Religionspädagogik.

Anna Alabd

Einblicke in die Forschung über die Herausforderungen der Autonomie von christlichen und muslimischen Frauen. Eine Analyse aus interreligiöser Perspektive

Zusammenfassung

Der Artikel soll einen Einblick in einen Forschungsprozess geben, der sich mit den Konzepten der persönlichen Selbstbestimmung und der moralischen Autonomie sowie deren Verbindung mit dem Geschlecht in der religiösen Tradition des Christentums und Islams im Licht interreligiöser Ethik beschäftigt. Dabei wird die herausfordernde Dimension der Autonomie von christlichen und muslimischen Frauen auf der Basis einer qualitativ-empirischen Studie thematisiert. Die Interviewpartnerinnen werden beispielsweise nach dem Umgang mit traditionellen geschlechterspezifischen Bildern in der eigenen Religion, zur Sexualmoral, zu moralischen Geboten und Verboten befragt. Dadurch können typische ethische Konflikte von Frauen identifiziert werden und die Differenz zwischen patriarchaler Tradition innerhalb der Religion und den Autonomieansprüchen der Frauen aufgezeigt werden. Der interreligiöse Dialog wird dabei als Rahmen für die Interviews sowie deren Analyse genutzt und intendiert durch die Behandlung der Thematik der *Autonomie von Frauen* eine Verbesserung des Alltagslebens von christlichen und muslimischen Frauen. Den hermeneutischen Schlüssel dafür bildet die interreligiöse Ethik, wie sie von Hansjörg Schmid entwickelt worden ist. So bildet interreligiöse Ethik die Schnittmenge in der Analyse und trägt durch die ausführliche Beschäftigung damit gleichzeitig zu einem besseren Verständnis der Religionen bei.

Abstract

The article aims to provide an insight into the research process dealing with the concepts of personal self-determination and moral autonomy and their connection with gender in the religious tradition of Christianity and Islam in the light of interreligious ethics. In doing so, the challenging dimension of autonomy of Christian and Muslim women is addressed on the basis of a qualitative-empirical study. The interview partners are asked, for example, about how they deal with traditional gender-specific images in their own religion, about sexual morality, moral commandments and prohibitions. In this way, typical ethical conflicts of women can be identified and the difference between patriarchal tradition within the religion and the autonomy claims of women can be shown. The interreligious dialogue is used as a framework for the interviews and their analysis and intends to improve the everyday life of Christian and Muslim women by addressing the issue of women's autonomy. The hermeneutic key for this is interreligious ethics as developed by Hansjörg Schmid. Thus, interreligious ethics forms the intersection in the analysis and at the same time contributes to a better understanding of the religions by dealing with it in detail.

Resumen
El artículo aborda la cuestión de la ética interreligiosa, sus oportunidades y también sus desafíos. La ética interreligiosa constituye la base de un estudio sobre la autonomía de mujeres cristianas y musulmanas, el cual forma parte de un proyecto de tesis doctoral más amplio. El estudio incluye interrogantes sobre cuáles son las imágenes tradicionales de género en la propia religión, sobre moral sexual, o sobre mandamientos y prohibiciones morales, entre otras. Ello permite identificar conflictos éticos característicos de las mujeres en un contexto interreligioso y arroja diferentes conceptos en torno a la autonomía personal y moral. El diálogo interreligioso fue y es empleado como marco para realizar las entrevistas y para su análisis; asimismo, busca mejorar la vida cotidiana de las mujeres cristianas y musulmanas abordando la cuestión de la autonomía de las mujeres. Este artículo tiene por objeto mostrar la búsqueda de conceptos en torno a la autodeterminación personal y la autonomía moral, así como su conexión con el género en las tradiciones religiosas del cristianismo y el islam a la luz de la ética interreligiosa.

Keywords: Interreligious ethics, autonomy, gender justice in Christianity and Islam.

Für die theologische Ethik stellen sich im Bereich der Genderthematik noch viele Herausforderungen:[1] Angefangen von der Frage nach dem Selbstbestimmungsrecht von Frauen, der Auflösung binärer Geschlechtervorstellungen und den Ansichten zur Geschlechternatur, sowie verschiedenste bioethische Fragen. Wenn in der jeweiligen theologischen Ethik klassische Geschlechterrollenvorstellungen oder Auffassungen über Geschlechteridentitäten und traditionelle patriarchale Lesarten aufeinandertreffen, können aktuelle Fragen aus der Lebenswirklichkeit von Frauen weder ernst genommen noch geklärt werden.

---

[1] Ausgenommen ist hiervon natürlich die feministisch-ethische Forschung, in der auch diese Thematik behandelt wird.

Anna Alabd
Einblicke in die Forschung über die Herausforderungen der Autonomie von christlichen und muslimischen Frauen. Eine Analyse aus interreligiöser Perspektive

Einen Lösungsversuch kann die interreligiöse Ethik darstellen. Der Grund dafür liegt in der Berücksichtigung der Tatsache, dass postmoderne Gesellschaften in Bewegung sind[2] und es deshalb interdisziplinäre Perspektiven braucht. Eine pluralistische Gesellschaft zeichnet sich durch eine ständige Bewegung fließender kultureller und religiöser Traditionen aus, von denen jede eigene moralische Wertesysteme vorgibt, welche sich gleichzeitig gegenüberstehen und gegenseitig inspirieren. So lässt sich Ethik als der Versuch beschreiben, einerseits zwischen der Vielfalt partikularer Moralvorstellungen, die schon immer ein kulturelles Phänomen waren, und in der Suche nach gemeinsamen universellen moralischen Grundlagen andererseits, wie zum Beispiel gemeinsame menschliche Erfahrungen, gemeinsame menschliche Verwundbarkeiten und Rechte, zu vermitteln. Die Suche nach diesen gemeinsamen ethischen Grundlagen im Rahmen eines säkularen Staates ist für demokratische Gesellschaften heute von wesentlicher Bedeutung. Religionen bieten moralische und spirituelle Ressourcen, die zu einer friedlichen Gesellschaft beitragen können. Dies ist nicht nur eine Herausforderung für die offiziellen Vertreter:innen der Religion, von denen die meisten Männer sind. Dies ist auch eine Angelegenheit für Frauen, die sich als Teil einer religiösen Tradition verstehen.

Geschlechterordnungen sind tief in den Religionen verwurzelt und religiöse Vorstellungen sowie Normen prägen auch Geschlechterkonstruktionen. Sie weisen in ihren verschiedenen Dimensionen unterschiedliche geschlechtsspezifische Prägungen auf. Konkret kann dies bedeuten, dass beispielsweise der Zugang zu religiösem Wissen, Ämtern oder Rollen innerhalb religiöser Institutionen vom Geschlecht abhängig ist. Auch rituelle Praxis, Verhaltensnormen, Sexualmoral und anderes kann in den Religionen eine geschlechtsspezifische Konnotation aufweisen.[3]

> Bilder idealisierter Männlichkeit und Weiblichkeit, geschlechtsspezifisch geprägte Handlungserwartungen sowie die Sexualmoral werden durch religiöse Vorstellungen festgeschrieben, infrage gestellt oder auf der Grundlage einer Re-Lektüre ‚heiliger' Schriften an soziale Wandlungsprozesse gekoppelt.[4]

---

[2] Vgl. Karl-Wilhelm Merks, *Grundlinien einer interkulturellen Ethik. Moral zwischen Pluralismus und Universalität* (Academic Press Fribourg: Fribourg / Herder: Freiburg 2012), Studien zur theologischen Ethik 132, 278-280.

[3] Vgl. Edith Franke und Verena Maske, „Religionen, Religionswissenschaft und die Kategorie Geschlecht/Gender," in: Michael Stausberg (ed.), *Religionswissenschaft* (De Gruyter: Berlin / Boston 2012), 125-131, hier 121.

[4] Marita Günther und Verena Maske, „Religionswissenschaft: Macht – Religion – Geschlecht. Perspektiven der Geschlechterforschung," in: Beate Kortendiek et al. (ed.), *Handbuch Inter-*

Anna Alabd
Einblicke in die Forschung über die Herausforderungen der Autonomie von christlichen und muslimischen Frauen. Eine Analyse aus interreligiöser Perspektive

Je nach Kontext, historischen Entwicklungen oder Strömungen zeigen sich Geschlechterkonstruktionen in den religiösen Traditionen auf unterschiedliche Wirkungsweisen. Das Verhältnis kann hier sehr unterschiedlich gestaltet sein und reicht von restriktiven Begrenzungen zu emanzipatorischen Erweiterungen der Handlungsspielräume. Insbesondere jedoch sind abrahamitische Religionen wie das Judentum, das Christentum und der Islam patriarchal geprägt und weisen eine Differenz zwischen ihrer Tradition und den Autonomieansprüchen von Frauen auf. Dennoch finden sich in diesen religiösen Traditionen auch Ansätze für eine geschlechteregalitäre Gesellschaftsordnung, die in der feministischen Frauenbewegung zumeist innerreligiös auch weiterentwickelt wird.[5]

So erleben sich viele christliche und muslimische Frauen zwischen der Sehnsucht nach Sicherheit und moralischer Orientierung innerhalb ihrer Religionsgemeinschaft und dem Bestreben nach Freiheit im persönlichen Leben, beispielsweise in der Partnerwahl, der Familiengründung oder der Suche nach sexueller Identität, hin- und hergerissen.[6] Denn diese Fragen berühren die individuelle verantwortliche Entscheidungsfindung und die moralischen Leitlinien der eigenen Glaubensgemeinschaft, deren normativen Ordnungen von der persönlichen Präferenz abweichen können.[7]

Im Folgenden möchte ich die interreligiöse Ethik im Sinne eines hermeneutischen Schlüssels für diese Problemkonstellation vorstellen, wie sie Hansjörg Schmid entfaltet hat. Die Bedeutung der interreligiösen Ethik besteht darin, einen Weg aufzuzeigen, wie aus einer interreligiös-vergleichenden Forschung eine Alltagsrelevanz für religiöse Frauen erwachsen kann, die in einer Spannung zwischen traditionellen Frauenbildern und modernen Autonomiebestrebungen stehen.

Interreligiöse Ethik und ihre Herausforderungen

Zur Thematik der interreligiösen Ethik gibt es insgesamt relativ wenig Forschung. Hansjörg Schmid kann hier als ein Vorreiter der interreligiösen Sozialethik genannt werden. Da weder von *der* christlichen noch *der* islamischen

---

disziplinäre Geschlechterforschung (Springer: Wiesbaden 2019), Geschlecht und Gesellschaft 65, 552-559, hier 552.

[5] Vgl. Günther und Maske, „Religionswissenschaft," 552.

[6] Vgl. unveröffentlichte Interviews von Frau Samira im Oktober 2021, Frau Amina im September 2021, Frau Marina, Mai 2021.

[7] Vgl. Angelika Walser, „Die religiöse Identität von Frauen im Spannungsfeld von Zugehörigkeit, Autorität und Autonomie," in: *Interdisciplinary Journal for Religion and Transformation* 5 (2017) 27-54.

Ethik gesprochen werden kann, sondern jeweils von einer Pluralität an Positionen, stellt sich in diesem Zusammenhang die Frage nach dem *Warum* von interreligiöser Ethik.

Religionsbasierte Ethik versucht auf der Basis ihres Gottesbezugs zu weltlicher Urteilsbildung beizusteuern. Notwendig ist dafür eine aus der theologischen Reflexion resultierende Selbstbeschränkung der Religion, die auch für den Dialog eine Voraussetzung darstellt.[8] Daran anknüpfend intendiert die interreligiöse Ethik, einen angemessenen Rahmen zu schaffen, in dem Diskurse stattfinden können, die den Status quo spätmoderner Gesellschaften einholen: Wir leben in einer globalisierten Welt, in der in westlichen Gesellschaften die gesellschaftliche Pluralisierung von Lebensweisen, Weltanschauungen und Religionen zum Normalfall geworden sind. Interreligiöse Ethik setzt sich konstruktiv mit anderen Religionen und ihren ethischen Positionen auseinander, um zu einer interreligiösen Verständigung beizutragen. Dabei soll sich interreligiöse Ethik nicht auf bloßes Suchen von Gemeinsamkeiten beschränken, sondern eine Öffnung für gemeinsame Such-, Lern- und Entdeckungsprozesse herbeiführen.[9]

Hermeneutik der Asymmetrie als Voraussetzung für Lernprozesse
Der *State of the Art* verlangt danach, Asymmetrien zu betrachten und diese ernst zu nehmen. Dies bildet die Grundvoraussetzung einer Annäherung an die interreligiöse Ethik und ermöglicht in Folge Lernprozesse.

Eine strukturelle Asymmetrie ist, dass es in den meisten muslimischen Konfessionen anders als in den meisten christlichen keine Normierungsinstanzen gibt und daher größere Pluralität auftritt. Wobei es auch hier zu erwähnen gilt, dass es seitens des protestantischen Christentums keine Allgemeinverbindlichkeit gibt. Bei Kooperationen müssen daher die Ansätze und Strukturen zu Beginn geklärt werden. Hier können die Religionen beziehungsweise Konfessionen als Motivationskräfte wirken und zu Zielbestimmungen beitragen,

---

[8] Vgl. Reiner Anselm, „Ausblick: Wie lässt sich der Pluralismus in der Ethik aufrechterhalten?," in: Sarah Jäger und Reiner Anselm (ed.), *Ethik in pluralen Gesellschaften* (Springer: Wiesbaden 2019) Grundsatzfragen 3, 141-153, hier 151.
[9] Vgl. Hansjörg Schmid, *Interreligiöse Sozialethik. Perspektiven für eine Theologie im Plural*, Beitrag geht auf einen Vortrag in der Philosophisch-Theologischen Hochschule St. Augustin am 20.6.2013 anlässlich der Verleihung des Preises „Theologie interkulturell" zurück. Die Vortragsform wurde weitgehend beibehalten. https://core.ac.uk/display/-147103864?utm_source=pdf&utm_medium=banner&utm_campaign=pdf-decoration-v1, 13. Mai 2022), 1-13.

während die säkulare Gesellschaft und ihre Mechanismen einen Rahmen für Allgemeingültigkeiten schaffen kann.[10]

Schmid nennt als eine weitere wichtige strukturelle Asymmetrie die Bausteine, welche für die jeweilige Ethik bereitstehen. Während christliche Ethik von der Geschichte der Moderne und den Auseinandersetzungen ihrer Ideologien geprägt ist, befindet sich eine islamische Ethik als systematische Ausarbeitung noch in ihren Anfängen. Da zumeist andere Grundlagen bestehen, braucht es hier eine Zurückhaltung bei Gleichsetzung und Parallelisierung.[11]

In der Methodik und der Ausrichtung müssen individualethische und sozialethisch-strukturelle Zugänge miteinander in Beziehung gesetzt und diskutiert werden. In diesem Zusammenhang stellt sich auch die Frage nach der Vernunftorientierung. Die Position, welche die Vernunft in der Argumentation der ethischen Diskussionen einnimmt, muss zuvor geklärt werden, denn von islamischer Seite beispielsweise kann vernunftorientierte Argumentation sehr unterschiedlich verstanden und angewendet werden.[12] Aber auch das Spektrum an christlichen Positionen ist sehr heterogen und braucht daher eine Grundsatzdiskussion des Verhältnisses von Vernunft und Offenbarung in der interreligiösen Ethik. Eine weitere Frage, deren Antwort im gemeinsamen Diskurs liegen kann, lautet, wo die Grenzen der Anpassung und Veränderung liegen. Denn ein Antwortprozess braucht einen ergebnisoffenen Vergleich, ohne einzelne Entwicklungslinien zu einem übergreifenden Maßstab zu erheben.[13]

Interreligiöse Ethik als vergleichende Ethik?

In der interreligiösen Ethik braucht es methodisch-hermeneutische Überlegungen und kritische Auseinandersetzung zum Vergleichen, da sie ein wichtiger Bestandteil ihrer Arbeitsweise sind. Der Alltag ist durchzogen von permanenten Vergleichen. Neues und Besonderes kann nur als solches erkannt werden, weil das menschliche Denken und die menschliche Sprache in Form von impliziten und expliziten Vergleichen strukturiert sind. Vergleiche ermöglichen die Bildung von individuellen und kollektiven Identitäten. Indem andere Überzeugungen mit dem Eigenen in Relation gesetzt werden, kann Sicherheit und Orientierung gewonnen werden. Es setzt also auch die Begegnung mit

---

[10] Vgl. Anselm, „Ausblick," 142-143.
[11] Vgl. Hansjörg Schmid, *Islam im europäischen Haus. Wege zu einer interreligiösen Sozialethik* (Herder: Freiburg im Breisgau 2012), 533-534.
[12] Siehe die verschiedenen Positionen der Rechtsschulen.
[13] Vgl. Schmid, *Islam im europäischen Haus,* 534-536.

anderen Weltanschauungen und Religionen Vergleiche voraus. Bei solchen qualitativen Vergleichen ist der Spielraum von Interpretationen in der Regel noch breiter als in Fällen, bei denen quantitative Vergleichsmaßstäbe herangezogen werden. Beim Vergleich handelt es sich um eine Methode, bei der zwei oder mehrere Gegenstände bewertend in Beziehung gesetzt werden. Dabei muss sich ihre Vergleichbarkeit sinnvoll begründen lassen. Voraussetzung dafür sind Nicht-Identität und Vorhandensein gemeinsamer Eigenschaften, also ein Mindestmaß an Differenz wie an Ähnlichkeit.[14]

Das wissenschaftliche Arbeitsinstrument des Vergleichs wird oft kritisch betrachtet, da religionstheologische Entwürfe häufig pauschal vergleichen und damit weitreichende Urteile über andere Religionen fallen. Viel effizienter sind Diskussionen von Detailvergleichen und damit einhergehende vielfältige Deutungsmöglichkeiten.[15]

Beim Vergleich entsteht die Gefahr einer Dekontextualisierung und Vereinfachung von Komplexität.[16] Damit können Vergleiche instrumentalisiert werden, weil sie voreingenommen oder interessensgeleitet sind. Anderseits ist ein Vergleich ohne Interessen nicht möglich, weshalb er eine kritische Reflexion der eigenen Standortgebundenheit sowie der damit verknüpften Ziele erfordert. Aber auch der:die Beobachtende erweist aufgrund seiner:ihrer Standortgebundenheit einen „blinden Fleck" auf, da er:sie sich beim Beobachten nicht selbst beobachten kann.[17] Ebenso braucht es ein bewusstes Mitreflektieren von bestehenden Machtdifferenzen, etwa wenn dominierende Gruppen, Schichten oder Kulturen in einer Gesellschaft Definitionshoheit über Minderheiten haben.[18]

Schmid schlägt vor, dass nicht Einzelnormen, sondern Prinzipien, wie etwa Gemeinwohl, Gerechtigkeit, Solidarität, in den Mittelpunkt des Vergleichs der beiden Sozialethiken gestellt werden sollen. Er lässt jedoch hierbei die Frage offen, welche Schnittmengen möglich sind beziehungsweise welche Sozialprinzipien in der ethischen Argumentation eingesetzt werden sollen. Ebenso unbeantwortet bleibt die Frage, ob eine Systematik der Prinzipien möglich ist oder ob es eine „normative Orientierung" für ein dynamisches Verständnis

---

[14] Vgl. ebd., 536-539.
[15] Vgl. ebd., 154-155.
[16] Vgl. ebd., 155.
[17] Siehe Niklas Luhmann mit seinem Verweis auf die erkenntnistheoretische Problematik des Vergleichs als Form des Beobachtens.
[18] Vgl. Schmid, *Islam im europäischen Haus*, 159.

von Prinzipien braucht.[19] Nichtsdestotrotz braucht es in diesem Zusammenhang in erster Linie eine grundlegende Begriffsdefinition dieser Prinzipien, um sie in einem Vergleich verwenden zu können. Hierbei ist weniger eine gleiche Grundlegung beziehungsweise Verwurzelung wichtig, sondern eine übereinstimmende Verwendung des Prinzips.

Deshalb erfolgt auch im Zuge des Dissertationsprojektes die interreligiöse ethische Analyse der Thematik *der Autonomie von christlichen und muslimischen Frauen* auf der Basis einer übereinstimmenden Verwendung verschiedener ausgewählter Prinzipien.[20] Folgende Prinzipien finden aufgrund der Analyse der Interviews bereits Anwendung: Würde, Autonomie/Selbstbestimmung, Freiheit und Gerechtigkeit.

Das Prinzip der Gerechtigkeit beispielsweise kann sehr unterschiedlich begründet werden. Hervorgehend aus der jüdischen Auslegungstradition wird Gott Gerechtigkeit sowohl im Christentum als auch im Islam zugesprochen. Im Islam wird Gerechtigkeit als einer der Namen Gottes genannt (al-Adl). Von daher kommt auch das Verständnis einer göttlichen Gerechtigkeit, nach der die Menschen leben und handeln sollen. Hier finden sich konkrete Weisungen im Koran, wie etwa, dass Arme und Schwache besonders geschützt werden sollen. Auch die Praxis des Propheten Muhammad hat große Auswirkung auf das Gerechtigkeitsverständnis von Muslim:innen. Dennoch haben sich über die Jahrhunderte hinweg unterschiedliche Theorien zur Gerechtigkeit entwickelt. Die Schule der Mutaziliten stellt beispielsweise das Prinzip der Gerechtigkeit Gottes in den Mittelpunkt.[21] In Judentum und Christentum wird Gerechtigkeit Gott als eine herausragende Eigenschaft (z. B. Dtn 33,22) zugeschrieben und beschreibt damit auch seine Fürsorge für sein Volk. Auch im Neuen Testament finden sich zahlreiche Verweise auf die Gerechtigkeit Gottes und seiner Zuwendung zu den Benachteiligten und Unterdrückten.[22] Christliche Theolog:innen und Philosoph:innen beschäftigten sich über die Jahrhunderte hinweg mit dem Begriff der Gerechtigkeit und entwickelten unterschiedliche Theorien.

---

[19] Vgl. ebd., 537.
[20] Die ausgewählten Prinzipien resultieren aus den Analysen der Interviews mit den Frauen.
[21] Vgl. Senol Korkut, „Gerechtigkeit (isl.)," in: Richard Heinzmann (Hg.), *Lexikon des Dialogs Grundbegriffe aus Christentum und Islam* (Freiburg im Breisgau 2016), 168-169, hier 168.
[22] Vgl. Martin Thurner, „Gerechtigkeit (chr.)," in: *Lexikon des Dialogs. Grundbegriffe aus Christentum und Islam* (Herder: Freiburg im Breisgau 2016), 168.

In der konkreten Umsetzung beziehungsweise Verwendung des Begriffes stellt sich somit die Frage nach der Vergleichbarkeit. Gerechtigkeit sowohl aus christlicher als auch aus muslimischer Perspektive kommt eine herausragende Rolle zu, wird als Gotteseigenschaft beschrieben und soll durch die Menschen zum Tragen kommen. Da dem Prinzip im Koran und in der Bibel gleichermaßen höchste Wichtigkeit beigemessen wird, kann es im interreligiösen ethischen Diskurs als vergleichendes Prinzip verwendet werden.

Relevanz der interreligiösen Ethik für mein Forschungsprojekt
(Inter-)religiöse Ethik in einer pluralen Gesellschaft braucht den Rahmen des Säkularen. Gräb verweist darauf, dass eine säkulare religionsneutrale Gesellschaft nicht nur negative Religionsfreiheit zulässt, sondern auch Freiräume für positive Religionsfreiheit ermöglicht. Damit können weltanschaulich-religiöse Vorstellungen in eine allgemein-säkulare Ethik einfließen, beziehungsweise in den Diskurs treten und ihre Potentiale aufzeigen und in die Gesellschaft einbringen.[23] So wie säkulare Gesellschaften und Religionen voneinander lernen können, können auch Muslim:innen und Christ:innen im Dialog über (sozial-) ethische Fragen sprechen und nicht nur voneinander, sondern auch miteinander lernen.[24] Was dies im Blick auf mein Dissertationsprojekt bedeutet, wird nun detailliert vorgestellt werden.

Einblicke in das Forschungsprojekt über die Autonomie von christlichen und muslimischen Frauen im Vergleich

Im Folgenden sollen erste Ergebnisse der Studie zur Autonomie von christlichen und muslimischen Frauen dargestellt werden. Die Studie ist Teil eines Dissertationsprojektes, das nach dem Begriff der Autonomie und Selbstbestimmung im Licht ethischer Konflikte fragt. Anhand von Fragen zum Umgang mit traditionellen geschlechtsspezifischen Bildern in der eigenen Religion, zur Sexualmoral, zu moralischen Geboten und Verboten und anderem soll eine Identifizierung typischer ethischer Konflikte von Frauen im interreligiösen Kontext erfolgen. Anhand dieser ethischen Dilemma-Situationen kann klar aufgezeigt werden, welchen Wert christliche und muslimische Frauen ihrer persönlichen Selbstbestimmung beimessen. Konkret wird beispielsweise danach gefragt, wie sie sich entscheiden, wenn ihre Selbstbestimmung etwa im Bereich der Sexualmoral in Konflikt mit moralischen Geboten und Verboten

---

[23] Vgl. Anselm, „Ausblick," 143-144.
[24] Vgl. Schmid, *Islam im europäischen Haus,* 537-538.

der eigenen religiösen Tradition gerät. Darüber hinaus wird durch die Studie versucht herauszufinden, ob und inwiefern christliche und muslimische Frauen die Ressourcen ihrer Heiligen Schrift und die eigene religiöse Tradition für eine Entscheidungsfindung in moralischen Konfliktsituationen als hilfreich beurteilen und wie sie mit tradierten Geschlechterrollen umgehen.

Forschungsdesign
In der Studie werden Frauen aus verschiedenen christlichen und muslimischen Konfessionen im Alter von circa 20-70 Jahren, die im deutschsprachigen Raum leben, interviewt. Neben personenbezogenen Daten wie Geburtsjahr, Ausbildung und Beruf, Konfession, Familienstatus und sexuelle Orientierung, die zur Einordnung dienen, werden auch Fragen zur religiösen Erziehung, dem religiösen Umfeld, zum Bereich der Sexualität und dem persönlichen Konzept der Selbstbestimmung erhoben. Es ist ein Ziel des Forschungsprojektes, Frauen zu befähigen, offen über kontroverse ethische Fragen zu sprechen. Wie bereits weiter oben beschrieben, wird anhand von Dilemmata erhoben, welche Konflikte im Umgang mit Normen der eigenen religiösen Tradition auftreten, ob und inwiefern es zum Konflikt mit dem je eigenen persönlichen Konzept von Selbstbestimmung kommt und wie das Dilemma letztendlich gelöst wurde. In der interreligiösen oder interkonfessionellen Begegnung können sich weitere Fragestellungen entwickeln und Begrifflichkeiten neu hinterfragt oder definiert werden. Der interreligiöse Kontext fungiert in diesem Zusammenhang als positive Ressource, da er gleiche oder ähnliche Strukturen über Religionen/Konfessionen hinweg aufzeigen kann und weiterführend übergreifende Lernprozesse anregt und auch zur Stärkung weiblicher Selbstbestimmung beiträgt.

Dafür eignet sich die Methode der *Grounded Theory* (GTM), die als Grundlage für den Umgang mit den Interviews gewählt wurde. Die Methode ist theoriegenerierend und erlaubt es, theoretische Ansätze zur Autonomie zu vergleichen und verschiedene Theorien, welche aus den Interviews abgeleitet wurden, zusammenzuführen. Gleichzeitig gestattet sie, Lebensrealitäten religiös verorteter Frauen zu beleuchten. Sie beinhaltet eine ständige Verbindung zwischen Aktion (Datengewinnung) und Reflexion (Datenanalyse und theoretische Reflexion).[25]

---

[25] Vgl. Jörg Strübing, *Grounded Theory. Zur sozialtheoretischen und epistemologischen Fundierung eines pragmatischen Forschungsstils* (Springer: Wiesbaden ⁴2021), Qualitative Sozialforschung, 125-129.

Problemhorizont

Die Problematik des Selbstbestimmungsrechts von Frauen zeigt sich ganz konkret daran, dass in der Fachliteratur, ausgenommen ist natürlich die feministische Forschung, überwiegend nicht mit oder von Frauen selbst gesprochen wird, sondern über diese.

Simone de Beauvoirs berühmte Worte aus dem Jahr 1949 scheinen immer noch großteils zu gelten: „Die Menschheit ist männlich, und der Mann definiert die Frau nicht als solche, sondern im Vergleich zu sich selbst: Sie wird nicht als autonomes Wesen angesehen."[26]

In gesellschaftlichen und religiösen Systemen, in denen die Lebensrealität von Frauen nicht wahrgenommen oder dargestellt wird, scheint es nicht erstaunlich, dass patriarchale Strukturen bis heute wirksam sind.[27] Auch wenn auf rechtlicher Ebene die Gleichstellung der Geschlechter weitgehend festgeschrieben ist,[28] erleben viele Frauen immer noch Misogynie und Androzentrismus: Konkret zeigt sich dies daran, dass an Frauen höhere moralische Anforderungen gestellt werden, sie im Durchschnitt deutlich weniger als Männer verdienen, den größten Teil der (unbezahlten) *Care*-Arbeit übernehmen, oft sexueller Belästigung am Arbeitsplatz und Gewalt im häuslichen Umfeld ausgesetzt sind.[29]

In diesem Zusammenhang muss auch die Rolle von Religionen als System der Erhaltung von Ungleichbehandlung und Diskriminierung erörtert werden. Aufgrund ihres Geschlechts erleben viele Frauen bis heute in ihrer religiösen Verortung Ausgrenzung, indem sie in Rollen gedrängt werden oder Aufgaben nicht übernehmen dürfen. Dabei dient der Differenzdiskurs auch zur Legitimation von Machtmissbrauch im Rahmen bestehender Geschlechterverhältnisse und der Tradierung einer patriarchalen Gesellschaftsordnung durch Religionen.[30]

Viele der Erwartungen, die an Frauen gerichtet sind, sind mit normativen Regelungen und patriarchalen Bildern verbunden. Ein wesentlicher Beitrag zur Veränderung ist das Wissen über die Perspektive der Betroffenen selbst.

---

[26] Simone de Beauvoir, *Das andere Geschlecht. Sitte und Sexus der Frau* (Rowohlt-Taschenbuch-Verlag: Reinbek bei Hamburg ^{19}2000), 12.

[27] Siehe Caroline Criado-Perez, *Unsichtbare Frauen. Wie eine von Daten beherrschte Welt die Hälfte der Bevölkerung ignoriert* (btb: München ^{6}2019).

[28] Ich beziehe mich hier auf den deutschsprachigen Raum.

[29] Siehe Criado-Perez, *Unsichtbare Frauen*.

[30] Anna Alabd, *„Für mich bedeutet eine Frau sein, dass ich ich bleiben darf." Die Autonomie von Frauen als Herausforderung für theologische Ethik im Christentum und Islam* (Masterarbeit, Paris Lodron Universität Salzburg 2020), 44.

Deshalb ist eine differenzierte Analyse von religiösen und geschlechtsspezifischen Konstruktionen notwendig, da sie soziale Wirklichkeit schaffen, die kritisierbar und veränderbar ist. Die Studie intendiert auf Basis der bereits genannten ethischen Position eine Untersuchung dieser Wechselwirkung, indem mittels biographischer Interviews Frauen selbst zu Wort kommen. Dabei wird die Verwobenheit von Geschlecht und Religion mittels dreier Ebenen der Dekonstruktion in der anschließenden Analyse aufgedeckt. Dieses Instrument stammt aus der geschlechtersensiblen Religionswissenschaft:

- Individuelle Konstruktionsprozesse: Wie sind religiöse und geschlechtsspezifische Sozialisations- und Identitätsbildungsprozesse miteinander verschränkt und wo zeigen sich Grenzen und Ausschlüsse hinsichtlich individueller Handlungsmöglichkeiten und Selbstverständnisse?
- Symbolische Konstruktionsprozesse: Welche Bilder von Männlichkeit und Weiblichkeit, welche Geschlechterordnungen werden durch religiöse Lehren und Praktiken transportiert und welche sozialen Konsequenzen ziehen sie nach sich?
- Strukturelle Konstruktionsprozesse: Wie tragen Religionen zur gesellschaftlichen Ordnung und strukturellen Arbeitsteilung bei, die häufig zugleich geschlechtsspezifische Implikationen aufweisen?[31]

Ziel der Studie
In der Studie sollen Frauen anhand ihrer Reflexion in den Interviews befähigt werden, offen über kontroverse ethische Fragen zu sprechen. Dabei geht es um ihre Selbstdefinition und Selbstwahrnehmung ebenso wie um ihr Verständnis von Traditionen. Die Auseinandersetzungen thematisieren die Suche nach befreienden Impulsen zur Verwirklichung der eigenen Lebenspläne von Frauen, wie sie sich selbst als autonome und verantwortliche moralische Subjekte erleben und dadurch in ethische Konflikte geraten. Diese stehen im Kontext der normativen Richtlinien ihrer Religion. Damit zeigt die Studie eine Diskrepanz der Lebensrealität von Frauen und dem (normativen) Rahmen auf, den die Religionsgemeinschaften für Frauen festlegen.

In diesem Zusammenhang ist die Klärung der Begrifflichkeiten Autonomie und Selbstbestimmung notwendig. Letzterer wird verwendet als Ausdruck der persönlich-individuellen Einstellung zur Lebensführung von Frauen, während Autonomie als allgemeiner normativer Leitbegriff angewandt wird. Begriffe

---

[31] Vgl. Günther und Maske, „Religionswissenschaft," 557.

wie „Geschlechtergerechtigkeit" oder „Autonomie" sind keine Begriffe der Bibel oder des Korans, deshalb braucht es hermeneutische Anstrengung, um die Welt der Heiligen Schrift für die Anliegen der Frauen von heute zu öffnen und zu vermitteln. Religiöse Frauen lesen heute ihre Heilige Schrift im Licht der Fragen, mit denen sie konfrontiert sind. Sie suchen darin befreiende Impulse für ihr eigenes Leben.

Ergebnisse

Die Interviews haben deutlich gezeigt, dass Autonomie – in einer weiten und offenen Bedeutung des Begriffs – ein zentrales Anliegen der Frauen im deutschsprachigen Raum ist, unabhängig davon, welcher Konfession sie angehören. Sie beeinflusst Selbstdefinition, Selbstfindung und Selbststeuerung, welche die amerikanische Moralphilosophin Diana T. Meyers als drei wesentliche Aspekte des Konzepts der persönlichen Autonomie nennt.[32] Ihr Ansatz betont, wie wichtig es für Frauen ist, ihre eigene Stimme zu entdecken und zu hören. Eine Teilnehmerin drückt das so aus:

> Selbstbestimmung bedeutet für mich, mir selber zu vertrauen, meine Gefühle vertrauen, meine Erfahrungen – oder ja auch meine Kenntnisse. […] Früher waren meine Gefühle nicht so wichtig – oder meine Träume. Aber ich habe das gelernt, dass ich an meine Träume glaube, dann kann ich das erreichen. Ich glaube, das ist auch Selbstbestimmung.[33]

In Zusammenhang damit kann der Ansatz von Herlinde Pauer-Studer genannt werden. Sie konstatiert personale Autonomie als Voraussetzung für moralische Autonomie, da Individuen sich für ein selbstbestimmtes Leben entscheiden müssen, um sich als moralische Subjekte im Sinne Kants verstehen zu können. Hierbei spielt natürlich der Freiheitsbegriff eine tragende Rolle:

> Soziale Freiheit ermöglicht auch die Autonomie personaler Identitätsfindung. Individuen ist es im Rahmen der skizzierten Einschränkungen überlassen, welche Art von Person sie sein wollen, welche Dinge ihnen erstrebenswert scheinen, auf welche Projekte sie Zeit und Energie verwenden. Soziale Freiheit schafft Raum für Autonomie im Sinne individueller Selbstverwirklichung und Selbstfindung.[34]

---

[32] Vgl. Angelika Walser, *Die Autonomie von Frauen in bioethischen Konfliktfeldern als Herausforderung für die Theologische Ethik* (Habil., Univ. Wien 2013), 185-188.
[33] Unveröffentlichtes Interview mit Frau Samira, Oktober 2021, Linz.
[34] Herlinde Pauer-Studer, *Autonom leben. Reflektionen über Freiheit und Gleichheit* (Suhrkamp: Frankfurt a.M. 2000), suhrkamp taschenbuch wissenschaft, 15.

Anna Alabd
Einblicke in die Forschung über die Herausforderungen der Autonomie von christlichen und muslimischen Frauen. Eine Analyse aus interreligiöser Perspektive

In den monotheisitischen Religionen wie im Christentum beziehungsweise in manchen christlichen Konfessionen finden sich große kulturgeschichtliche Tabus, auf denen Einschränkungen oder Ausschluss begründet werden. Konkret bezieht sich das beispielsweise auf die sogenannte weibliche „Unreinheit", etwa durch Menstruation oder Geburt.[35]

In der orthodoxen Kirche beispielsweise wurde das levitische Bluttabu auf kirchlichen Kontext übertragen.[36] So erzählt eine interviewte orthodoxe Frau über ihre Erfahrungen zur Menstruation, dass sie zu der jeweiligen Zeit keinen Kirchenraum betreten durfte. Während des Zusammenlebens mit ihrer Mutter hielt sie sich an die Regelung, später nach ihrer Eheschließung bewegte sie Folgendes, sich nicht mehr daran zu halten: „Ich glaube Gott hat die Frauen gemacht – so – es ist nicht verboten, ist nur eine schlechte Regel, gemacht von Männern."[37] Sie definiert ihre Selbstbestimmung als grundlegend für ihr Leben. Ihr Denkvermögen versteht sie als Grundlage ihrer Autonomie – die Fähigkeit eigenständig moralische Reflexionen zu generieren und basierend darauf Entscheidungen zu treffen. Dies nutzte sie auch in der Überlegung, warum sie aufgrund ihrer Menstruation Ausschluss vom Gottesdienst erlebte, und entschied in ihrer moralischen Reflexion, dass sie als Frau von Gott geschaffen wurde und deshalb ein Ausschluss nicht gerechtfertigt sei.

Im Kontext von Geboten und Verboten spricht eine interviewte Frau über ihr Verständnis der Praxis der Religion folgendermaßen:

> Ich achte darauf, dass ich mein Gebet verrichte, dass ich Koran lese. […] die Verbindung zu halten ist für mich wichtig. Aber für mich bedeutet ein Verbot – (denkt darüber nach) – ist das gut für dich, wenn du das tust? Gebot heißt für mich immer, es ist leichter für dich, wenn du das annimmst.[38]

Anhand von Fragen und Antworten wie diesen kann die grundlegende Annahme getroffen werden, dass sich Frauen in einer bewussten Auseinandersetzung mit ihrer religiösen Tradition befinden. In allen bereits geführten Interviews zeigen sich an unterschiedlichen Themen Spannungen zwischen Respekt und Kritik an der Tradition und religiösen Ritualen. Feststellen lässt sich auch

---

[35] Vgl. Günther und Maske, „Religionswissenschaft," 552.
[36] Vgl. Monica Herghelegiu, *Rolle der Frau in der Orthodoxen Kirche. Online Texte der Evangelischen Akademie Bad Boll*. https://www.ev-akademie-boll.de/fileadmin/res/otg/470108-Herghelegiu.pdf, 5. Mai 2022, 4.
[37] Unveröffentlichtes Interview mit Frau Marina, Mai 2021, Linz.
[38] Unveröffentlichtes Interview mit Frau Amina, September 2021, Salzburg.

eine Diskrepanz zwischen Frauen mit religiöser Bildung, das heißt Religionslehrerinnen oder Theologinnen, und „einfachen" gläubigen Frauen. Letztere stehen vor größeren Herausforderungen, ihr religiöses Empfinden zu verbalisieren, einzuordnen und mit Traditionen und religiösen oder kulturellen Praktiken zu brechen oder ihre Ablehnung zu argumentieren.

Resümee
Christliche und islamische Ethik gehen von der durch Gott geschenkten Freiheit des Menschen aus. Das heißt, wenn die Moralfähigkeit des Menschen gegeben ist, ist der Mensch zu mehr fähig, als sich nur nach Richtlinien Gottes oder anderer Autoritäten zu richten und danach zu handeln. Der Grund moralischen Sollens beziehungsweise der menschlichen Erkenntnis liegt demnach im Menschen selbst. Begründungen dafür sind in den Offenbarungstexten der Religionen zu finden. In der von Gott erschaffenen menschlichen Freiheit liegt auch der Verantwortungsbereich der Handlungen des Menschen.[39] Diese Freiheit wird Männern und Frauen zugesprochen. Die Begründung der Autonomie von Frauen kann im religiösen Kontext ebenso argumentiert werden wie die Begründung der Autonomie der Männer. Mittels der kritischen Analyse der feministischen Theologie und ihrer Methoden kann das Menschen-, aber auch Gottesbild, das in den Religionen vertreten wird, hinterfragt werden. Denn dieses wirkt sich auf den Umgang mit Frauen und ihrer Verortung in den Religionen aus.[40] Die Interviews haben gezeigt, dass Autonomie ein positiver Wert für Frauen ist und sie dadurch zu einem authentischen Lebensentwurf – auch in ihrer religiösen Verortung – gelangen, der individuell unterschiedlich ausgeprägt sein kann. Patriarchale Strukturen finden sich im Christentum und Islam ebenso wie in säkularen Systemen. Durch die Interviews und deren Aufbereitung können gemeinsame Lernprozesse initiiert werden, in denen Frauen nicht nur voneinander lernen, sondern auch miteinander kritische Reflexionen anstoßen, neue Denkprozesse starten und im Zusammenleben unterschiedlicher religiöser oder kultureller Herkunft anstelle von problematischer Differenz Bereicherung erleben.

---

[39] Vgl. Carola Wittig, *Reproduktive Autonomie. Über das Potential eines umstrittenen Begriffs* (Aschendorff: Münster 2018), Studien der Moraltheologie. Neue Folge 10, 165-168.
[40] Weitere Ausführungen dazu siehe Masterarbeit Anna Alabd, *Für mich bedeutet eine Frau sein, dass ich ich bleiben darf*.

Anna Alabd
Einblicke in die Forschung über die Herausforderungen der Autonomie von christlichen und muslimischen Frauen. Eine Analyse aus interreligiöser Perspektive

Anna Alabd hat Katholische Religion, Geschichte, Sozialkunde und Politische Bildung (BEd. Univ.) an der Paris Lodron Universität Salzburg und an der Katholisch-Theologischen Privatuniversität Linz (MEd.) studiert. Seit dem Wintersemster 2020/21 ist sie Doktorandin an der Paris Lodron Universität Salzburg im Fachbereich Religious Studies. Sie hat eine dreijährige Arbeitserfahrung als Projektverantwortliche für Interreligiösen Dialog im Dekanat Traun in Oberösterreich.

Seit Jänner 2021 ist Anna Alabd Mitglied des Doktoratskollegs PLUS gender_transkulturell.

Über das Bayerische Forschungszentrum für Interreligiöse Diskurse (BaFID) wurde sie im Oktober 2021 zur Stipendiatin der Hanns-Seidel-Stiftung e.V., Institut für Begabtenförderung. Ihr Dank gilt deshalb auch der Hanns-Seidel-Stiftung und dem Bundesminsisterium für Bildung und Forschung (BMBF) für die Förderung.

Anne-Claire Mulder

To Whom Do You Attribute Religious Authority? A Pilot Study.

Abstract
The text "To Whom Do You Attribute Religious Authority?" is the report of a pilot study into patterns of attribution of religious authority among participants of the seventh Synod-weekend of the (Dutch) Ecumenical Women's Synod. It must be situated in the broader discussion on changing patterns in (religious) authority and departs from the presupposition that authority is relational and attributed instead of linked to a position; an idea that is further developed in the Italian-German discourse on a symbolic in the feminine. Two questions guided this pilot study: 1) to whom – and for what reasons – do the participants of this Synod-weekend attribute religious authority, and 2) do they distinguish between women and men in the attribution of authority. The pilot study consisted of a questionnaire, followed by eight interviews, in which respondents to the questionnaire reflected upon their answers.

The answers indicate that the respondents prefer horizontally organised authority relations. Being inspired by the other, either by their wisdom or faith, and by their integrity, is an important impulse to trust and hence to attribute religious authority to this person. They also show an ambivalence between the paradigm of equality between the sexes and a practice of relating to women. The majority of respondents did not distinguish between women and men in the attribution of religious authority; the answers on the question who had inspired their faith indicated, however, that they were more inspired by women than by men in their life.

Resumen
"¿A quién atribuyes autoridad religiosa? Un estudio piloto" es el informe de un estudio piloto sobre los patrones de atribución de autoridad religiosa llevado a cabo entre las participantes del Séptimo Sínodo de Fin de Semana del Sínodo Ecuménico de Mujeres de los Países Bajos. El estudio se sitúa en el contexto de la actual discusión sobre los cambios en los patrones de reconocimiento de autoridad religiosa. Parte de la presuposición de que la autoridad es relacional y atribuida en lugar de vinculada a una posición, una idea que se halla desarrollada con mayor profundidad en el discurso italiano y alemán sobre lo simbólico en lo femenino. Dos cuestiones guían este estudio: 1) A quién, y por qué motivos, las participantes en el sínodo otorgan autoridad; y 2) si

al hacerlo, distinguen entre hombres y mujeres. El estudio piloto se valió de un cuestionario, al que siguieron ocho entrevistas individuales en las que las entrevistadas reflexionaban sobre sus respuestas al cuestionario.

Las respuestas indican que las participantes prefieren formas de organización horizontal en las relaciones de autoridad. El hecho de sentirse inspiradas por otra/o, ya sea por su sabiduría o su fe o bien por su integridad, es un impulso importante para confiar en esa persona y, consecuentemente, reconocerle autoridad religiosa. Las respuestas también muestran cierta ambivalencia hacia el paradigma de la igualdad entre los sexos frente a la práctica de relaciones femeninas. La mayoría de las que respondieron el cuestionario no distinguieron entre hombres y mujeres a la hora de atribuir autoridad religiosa. Sin embargo, sus respuestas a la pregunta sobre quién ha inspirado su fe indican que se sienten más inspiradas por mujeres que por hombres.

Zusammenfassung
Der Text „To Whom Do You Attribute Religious Authority?" ist ein Bericht einer Pilotstudie über die Muster der Zuschreibung von religiöser Autorität unter den Teilnehmerinnen des siebten Synodenwochenendes der (niederländischen) Ökumenischen Frauensynode. Der Bericht soll in die breitere Diskussion sich wandelnder Muster von (religiöser) Autorität eingeordnet werden und geht von der Annahme aus, dass Autorität relational und zugeschrieben statt an eine Position gebunden ist; eine Idee, die im deutsch-italienischen Diskurs über eine Symbolik im Weiblichen weiterentwickelt wird. Zwei Fragen leiteten diese Pilotstudie: 1) Wem – und aus welchen Gründen – schreiben die Teilnehmerinnen dieses Synodenwochenendes religiöse Autorität zu? und 2) Machen sie bei der Zuschreibung von Autorität einen Unterschied zwischen Frauen und Männern? Die Pilotstudie bestand aus einem Fragebogen, gefolgt von acht Interviews, bei denen die befragten Frauen über ihre Antworten reflektierten.

Aus den Antworten geht hervor, dass die Befragten horizontal organisierte Autoritätsbeziehungen bevorzugen. Sich von einer anderen Person inspirieren zu lassen, sei es durch ihre Weisheit oder ihren Glauben, sei es durch ihre Integrität, ist ein wichtiger Impuls, dieser Person zu vertrauen und sie somit als religiöse Autorität anzuerkennen. Sie zeigen auch eine Ambivalenz zwischen dem Paradigma der Gleichheit der Geschlechter und einer Praxis der Beziehung zu Frauen. Die meisten Befragten machen bei der Zuweisung religiöser Autorität keinen Unterschied zwischen Frauen und Männern; die Antworten auf die Frage, wer ihren Glauben inspiriert hat, zeigen jedoch, dass sie sich in ihrem Leben eher von Frauen als von Männern inspirieren ließen.

Keywords: Attributing authority, religious authority, empirical pilot-study, Dutch Ecumenical Women's Synod, sexual difference.

Introducing the Background of the Research-question

In 1990 the book *Sexual Difference. A Theory of Social-Symbolic Practice* by The Milan Women's Bookstore Collective was published.[1] It is both the reflection of a collective of Italian feminist philosophers on different important moments within the Italian women's movement, and a reflective cartography of the trajectory that brought this collective to a praxis of nursing authority relations between women. Central in their theory is the idea of sexual difference: the thesis that the difference between the sexes is an irreducible one; an irreducibility which has been effaced in and by the dominant symbolic order, with the effect that women "are forced to comply with models that do not match them."[2] Therefore women need a symbolic "in the feminine", in which this irreducible difference is developed in theory and practice so that women can wrap themselves in an (symbolic) envelope of images and practices that can direct their becoming. The book by the Milan Women's Bookstore Collective describes (among others) how the praxis of *affidamento* developed from the recognition and subsequent reflection that the voice of some had more weight than the voice of others in the group.[3] They concluded that authority is a quality of the relation between the subject and the other; that it is ascribed or attributed by the subject when the words, texts or actions of the other touch the desire of and open a new horizon for this subject; that characteristic for the "authority" is that she inspires, encourages, generates new ideas, challenges, shows unknown possibilities; that it is a relation marked by trust and entrustment: trust, that the one who attributes authority is willing to seriously consider the ideas and judgements of the "authority" and that the "authority" is willing to venture judgements, which are both aspects that illuminate that this relation has some asymmetrical characteristics.[4]

---

[1] The Milan Women's Bookstore Collective, *Sexual Difference. A Theory of Social-Symbolic Practice,* translated by Patricia Cicogna and Teresa de Lauretis (Indiana University Press: Bloomington and Indianapolis 1990).

[2] Luce Irigaray, *Sexes and Genealogies,* translated by Gillian C. Gill (Columbia University Press: New York 1993), 64.

[3] The Milan Women's Bookstore Collective, *Sexual Difference,* 110.

[4] See the Milan Women's Bookstore Collective, *Sexual Difference,* 108-150; and "Authority" in: Ursula Knecht, et al., *ABC des guten Lebens* (Christel Göttert Verlag: Rüsselsheim 2012), 25-27, here 25. See for the English translation: https://abcofgoodlife.wordpress.com/category/authority/ translated by Anne-Claire Mulder, Barbara Streidl and Derek Singleton. Several authors of this *ABC* were involved in translating texts of Italian philosophers as Luisa Muraro, Chiara Zamboni and Diana Sartori, who were part of the Milan Women's Bookstore Collective, and in the further reflection upon their ideas.

There has been little reception of these thoughts on authority within the English-speaking feminist discourse.[5] This may also be explained by the fact that these thoughts on authority differ from the dominant (English) discourse on authority. In that discourse, authority has been criticised as "hierarchical", "masculine" and as "power over", or discussed from the perspective of its demise due to processes as secularization, democratization, individualization and women's emancipation.[6]

I encountered this Italian discourse on authority through the German translations and reception of texts by Luisa Muraro, Diana Sartori or Chiara Zamboni, which generated a lively German-Italian discourse.[7]

These thoughts appeal to me because they imply shifting the centre of gravity of authority-relations from "the" authority to the one who attributes authority, thereby redressing the (hierarchical) power balance between the authority and the subject. It enables the generation of a more balanced relation in which the freedom of the subject to reflect upon the views of the other is respected. They highlight that underlying the act of attribution of authority to someone's words, notions, images, gestures or examples is the subject's recognition that these words are authoritative for her, because they offer direction for realising her desire. These ideas imply, moreover, that relations to established authorities or to authoritative ideas and interpretations of, for example, the good life, can change when different ideas and/or practices are authorized by the subject or collective. For authority relations are the result of this process of attribution and therefore in flux. And lastly, these ideas interest me because of their potential to rethink *religious* authority from a feminist perspective. Religious authority is currently predominantly understood as referring to the ordained ministry, evoking associations with masculinity and the power of men.[8]

---

[5] Apart from *Sexual Difference*, no other books have been translated into English.

[6] See for instance: Hilge Landweer and Catherine Newmark (eds.), *Wie männlich ist Autorität. Feministische Kritik und Aneignung* (Campus Verlag: Frankfurt 2018), 8-14. In the Dutch language area, one can perceive a cautious return of the subject-matter. See: Christien Brinkgreve, *Het verlangen naar gezag. Over vrijheid, gelijkheid en verlies van houvast* (Atlas Contact: Amsterdam/Antwerpen, 2012); Paul Verhaeghe, *Autoriteit* (De Bezige Bij: Amsterdam 2015).

[7] The authors mentioned belong to the Milan Women's Bookstore Collective. See also Anne-Claire Mulder "Religious Authority, Religious Leadership, or Leadership of a Religious Organisation – Same-Difference? An Effort in Clarification", in: *Journal of the European Society of Women in Theological Research* 24 (2016), 133-154, esp. 135-138.

[8] See Mulder, "Religious Authority", 140-151, for a description of the process whereby religious authority became vested in the ordained ministry.

However, these ideas about authority as attributed and relational intimates that religious authority is circulating and at work in all kinds of relations, which means that anyone can be experienced as a religious authority by someone or a group.[9]

These different interpretations of authority raise general questions as "to whom is religious authority attributed and what are the reasons to do so?", "what images, ideas, relational dynamics are considered to be of importance for assigning authority to someone else?" Or "what relational dynamics might be distinguished in the process of attribution of religious authority?" And, finally, the more specific question of whether sexual difference and gendered relations play a role in these processes. Would women consider the gender of the authority to be of importance in assigning religious authority, and if so, why?

These questions motivated me to set up a pilot study to explore the questions to whom feminist, religious women would attribute religious authority.

The Research Design
There is little empirical research on the process of attribution of religious authority and even less on what women consider to be of importance in assigning religious authority to another.[10] I therefore decided to set up a pilot study – an often-used instrument before a larger study is set up – to explore the question to whom women would attribute religious authority and why. I used a questionnaire that focussed both on what ideas, words or practices women would consider important in attributing authority and the relational dynamics of this process. The questionnaire was therefore of an exploratory nature: a try-out of these ideas about the attribution of authority among a group of grass-root women belonging to the Dutch women-and-faith movement. Instead of pre-testing the questions of the questionnaire, this pilot study was followed up by interviewing eight women who had filled in the questionnaire, in which the interviewees were asked to reflect upon their own answers to the questionnaire

---

[9] See Mulder, "Religious Authority", 153.
[10] One of the few empirical studies of this process of attribution of authority among women is Sahar Noor's study *Creating a Female Islamic Space. Piety, Islamic Knowledge and Religious Authority among Born-Muslims and Converts to Islam in the Netherlands and Belgium* (Global Academic Press: Vianen 2018). The reflections in *Sexual Difference* upon the personal and group-experiences with the dynamics of authority relations might be considered "auto-ethnography" *avant la lettre*.

in order to get a picture of their interpretation of these questions and thus a fuller interpretation of the results.[11]

The questionnaire was distributed among the participants of the *Seventh Synod-weekend of the Oecumenische Vrouwensynode (Ecumenical Women's Synod)* in 2017, a two days symposium of lectures, workshops and discussions. The Dutch *Ecumenical Women's Synod* is a feminist network organisation established in 1987 after the first Synod. Participants of these Synod-weekends have a strong interest in feminist theology and often a (long) history of participating in grass-root women-and-faith groups. Thus, as feminists, they have a similar political interest in justice in areas such as gender, culture, age and sexuality as the Italian-German authors,[12] but as religious grass-root women, they differ from them in religiosity, education and nationality. This made them an interesting group of respondents for this pilot study in exploring what women would consider to be of importance in assigning religious authority to another and why.

The Questionnaire
The overall question in the questionnaire was: "To whom do you attribute religious authority?" This main question was divided into five sub-questions, making up five sections of the questionnaire. I used different modes of questioning: open questions asking for associations, statements to which one had to agree or disagree on a five-point scale and lists of statements allowing for multiple answers.

Section 1 consisted of two open questions asking for associations with "religious authority" and "speaking with authority" respectively.

Section 2 was devoted to the question "When do you attribute religious authority to someone." This section was divided into three parts. In part 2a, I asked "When do you attribute religious authority to someone" followed by ten statements listing qualities, attitudes and modes of behaviour which might be a reason for attributing religious authority. The respondents could indicate their agreement or disagreement on a five-point scale. In parts 2b and 2c, I asked "When do you attribute religious authority to women/men", respectively, followed by the same statements used in 2a. This time the respondents could choose multiple statements, fitting their ideas of what is important in

---

[11] Sharlene Nagy Hesse-Biber (ed.), *Feminist Research Practice. A Primer* (Sage Publications Inc.: Thousand Oaks, California ²2014) 314, 366.
[12] See https://www.vrouwensynode.nl/vrouwensynode/, 6 March 2022.

(a) religious authority. These two questions were directed at charting whether respondents would make a distinction between a woman and a man in attributing religious authority.

Section 3 focussed on the question of who had inspired the faith of the respondents. I presented a gendered list of persons ranging from their own mother and father to writers and mystics.

In Section 4, I wanted to know how the respondents relate to the one to whom they attribute religious authority, a question that addresses the qualities that characterise the relational dynamic within an authority relation. In 4a, I formulated five statements which described this relation. The respondents could indicate their agreement or disagreement with these statements on a five-point scale. Like the set-up of section 2, and for the same reason, I asked in 4b and 4c, "How do you relate to the woman (4b)/the man (4c) to whom you attribute religious authority."

Section 5 consisted of a series of summing questions, offering a list of persons and/or ministries to whom one would attribute religious authority.

The Interviews

The results of the pilot study raised a number of questions about the reasons behind the respondents' answers. How had they interpreted the different statements? What difference did it make whether an "authority" is a woman or a man in attributing authority? In what way had their life experience influenced their answers? To gain more in-depth understanding of the answers, especially of those in sections two and four, I interviewed eight respondents to the questionnaire and asked them to reflect upon their answers of three years before.[13]

The interviewees – who chose their own pseudonym – formed a representative mix of the respondents of the questionnaire: at the time of the interview, they were between 31 and 86 of age, five being over 65; three identified themselves as Roman Catholic, five belonged to one of the Protestant churches in the Netherlands. Their social background was mixed.

---

[13] The eight interviewees had indicated on the questionnaire to be interested in participating in follow-up research. Each received her own filled-in questionnaire. Despite the time-gap most of the interviewees answered that they still agreed with their answers. Due to the Covid-19 restrictions, the interviews were conducted by telephone or Zoom, which may have had an impact on the interviews but in ways unknown to me.

The Results[14]
(About) the respondents to the questionnaire
32 participants – about 25% – of the Seventh Synod of the *Oecumenische Vrouwensynode* returned the questionnaire. Of those 32 women, 18 identified themselves as Protestant, nine as Roman Catholic and five as otherwise affiliated. At the time of the Synod, ten of the respondents were aged between 20 and 40, eight between 41 and 65, 14 over 66. This age structure roughly mirrors the age structure in the Dutch churches and the ecumenical women's movement. The smaller number of respondents of the "middle" generation reflects the effect of secularization and the influence of secular feminism on church affiliation – many women of that generation left the church because of its patriarchal character. The relatively high number of young respondents is due to the number of young female theologians, both students and graduates, who filled in the questionnaire.

Section 1) What are your associations with "religious gezag/authority" and with "speaking with gezag/authority"
The first section of the questionnaire asked for the associations with the notion "religious *gezag*" and "speaking with (religious) *gezag*". The word "gezag" is one of the two Dutch words for authority, the other being "autoriteit". *Gezag* is derived from the verb *zeggen* (meaning "to speak") and is related to another Dutch word, *gezeggen*, which has connotations of "judging, assessing, prescribing."[15] I used *gezag* because I wanted to know whether the associations with *gezag* would differ from those with "authority".[16]

Ad 1a. Associations with "religious *gezag/authority*".

The question "what are your associations with *religieus gezag*?" showed a broad spectrum of negative associations, referring to

– positions of religious leadership such as pope, bishops, ministers;
– sources of authorities such as Bible/Scripture, Christ, tradition;
– institutions such as church, synod, etc.;
– qualifications as power, domination/dominating, violence/overpowering.

---

[14] An overview of the results can be found in the appendix.
[15] Marlies Phillipa et al., "Gezag", in: *Etymologisch Woordenboek van het Nederlands* (Amsterdam University Press: Amsterdam 2018). https://www.etymologie.nl/ 16 October 2021.
[16] In section 5 of the questionnaire, I asked for the associations with "religious authority". A comparison of the answers given in section 1 and 5 shows that most respondents gave similar responses to each question. More than one wrote "similar to *gezag*" or "is there a difference between *gezag* and authority?"

The respondents also offered more positive associations like "inspiration", "passionate", "charisma", "wisdom", "empathy", "carrying responsibility"; or "someone in whom I recognize the 'spirit of wisdom' and whom I do not catch at 'trickery' or guru-language." These "positive" associations reappeared in different guises in the other answers to the questionnaire and give a hint of what the respondents consider important in "a religious authority".

The reflections of the interviewees upon their own associations shed some light on the critical picture of religious authority in the answers given by the respondents.

For Talitha (38, Protestant), "religious authority" evoked associations with the orthodox ministers she knew in her youth, who seemed to be elevated above ordinary human beings, only had a surname and lived in big houses. "If such a minster nodded at you, you might enter heaven, perhaps…".[17]

Sara (86) and Francisca (73), both Catholic, indicated that they had become even more critical of "religious authority" than they had been in 2017 due to the developments in the (Dutch) Roman Catholic Church, especially of its stand on homosexuality and its increasingly authoritarian attitude. Francisca says: "…in particular this authoritarian authority destroys many things. Those men still think that they have a monopoly on wisdom and that they have a God-given ordination."[18]

These quotes colour the associations with masculinity and patriarchal power evoked by the words "religious authority" and elucidate the often-emotional reactions of the respondents.

Ad 1b. Associations with "Speaking with authority".

This question, too, produced a wide range of words and images: some echoing the negative associations of 1a, and many which suggest positive associations with "speaking with authority". Participants referred to persons such as Jesus, a favourite aunt, fellow-(religious)sisters; to qualities such as powerful, honesty, authenticity, trustworthiness and being knowledgeable, or associated it with a well underpinned, nuanced argument. They mentioned modes of speaking, for example, "with humour, based on experience", or "with awareness of one's position (in society)". Some respondents presented both a negative and a positive image, for example, "I hear fire-and-brimstone sermons" and "(a) woman's voice – SO different." One wrote: "Giving direction,

---

[17] Interview with Talitha: 2 December 2020. All the answers of the respondents have been translated by the author.
[18] Interview with Francisca, 3 November 2020.

offering direction, speaking truth, passing on truth (can be both positive and negative)."

Katinjo (70, Remonstrants) wrote in 2017 that it depends on who speaks, thereby avoiding an "either-or" opposition. Reflecting upon this association, Katinjo says in 2020:

> It is not sensible, of course, but when the archbishop starts to contend something, then I bristle, like "that is nonsense". That is of course not true. On the other hand, there are moments when I think "O, when s/he says it, then it'll be true, I guess." That is of course not the case, either. You should always try, to look at what has really been said and to distinguish it from who has said it, but I find that often rather difficult.[19]

Katinjo's critical self-reflection highlights the complex dynamics of attributing authority. It illuminates that rational deliberation is only a part of this process, but that preconceptions, previous experiences, attraction and longing for inspiration or meaning play an (important) role, too. This will become more explicit in the answers to the question of section two.

Section 2) When do you attribute religious authority to someone?
The overall question of this second section was: "When do you attribute religious authority to someone". The first part (2a) opened with the sentence: "I attribute religious authority to someone if...", followed by ten statements with which one could agree or disagree, using a five-point scale (disagree, partly disagree, neutral, partly agree, agree). In 2b and 2c, I asked, "when do you attribute religious authority to women/men", respectively. The same statements as in 2a were offered, but multiple answers were possible. The statements offered were partly based on ideas from the Italian-German discourse about attributing (religious) authority to someone else (inspiring, offering direction, etc.) and partly reflected more traditional ideas about the qualities and attributes of (a) religious authority, such as learning and acting from the Gospel, as well as on the many conversations with friends and colleagues about the attribution of religious authority.

The results of this section are presented as follows: the statements that ended in the top three and bottom two of the lists are presented first, followed by (some of) the interviewees' reflections on these statements.

---

[19] Interview with Katinjo, 10 November 2020.

Ad 2a. When do you attribute religious authority to someone? The answers to this question produced the following top three and bottom two statements wherewith the respondents agreed:

1. (if) this person has wisdom and speaks wise words.[20]
2. (if) the views of this person about God and the good life inspire me.
3. (if) someone's spirituality corresponds with the acts of this person.
9. (if) you can notice in the sermons that the person is learned.
10. (if) someone is in a position of religious authority.

The choices of the interviewees corresponded with the choices of the respondents. They would attribute authority to someone if this person had wisdom and spoke wise words, too, although Martha (31, Protestant) remarked critically that the word wisdom (*levenswijsheid*) evokes associations with elderly persons,[21] a reflection affirmed by Francisca. She explained that she experienced this wisdom in elderly people: "Although not only in elderly people, but for the time being, yes (...) and in some of the books I read."

The majority of the interviewees would also attribute religious authority "if the views of this person about God and the good life inspire me". They gave various reasons. Martha emphasized the word "views" in this thesis because these "can come from anyone", subsequently mentioning two young theologians who inspired her.

Reflecting upon the statement "if someone's spirituality corresponds with the acts of this person" (third in this top three), Sara said that "I need to see it in acts" because faith in itself is not inspiring, neither can you be certain of it.[22] Elisabeth (59, Protestant) used the words "congruence" and "continuity" to describe her position:

> I think that for me the continuity (...) is caused by what a person says about faith and how that person engages in relations. And when I experience a large incongruence between these two, then I find it difficult to attribute authority to that person – at least, consciously.[23]

---

[20] In the Dutch version of this statement the word *Levenswijsheid* – wisdom acquired through life-experiences – was used instead of wisdom. However, the English language knows only the word "wisdom" for *wijsheid* (wisdom) and *Levenswijsheid*.
[21] Martha, 18 November 2020.
[22] Sara, 9 November 2020.
[23] Interview with Elisabeth, 2 November 2020.

Chaja (71, Protestant) reflected critically on this statement, however: "Well, what kind of person comes to mind? For if the person is Trump and his spirituality matches his acts, I won't attribute authority to him, you see. Thus, it also depends on who it is and what his spirituality is."[24]

The interviewees as a group were more negative about the statements which ended in position 9-10 on the list – "... if you can notice in the sermons that the person is learned" and "if someone is in a position of religious authority" – than the respondents as a group. For Sara and Francisca, it did not matter at all whether someone had studied or not. Francisca – and Martha too – pointed to the implicit hierarchy between educated and uneducated in this statement; Francisca referred to the ordinary persons, who are such a source of inspiration for her, whereas Martha explained that the implicit hierarchy in this statement was intertwined with the opposition between "book learning" and "(practical) wisdom and compassion." Elisabeth, on the other hand, valued the (theological) education of the religious authority. She had participated for a long time in evangelical and missionary movements and had missed the challenge and fortifying power of a sermon by someone who had studied the Bible.

None of the interviewees would grant someone religious authority based on this person's position of religious authority. Francisca, who was mixed up in a struggle with the new priest of her parish, who had forbidden her to act as lay preacher, told him: "'Who are you to forbid me to do this. I will do it, all the same'. And I do just that." Chaja, who had circled "neutral" in the questionnaire, pointed out that people in these positions can be both good and nasty. She subsequently told a story about her experience with the nasty, painful side of church authorities, which colours her choice for "neutral". These authorities claimed the authority to say to her: "You have to stop as minister (and when) they say that, you can whistle for it". Both stories recall the negative associations with religious authority in the previous section.

As indicated in the above, sections 2b and 2c focussed on the attribution of religious authority to women (2b) and men (2c), respectively. In the following, I will first present the answers to both questions and will discuss the outcomes of both sections afterwards.

---

[24] Chaja, 9 November 2020.

2b When do you attribute religious authority to women?
The table below lists the statements with the highest and the lowest score. Three of the statements were circled equally often.

1. Someone's texts about God and the good life make me think.   25×
2. This person has wisdom and speaks wise words.   21×
2. The views of this person about God and the good life inspire me.   21×
2. The faith of that person inspires me.   21×
9. You can notice in the sermons that the person is learned.   5×
10. Someone is in a position of religious authority.   4×
11. Other:
    – If women position themselves as unconventional and enthusiastic.
    – An attitude to life like connectedness with fragile life and, from there, giving shape to faith/spirituality.

The option "Other" produced five sentences, three of which corresponded with the qualities mentioned in the questionnaire, and two referred to other qualities which induce the attribution of religious authority.

2b When do you attribute religious authority to men?

1. Someone's texts about God and the good life make me think.   22×
2. This person has wisdom and speaks wise words.   21×
3. The views of this person about God and the good life inspire me.   20×
4. The faith of that person inspires me.   19×
9. Someone is in a position of religious authority.   5×
10. You can notice in the sermons that the person is learned.   4×
11. Other:
    – If men position themselves as progressive and enthusiastic.

Ad 2b and 2c. When do you attribute religious authority to women/men?
The answers on 2b and 2c differ from those on 2a. Due to the possibility of choosing more than one statement, the order of importance of the statements was reshuffled. In general, respondents circled more statements when thinking of "women" (2b) than when thinking of "men" (2c), including the answers on "statement" 11: Other, which produced five answers in 2b and only two in 2c, which, moreover, strongly resembled two of the statements in 2b.

The reshuffling explains the fact that the statement "(if) someone's texts about God and the good life make me think", which was in fifth place in 2a, ended in the first position in 2b and 2c. The order of the first four statements in 2b and 2c is the same, though, the only difference being that these statements were chosen more often in 2b than in 2c.

This similarity suggests that the respondents do not make a distinction between women and men in the attribution of religious authority with respect to the qualities mentioned in these statements. This apparent gender indifference was affirmed by a closer inspection of the answers on 2b and 2c, which showed that 19 respondents had circled the same statements for women as for men, whereas 13 respondents had not.

Among the interviewees, four did not distinguish between women and men, while four others did. When asked why she did not make a distinction between women and men, Hannah (68, Catholic) answered that she interprets religious authority in a gender-neutral manner, that is, she assesses them on aspects such as trustworthiness. She added that she was very much aware of the scandal of underestimating women in ecclesial institutions, but that she considered that a different story.[25] Katinjo also affirmed that she did not distinguish between women and men in attributing religious authority, because "each time I think about it myself. (...)" adding "at least that is what I think."

Four interviewees had made a distinction between women (2b) and men (2c) in their answers. Elisabeth explained that congruence between what someone says about their faith and what someone expresses of that faith in their life – the manner in which that person enters into relations – was important to her. She said:

> And I did see that specifically with a number of women in my life and specifically not with a number of men in my life (...) There are of course, in any case, not very consciously, surely men. When I think of C.S. Lewis, whose faith has indeed inspired my faith, that is a man.[26]

Martha affirmed that she indeed would sooner assign religious authority to women than to men. Reflecting upon the statement "when someone has wisdom and speaks wise words", she expressed the idea that women are more sincere and that it is more a trick for men. She, therefore, took it less seriously in a man. And addressing the statement "when someone acts according to the Gospel",

---

[25] Interview with Hannah, 4 November 2020
[26] Afterwards, Elisabeth added in an email that her faith was primarily influenced by C.S. Lewis' *Narnia Chronicles*.

she also favoured women. Experiences with the chairman of a diaconal institution about "living according to the Gospel" left her with the impression of a fraternity and hypocrisy, whereas "women are in a different position, so that it comes out of conviction (...), it feels more rooted in experience then."

Francisca was surprised that she had circled the statement about granting authority to someone "if his vision of God and the good life inspired her" in 2c only. Reflecting upon it, she said: "When do I attribute religious authority to women... You know, I do not see them that often, (...) but maybe that is not quite true." During the interview, a woman came to mind, "someone who could get to your very core." She attributed her choice in the questionnaire, therefore, to the importance that Franciscus's texts – and Clara's – and the Franciscans in her local parish have had for her faith.

Taken together, these answers of the interviewees point to the importance of experience in the attribution of religious authority, something that is revealed in their stories about particular persons or incidents who inspired their faith. This issue is the subject matter of section three.

Section 3) Who has inspired your faith during the course of your life?
In the theoretical expositions on authority, inspiration is mentioned as an important element of the authority relation.[27] As faith is not static but changes over time, I asked, "who has inspired your faith during the course of your life?" I offered a list of 24 female or male figures and sources of inspiration which might have influenced the faith of the respondents because I was interested to see whether sexual difference had played a role in this process. Table 1 shows "the top ten sources of inspiration of faith" of the respondents.

That the women's movement leads this list may not come as a surprise, considering that the respondents were attendees of the seventh Synod of the Ecumenical Women's Synod and have been influenced by the oecumenical women-and-faith grass-root groups of the 1980s and 1990s. It also illuminates the importance of this movement for the respondent's faith.

The mother as a source of inspiration for one's faith can be explained in different ways: as arising from the (close) mother-daughter relation[28] and/or because of the (important) role of the mother in the (faith) development of younger children. The high ranking of the male pastor can be explained in

---

[27] See among others: Knecht et al., *ABC des guten Lebens*, 25.
[28] Margaret Whitford, "Mother-Daughter relationship", in: Elisabeth Wright, *Feminism and Psychoanalysis. A Critical Dictionary* (Blackwell: Cambridge 1992), 262-266.

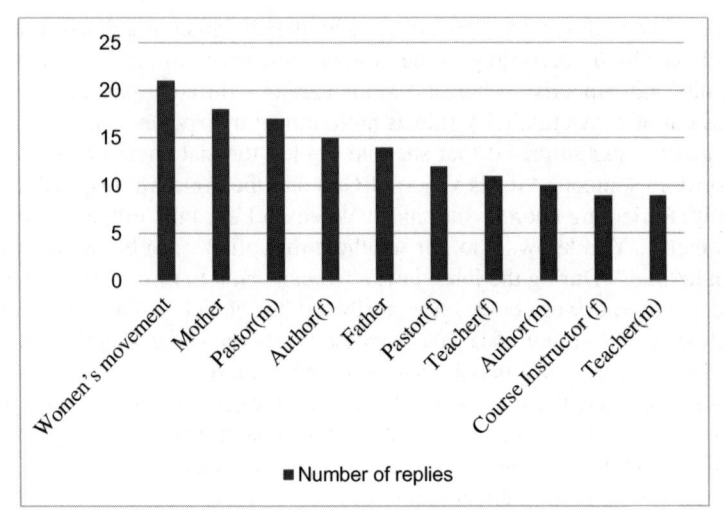

[Bar chart showing "Number of replies" for sources of religious authority, in descending order: Women's movement (21), Mother (18), Pastor(m) (17), Author(f) (15), Father (14), Pastor(f) (12), Teacher(f) (11), Author(m) (10), Course Instructor (f) (9), Teacher(m) (9).]

Table 1

more than one way, too: firstly, until far into the seventies of the last century, there were only male ministers in the mainline Protestant churches – today their number is still higher than that of female ministers – and in the Catholic Church this is still the case. But this ranking might also be part of the "gender indifference" referred to in section 2, although the high number of female figures that have inspired the faith of the respondents belies this suggestion.

To further explore the possible distinction the respondents might have made between female and male sources of inspiration, I made an inventory of the sex of the persons each respondent had circled. As it turned out, 60% of the respondents marked more women than men as sources of inspiration. Table 2 shows the results of this inventory.

I also found recurring combinations of inspirational figures such as mother and teacher(f), mother and minister(f) or mother and member of faith community(f). This might suggest a transference of the mother-daughter relation to other female inspirational figures.

The interviewees followed this pattern of the respondents. The women's-and-faith movement was also very important in their lives, especially in the lives of the older respondents. Sara, for instance, re-entered school through the educational programs for women set up by the government in the 1970s and eventually went to study theology. Women formed the majority on their lists

sex of source of inspiration

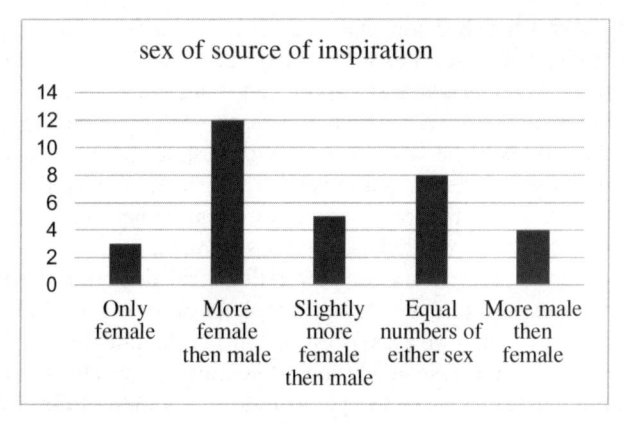

Category	Count
Only female	3
More female then male	12
Slightly more female then male	5
Equal numbers of either sex	8
More male then female	4

Table 2

of inspirational figures, too. During the interviews, they would sometimes add names of women – and men – that came to mind in the conversation. Their stories illuminate the role of inspirational figures and texts in their lives. I will give three examples.

Francisca, who was taken from school in her early teens to help the family financially, said that the books and examples of Simone de Beauvoir and Marguerite de Yourcenar had inspired her to keep fighting for herself and for what she wanted in her life. Later on, the local women-and-faith group and its courses were a source of inspiration. With them, she went to feminist theological lectures in Nijmegen, "an enormous experience". She also pointed to the Franciscan priest(s) in her local parish as an important source of inspiration for her faith and attitude. They encouraged her to become a lector and later on a lay pastor and taught her: "Do it, but do it with your heart and sensibly".

Talitha was raised in an orthodox Protestant milieu. When her mother went to a more liberal church, she encountered a different style of theology and of being a minister than she was used to. "In that church, I learned so many different things (...) I could raise questions that (...) generated new questions. That has kindled my theological consciousness." Of two other sources of inspiration, a female teacher and a female parishioner, "a heroine", she says: "They took time, attention, care. (...) They helped me in growing up." These experiences have influenced her own ministry with elderly people. She wants "to give a voice to those who have no voice. And to listen. Because it has revived me so much."

Hannah related that her aunt has been the central figure in her religious education, an input that still keeps her afloat, inspiring her in the literal sense of the word: that you receive inspiration, that it becomes alive through someone else. Following her aunt's example, Hannah decided to be baptized in the Catholic Church when she was 45 years old, despite the weird questions or strange remarks she received. With respect to the latter, her brother's not caring about the sceptical and critical reactions when he became a member of a Buddhist movement encouraged – inspired – Hannah, too.

All three stories pivot around an inspirational relation. But the nature and the content of this inspiration differed: it took the form of receiving (a) direction, of encouragement – you can do it –,[29] of non-hierarchical behaviour, of a listening ear – evoking Nelle Morton's "hearing to speech" –,[30] of a long-term affective relation, of an example to follow. All these different forms of the inspirational relation suggest that the character of authority relations is dynamic and adaptive. This is the subject matter of section 4.

Section 4) The relation to the one to whom you attribute religious authority
This section of the questionnaire was structured similarly to section 2: one part (4a) with five statements about qualities that mark the relation to a "religious authority". The respondents could indicate their disagreement or agreement on a five-point scale. The two other parts (4b and 4c) were directed at the relation to the woman or man to whom one would attribute religious authority, with the option to give multiple answers. The qualities mentioned in the statements were partly derived from the Italian-German discourse on authority – inspire, trust, entrust – and partly from more hierarchical (religious) authority relations: follow and obey.

Ad 4a. How do you relate to the person to whom you attribute religious authority?

The answers of the respondents produced the following order of statements:

1. I trust the speech/the words of the one to whom I attribute religious authority.
2. The one to whom I attribute (religious) authority inspires me in my choices.
3. I entrust myself to the advice of the one to whom I attribute religious authority.

---

[29] The Milan Women's Bookstore Collective, *Sexual Difference*, 114-115.
[30] Nelle Morton, *The Journey is Home* (Beacon Press: Boston 1985), 204-205.

4. I try to follow the example of the one to whom I attribute (religious) authority.
5. I obey the directions of the one to whom I attribute religious authority.

These answers indicate that the respondents see the relation with a religious authority as marked by trust. None disagreed, and a large majority agreed to this statement. The statement "inspires me in my choices" could also count on approval. "Obeying", however, was met with disapproval: 14 respondents fully disagreed, and eight partly disagreed with this statement. The other two statements – about entrustment and following – received a more ambivalent response; many respondents chose "neutral".

Ad 4b and 4c. How do you relate to the woman/man *to whom you attribute religious authority?*

The answers on the sub-sections 4b and 4c showed some variation to 4a. The option to give multiple answers explains that "trust" was favoured over "inspiration" in 4b, whereas in 4c these two changed places again, aligning 4c with 4a. This reshuffling is also caused by the same pattern as in section 2, namely that respondents circled fewer statements in 4c than in 4b.

In both sub-sections, "following" and "entrustment" were seen as less important and "obeying" was widely rejected. Only one of the 31 respondents indicated that she would obey the directions of the woman or man to whom she attributed authority.

In this section, another pattern was repeated, too, namely that 19 of the respondents circled the same statements in 4b and 4c, which suggests that they considered these qualities important markers of an authority relation irrespective of the sex of the "religious authority".

The interviewees followed this pattern: six did not distinguish between women and men in section four, whereas two did. None would "obey" the persons they granted religious authority. In their reflections, they mused in particular upon the words "trust" and "entrustment".

Chaja concurred that she would trust the one to whom she attributed religious authority irrespective of their sex. In the questionnaire, however, she had written a comment in the margin: "Sometimes, not always, depends". In the interview, she explained that trust can get lost, for instance when the words of the authority clash with (changed) convictions or values or with a changed frame of reference. That would cause a breach in the relation with the authority.

Speaking from a wide experience with hierarchical authority relations in the Ministry of Education, Katinjo described "trust" as a quality that is closely connected to personal integrity, honesty and the willingness to show one's vulnerability. Reflecting on "entrustment", she explained that a recent experience of a broken relation with a friend and coach had taught her how closely connected trust and entrustment are, how her loss of trust in the other was made worse because she had entrusted herself to this person.

Talitha mused that the word "entrustment" indicates a close relation; that she might have entrusted herself to the two women who supported her in her teens. "But how is that with a man? Yes, my old minister has inspired me very well in my choices. (...but) I find it always very difficult to trust men. (...) That is the difference between men and women for me."

For Martha, the statement "I trust the words of the one I grant authority" evoked associations with "blind trust", which made her weary because everyone makes mistakes. But in her view, "entrustment is different (...) Entrustment is about the trust that the other has my best interest in mind", about recognizing the trustworthiness of what someone says. She added that this belief in the good intentions of the other would bring her to follow the advice of the other so that "(...) yes, in that sense, entrustment also has an element of following, of obeying in it", although she admits that she would sooner entrust herself to a woman than to a man – other than her father.

Taken together, these stories illuminate the affective side of authority relations and the role of trust and entrustment in these relations, the emotional "attachment" to the "authority" and the (high) stakes in these relations.

Section 5) Concluding question – who has religious authority according to you?
This section can be seen as a summary and check of the issues discussed in the previous sections, especially in section one. Seven options were offered, of which the respondents could choose more than one. They could also offer their own answers. The option "Someone with wisdom" was by far the most popular (15×), closely followed by the options "An inspired/enthusiastic person" and "A theologian (f/m)" (both 11×). The option "Other" rendered two statements that referred to wisdom, too: "Wisdom based on broad life-experience of micro-macro" and "A wise person with knowledge, ability to reflect on her/his self and the world." These answers affirm the previous responses in the questionnaire, indicating that wisdom and inspiration are important qualities in the attribution of religious authority.[31]

---

[31] The options "prophet", "minister" and "bishop" were circled seven times each. It is not clear whether the respondents thought of their authority in relational or in factual terms as persons in a position of authority.

Conclusion

In this pilot study, I have explored two questions: a) to whom do female participants of the Seventh Synod-weekend of the Ecumenical Women's Synod attribute religious authority, and b) do these participants make distinctions between women and men in this process? These questions arose from two distinct discussions about authority and authority relations, notably the more general discussion on the loss of (religious) authority, through secularization, democratization, individualism and emancipation/feminism, and the discussion about the necessity of developing authority relations between women to advance their (collective) subjectivity and ideas about the good life for all. Both discourses presuppose that traditional forms of authority relations do not meet the current needs. Moreover, the Italian-German discourse offers a praxis of authority relations departing from the idea that authority is attributed. The study affirms that the authority of those "in authority" – holding a position with legitimized authority – has lost much of its credibility. This is apparent in the associations of the respondents with "religious *gezag*/authority" and the other answers on the questionnaire. These manifest an anti-hierarchical position towards authorities and a rejection of male authorities in particular. The latter was sometimes caused by painful personal experiences with male power.

This position vis-à-vis authority is not surprising considering the background of the respondents – participants of the Seventh Synod-weekend of the Ecumenical Women's Synod. Two-thirds of the respondents indicated that their faith was inspired by the women's (-and-faith) movement, which has a critical attitude to traditional authority/authorities. In the interviewees' life stories, this influence of feminism and feminist theology was also noticeable. More than one story reads as a story of emancipation, struggling with authoritarian fathers, with difficult partner relations, with violence. Their stories show that this struggle for the freedom to think and decide for oneself is often carried over in a struggle with religious authorities – think of Francesca's struggle with the new pastor of her parish – taking the form of a struggle for non-hierarchical forms of relation in which recognition of equality, respect for the freedom of the subject, autonomy in relation and free assent to the point of view of another are important characteristics.[32] In their reflections on authority, the interviewees insisted, for instance, on their freedom to decide

---

[32] Brinkgreve, *Het verlangen naar gezag*; Verhaeghe, *Autoriteit*.

for themselves whether to assent or not to the words, texts and views of someone else. They also advocated the importance of acknowledging the wisdom of "ordinary" people.

"Inspiration" is a recurring word in this process. The answers in the questionnaire show that the respondents find inspiration in texts, visions and conversations about God and the good life. The interviewees clarify that this inspiration takes the form of being touched or moved by these texts, views and words: they offer direction, encourage and affirm the subject, open different horizons, and present challenging ideas. Thus, being inspired by the other affects the perception and valuation of these inspirational sources. The high score of a quality such as wisdom and of speaking wise words in sections two and five suggests that people who inspire the subject are perceived as persons with wisdom, turning this person into someone to whom one would attribute authority.

Another form of inspiration that can affect the relation between subject and other is the experience of being listened to. Nelle Morton already pointed to the inspirational and transformative power of listening when she coined the expression "hearing someone (in)to speech".[33] Francisca referred to this power when she remarked that "it is a tremendous source of inspiration, when someone sees something in you that you haven't seen yourself, and (when) you open yourself to it." It means that this person stimulates the subject to "Go ahead", encouraging, and authorizing this subject in her desire. By doing that, this person becomes an authority herself[34] because she does what authority is about etymologically, namely to increase or enlarge.[35] Thus, (an) authority can become a religious authority by inspiring someone "to grow" or "to become": realizing the fullness of what she is capable of being,[36] incarnating an aspect of being in the image of God.

The next topic I want to draw attention to is the importance participants attached to the "congruence" between words and deeds, especially in those to whom the respondents attribute religious authority. Sara formulated this succinctly when she said: "I have to see it in deeds." This point of view corresponds with research by social psychologist Naomi Ellemers in her book *Morality and the Regulation of Social Behaviour*. She argues, first, that moral-

---

[33] See note 30.
[34] The Milan Women's Bookstore, *Sexual Difference*, 126.
[35] https://claritydaily.org/etymology/2017/1/4/authority, 28 October 2021.
[36] Irigaray, *Sexes and Genealogies*, 61.

ity is often considered more important for the group identity than competence or friendliness,[37] and secondly, that the perception of someone's moral character is central to the establishment of a relation of trust.[38] Thus, the group's cohesion is, to a large extent, determined by a shared morality (or worldview) and a shared trust that members will act accordingly.

The participants' answers indicate that they see the continuity between words and deeds as a form of moral behaviour that would point to a shared morality or understanding of what is "the good" or "the good life" and thereby induces trust. It explains why the respondents mention "trust" as an important element of the relation with the person or author to whom one grants authority, pointing to this idea of shared morality and the expectation that the other will act according to that morality. Chaja remarked that when this idea of a shared morality got lost – for instance, by a (gradual) change in worldview or because one had encountered persons with a different outlook on life which had become authoritative for the subject – the trust in the other would be affected, too. This elucidates why some interviewees – especially those with negative experiences with men and/or religious authorities – indicated that they doubted a shared morality with men. Their negative experiences had affected their trust in such an idea.

This brings me to the second question of this pilot study: do participants make a distinction between women and men in the attribution of authority? The answers in sections two and four suggest that the majority of the respondents do not make a distinction because only 13 (of the 32) respondents did. This may have been a choice of principle,[39] which seems plausible considering that for many the women's movement is foremost an emancipation movement. This option is supported by four of the interviewees, who indicated that they do not make a distinction between men and women. However, these statements were sometimes followed by sentences that undermined them. Sara, for instance, said: "I do not distinguish between man and woman. It can be anyone with a good story (…) a story I can relate to", but then continued, "I am thinking of Catharina Halkes…". It suggests that she endorses the principle of

---

[37] Naomi Ellemers, *Morality and the Regulation of Social behaviour. Groups as Moral Anchors* (Routledge: London and New York 2017), 43-44.
[38] Idem, 89.
[39] It might also be induced by the use of the plural "women" and "men" in that statement, which might have been understood as referring to the categories "women" or "men" rather than to individuals.

equality to emphasize that women are as able as men in telling a good story. Other interviewees used "disclaimers" such as "as far as I know", suggesting that they took into account that they might differentiate between women and men unconsciously. One of the respondents wrote the following in the section *Remarks* at the end of the questionnaire:

> My principle is that I do not distinguish between women and men when attributing *gezag*. But I think that I nevertheless do that unconsciously. In the case of male ministers (small example), I tend to address someone politely with *U* (You), while I call women by their first name. But that has maybe sooner something to do with *authority*.

This comment points to a dissonance between espoused and operant ideas about attributing religious authority and illuminates that ingrained patterns of authority relations are not easily shed. These examples suggest that the respondents might make more distinctions between women and men in the attribution of authority than they are aware of, and that their answers to the questionnaire are indeed inspired by the strength of the equality principle between the sexes.

As already mentioned, both in sections two and four a large minority of the respondents (13) did make a distinction between women and men, mostly by circling less of the statements for men than for women. In their reflections, those interviewees who made a distinction indicated that they had thought of specific persons when answering the questions – so they had not understood the question as referring to "women" or "men" as categories. But they also explained their choices – sometimes almost apologetically – by referring to negative experiences with men, which suggests that they, too, were caught in a paradigm of equality. Their answers therefore raise the question of whether only negative experiences with men lead to a distinction between women and men in the attribution of authority. In my view, the answer must be "no". The answers to the question "who has inspired your faith" hint at a different pattern in the attribution of authority to women and men. For the majority of the respondents not only mentioned more women than men as inspirational figures in their lives, but their answers also showed a chain of women who had constituted important sources of inspiration. It highlights the importance of the relation to another woman or women for orientation and direction. This is affirmed by the authoritative character of women's texts on God and the good life in 2b. Although this is far from what is understood by the notion of "a symbolic in the feminine", it suggests that for many respondents, the relation to other women constitutes a "wrap", a shared horizon of values which inspires trust in the other.

Could the preference of the respondents for wisdom (and wise words), a notion that has strong feminine connotations, be explained as an expression of this orientation toward other women? It is one of the issues that asks for further exploration. Other issues that need further exploration could be the authority relations between women, for instance, between hetero- and queer women,[40] or between the white women of the Ecumenical Women's Synod and (migrant) women of colour, and of course, the issue to whom women and men outside the circle of the Synod would attribute religious authority.

This pilot study has its limitations, as all pilot studies have. It has explored the question to whom women within the Ecumenical Women's Synod's circle would attribute religious authority. This exploration has charted some trends in this process, such as a strong rejection of hierarchical authority relations in favour of more "horizontal" relations, the important role of inspiration, of being touched by the words and the example of the other in the attribution of religious authority, and the importance as well as the difficulties of trust in an authority relation. It has also shown that the question of whether the respondents distinguish between women and men in the attribution of religious authority is not easily answered due to an ambivalence between principle and practice, between espoused and operant views perhaps, and to the interpretation of the gravity of inspiration and orientation in the attribution of authority. Both issues need further exploration.

Anne-Claire Mulder, PhD, is associate professor for Women's and Gender studies theology in the section of practical theology at the Protestant Theological University in the Netherlands. She wrote her PhD on the philosophy of Luce Irigaray. Her current research is devoted to processes of attribution of religious authority.

---

[40] One of the "remarks" mentioned the hetero-normative character of the questions.

Appendix: Results of questionnaire "To whom do you attribute Religious Authority?"

Section 1.

1a *What are your associations with the words "(religious) gezag/authority?*

Positions of authority	Sources of authority	Institutions	Symbols
Pope (7×)	God	Church (3×)	Pulpit (2×)
(Arch)bishop (4×)/ Church-dignitaries	Christ (2×)	Synod	Beard
Ministers (4×)	Scripture/ Word of God	Ordained ministry	
Church-leaders; authorities (male-hetero)	Apostles; prophet; Desert-fathers	My (religious) society JMJ	
Parents/family	Tradition (2×)	Established order	
Imam/ khalif	Rules/ discipline	Institutional setting	
Monks/nuns	Dogmatics	System of exclusion	
	Learning/scholarship	Wrong policy of ordination	
	Liturgy		

Qualities (neg)	Qualities (pos)	Relation (neg)	Relation (pos)
Power (7×) (1× which corrupts)	Inspiration/al, inspired/ (3×)	Distrust (2×)	Says things that matter, Confronts me with myself
Negative (6×)	Charisma (2×)	Being watchful/ wary	Strikes deeper layers
(Speaking) From above (4)	Saying something essential	Resistance and distaste	Offers me wisdom and insight
Severe/Rigid (4×)	Wisdom		
Oppression (3×)	Empathy		
Violence, overpowering	Honest		
Authoritarian	Connection		
Traditional/ Conservative	Carrying responsibility		
Thinking in terms of black and white	Giving direction		

Sentences about persons with authority
Generally acknowledged authority, for example on the bases of (ancient) knowledge and wisdom.
Someone with a message about religion/spirituality which transcends him/her and who is an example for large groups of people.
Someone in whom I recognize "a spirit of wisdom" and whom I do not catch on tricks or guru-language.
Leading the relations God- Human-beings-world.
Special, strong women, whether or not ordained/special, strong men whether or not ordained.
Someone with a religious background appointed to carry responsibility.

1b. *What are your associations with the words "Speaking with (religious) authority"?*

Qualities (neg)	Qualities (pos)	Mode of communicating
Authority/Authoritarian	Inner power/Power	Offering direction/Pointing in direction
Without doubt/Convinced	Honest, trustworthy	Humour and sense of perspective
Big words/Academic/Self-assured	Well-founded, nuanced argument	Acknowledging/Being aware of one's position (in society)
"Speaking from an institutional position"	"Speaking from an authentic, inner conviction"	Not whispering, not hidden, visible
	Professional	
	Hands-on expert	
	Aged	
	Animated, inspiration, something essential	

Institutional	Persons	Symbols	Voice
A mandate (2×) Institute behind you	Jesus (2×)	Shoulders held back	Clear voice
Calling??/Representing someone/God	My dearest aunt	Man with beard (white, 50+)	Fire-and-brimstone sermons
Temple	Some fellow sisters	Gown	Women's voice-SO different
		Headmaster	

Sentences
Do not accept without further ado
RUN AWAY – and start doing something better
Attributing authority oneself to the speaking
Getting authority by one's words

Section 2. When do you attribute religious authority to someone?

2a. *Ten theses about the question when you attribute religious authority to someone I attribute authority to someone if...*

1. this person has wisdom and speaks wise words.

Disagree	Partly disagree	Neutral	Partly agree	Agree
0×	1×	1×	6×	24×

2. the views of this person about God and the good life inspire me

Disagree	Partly disagree	Neutral	Partly agree	Agree
0×	1×	3×	7×	21×

3. someone's spirituality corresponds with the acts of this person.

Disagree	Partly disagree	Neutral	Partly agree	Agree
0×	0×	3×	8×	20×

4. the faith of that person inspires me.

Disagree	Partly disagree	Neutral	Partly agree	Agree
0×	1×	3×	10×	18×

5. someone's texts about God and the good life make me think.

Disagree	Partly disagree	Neutral	Partly agree	Agree
1×	0×	3×	10×	17×

6. this person me directs how to deal with others out of one's spirituality.

Disagree	Partly disagree	Neutral	Partly agree	Agree
0×	0×	6×	11×	13×

7. someone acts out of the Gospel.

Disagree	Partly disagree	Neutral	Partly agree	Agree
3×	2×	6×	11×	10×

8. I gladly sing someone's religious hymn-texts.

Disagree	Partly disagree	Neutral	Partly agree	Agree
4×	4×	10×	9×	5×

9. you can notice in the sermons that the person is learned.

Disagree	Partly disagree	Neutral	Partly agree	Agree
7×	3×	8×	11×	3×

10. someone is in a position of religious authority.

Disagree	Partly disagree	Neutral	Partly agree	Agree
10×	4×	7×	4×	0×

2b. *When do you attribute religious authority to* women*?* (Multiple answers possible)
    2. Someone's texts about God and the good life make me think.   25×
    3. This person has wisdom and speaks wise words.   21×
    2. The views of this person about God and the good life inspire me.   21×
    3. The faith of that person inspires me.   21×
    5. Someone's spirituality corresponds with the acts of this person.   20×
    6. This person directs me how to deal with others out of one's spirituality.   17×
    7. I gladly sing someone's religious hymn-texts.   10×
    8. Someone acts out of the Gospel.   10×
    12. You can notice in the sermons that the person is learned.   5×
    13. Someone is in a position of religious authority.   4×
    14. Other:
        – Creative handling of the religious tradition.
        – Getting to know someone as (a) wise (person) in daily life.
        – Someone has to say something spiritual.
        – If women position themselves as unconventional and enthusiastic.
        – An attitude to life as connectedness with fragile life and giving shape to faith/spirituality from there.

2c. *When do you attribute religious authority to* men*?* (Multiple answers possible)
    5. Someone's texts about God and the good life make me think.   22×
    6. This person has wisdom and speaks wise words.   21×
    7. The views of this person about God and the good life inspire me.   20×
    8. The faith of that person inspires me.   19×

9. Someone's spirituality corresponds with the acts of this person. 17×
10. This person directs me how to deal with others out of one's spirituality 16×
11. Someone acts out of the Gospel. 10×
12. I gladly sing someone's religious hymn-texts. 9×
12. Someone is in a position of religious authority. 5×
13. You can notice in the sermons that the person is learned. 4×
14. Other:
    - If men position themselves as progressive and enthusiastic.
    - An attitude to life as connectedness with fragile life and giving shape to faith/ spirituality from there.

Section 3. Who has inspired or influenced you during your life? (More answers possible)

Women's movement 21×	Mother 18×	Minister/Pastor (m) 17×
Author (f) 15×	Father 14×	Minister/Pastor (f) 12×
Teacher (f) 11×	Author (m) 10×	Course leader (f) (9×)
Teacher (m) 9×	Aunt 8×	Member (f) of faith-community 7×
Grand-mother 7×	Grandfather 7×	Peace-movement 6×
Sister 5×	Green Churches 5×	Refugee work 5×
Member (m) faith-community 4×	Female mystic 3×	Brother 3×
Uncle 2×	Male mystic 2×	

3b *Which authors have inspired you?*

Catharina Halkes (3×)	Johanna van Moorsel	Henri Nouwen 2×
Catherine Keller	Maria de Groot	Kees Waaijman
Nadia Bolz-Weber	Vandana Shiva	Prof. Bleeker
Sanny Bruijns	Chung Hyung Kyung	Bevrijdingstheologen
Marjorie Procter Smith	Schüssler-Fiorenza	Moltmann
Ruth Duck	Marilynne Robinson	Hein Blommestijn
Dorothee Sölle	Judith Butler	Frans Maas
Audre Lorde	Etty Hillesum	CS Lewis (oa)
Linda Rood		Levinas
Shirly Mocain		

3c *Which mystics have inspired you?*

| Etty Hillesum (2×) | Kierkegaard | Karmel spiritualiteit |
| Hildegard van Bingen (2×) | Rumi | Taizé |

3d *Other:*

| Colleagues 2× | Friends (F + M) | Beloved |
| Great-aunt | Politicians | Franciscans |

Section 4. Theses about your relation with the one to whom you attribute religious authority to

1. I trust the speech/the words of the one to whom I attribute religious authority.

| Disagree | Partly disagree | Neutral | Partly agree | Agree |
| 0× | 0× | 3× | 12× | 17× |

2. The one to whom I attribute (religious) authority inspires me in my choices.

| Disagree | Partly disagree | Neutral | Partly agree | Agree |
| 0× | 0× | 7× | 14× | 11× |

3. I entrust myself to the advice of the one to whom I attribute religious authority.

| Disagree | Partly disagree | Neutral | Partly agree | Agree |
| 0× | 2× | 10× | 11× | 8× |

4. I try to follow the example of the one to whom I attribute (religious) authority.

| Disagree | Partly disagree | Neutral | Partly agree | Agree |
| 2× | 4× | 12× | 9× | 5× |

5. I obey the directions of the one to whom I attribute religious authority.

| Disagree | Partly disagree | Neutral | Partly agree | Agree |
| 14× | 1× | 7× | 3× | 1× |

4b *How do you relate to the* woman *whom attribute religious authority to?*

1. The one to whom I attribute (religious) authority inspires me in my choices. 27×
2. I trust the speech/the words of the one to whom I attribute religious authority. 23×
3. I try to follow the example of the one to whom I attribute (religious) authority. 10×
4. I entrust myself to the advice of the one to whom I attribute religious authority. 9×
5. I obey the directions of the one to whom I attribute religious authority. 1×

4c *How do you relate to the* man *whom you attribute authority to?*

1. I trust the speech/ the words of the one to whom I attribute religious authority. 22×
2. The one to whom I attribute (religious) authority inspires me in my choices. 20×
3. I try to follow the example of the one to whom I attribute (religious) authority. 8×
4. I entrust myself to the advice of the one to whom I attribute religious authority. 6×
5. I obey the directions of the one to whom I attribute religious authority. 1×

Section 5. Concluding question – who has religious authority according to you?

1. Someone with wisdom 15×
2. An inspired/enthusiastic person 11×
3. A theologian (f/m) 11×
4. A prophet 7×
5. A minister 7×
6. A bishop 7×
6. Someone of strong faith 6×
7. Other:
   a. A loved friend (f).
   b. Someone of sincere faith and vulnerable heart.
   c. Wisdom based on broad life-experience of micro-macro.
   d. Ecological farmers (f/m) and people connected with the grass-roots.
   e. Someone who can lead in the relation God-human-world.
   f. A wise person with knowledge, ability to reflect on her/his self and the world.
   g. Theological education important.

Remarks by respondents at the end of the questionnaire
- These are difficult questions. (3×)
- "My principle is that I do not attribute authority differently to women and men. But I think that I nevertheless do that unconsciously. In the case of male ministers (small example), I tend to say You, while I call women by their first name. But that has maybe sooner something to do with authority."
- I thought the questions pretty nice. However, the affairs of faith and attitude to life go deeper for me than women's emancipation. I may have been lucky that I women as models.
- From my "minority" position as lesbian, I have difficulties with the fact that the male-hetero way of thinking was employed normatively.
- I notice that the measure of authority I attribute depends on the person. An official title/role or not makes a difference in the respect that he/she minister and chosen inspirator is. Preferably changing positions.
- I give (religious) authority to people who showed that they know how societal exclusion works. Further everyone can be a partner in dialogue.
- Difficult to distinguish between formal authority and positive or negative forms of authority in this questionnaire.
- I noticed that the associations with religious authority were no associations of personal attribution. Speaking with authority was, though. There is for me a big difference between religious authority and authority, which has the connotations of business-structures, government, politics.
- About section four: I also attribute religious authority to/acknowledge religious authority to people with convictions which are opposite to mine.

Round Table

African Female Theologians Telling Stories: 'Connected but Disconnected'

Abstract
The most well-known voices on the Dutch theological landscape are generally those of Dutch citizens with a European background. As African women theologians, we have had to navigate the space of "insider-outsiders" as we engage the Dutch and Flemish theological and academic landscapes. African Female Theologians in Europe (AFTE) was formed to help support the visibility of theologians who experience being "outsider-insiders". It is a space designed to specifically recognise and support the contribution of women theologians in the Netherlands and Belgium. In June 2021, AFTE organised its first symposium in order to explore the theme "Connected but Disconnected". The symposium sought to critically explore how African Female Theologians (as insiders-outsiders), in discussion with some Dutch sisters, negotiate the (dis)connections we encounter as we participate in Dutch/Flemish theological discourse. This special collection of essays presents some of the discussions that took place at this first symposium.

Zusammenfassung
Die bekanntesten Stimmen der niederländischen theologischen Welt sind im Allgemeinen die Niederländischen mit ihrem europäischen Hintergrund. Als afrikanische Theologinnen mussten wir uns durch den Raum der „Insider-Outsider" bewegen, während wir uns auf die niederländisch/flämische theologische und akademische Welt einließen. Die Vereinigung *African Female Theologians in Europe* (AFTE) wurde gegründet, um die Sichtbarkeit von Theologinnen zu unterstützen, die das „Insider-Outsider" erleben. Dies ist ein Raum, der speziell dazu gedacht ist, den Beitrag von Theologinnen in den Niederlanden und Belgien zu würdigen und zu unterstützen. Im Juni 2021 organisierte die AFTE ihr erstes Symposium zum Thema „Connected but Disconnected". Das Symposium wollte kritisch untersuchen, wie afrikanische Theologinnen (als Insider-Outsiders) im Gespräch mit einigen niederländischen Schwestern die (Dis-)Verbindungen aushandeln, denen wir bei der Teilnahme am niederländisch/flämischen theologischen Diskurs begegnen. Diese spezielle Aufsatzsammlung stellt einige der Diskussionen vor, die auf diesem ersten Symposium stattfanden.

Round Table
African Female Theologians Telling Stories: 'Connected but Disconnected'

Resumen
Generalmente, las voces mejor conocidas en el panorama teológico holandés son las de los holandeses que tienen un trasfondo europeo. Como mujeres teólogas africanas que habitan el contexto teológico y académico holandés/flamenco, nos vemos obligadas a navegar el espacio existente entre el estar dentro y el estar fuera. Teólogas Africanas en Europa (AFTE, por sus siglas en inglés) se formó para dar apoyo y visibilidad a las teólogas que experimentan esta tensión. Se trata de un espacio específicamente pensado para reconocer y fomentar las contribuciones de teólogas africanas en los Países Bajos y Bélgica. En junio de 2021, AFTE celebró su primer simposio con el objetivo de explorar el tema "Conectadas. Desconectadas". El simposio pretendía explorar críticamente, y en discusión con algunas teólogas hermanas holandesas, cómo las teólogas africanas, en tanto experimentamos el estar dentro y fuera simultáneamente, negociamos las (des)conexiones que encontramos al participar en el debate teológico holandés/flamenco. Esta especial colección de textos presenta algunas de las discusiones que tuvieron lugar en este primer simposio.

Keywords: Insider/outsider, (dis)connectedness, female theologians, African, Europe.

Introduction

This special collection of essays was initially presented at the Inaugural Symposium of the African Female Theologians in Europe under the auspices of the *Netherlands School for Advanced Studies in Theology and Religion* (NOSTER) in June 2021. Due to the Covid-19 pandemic, the event was held virtually and was attended by invited speakers and participants from around the Netherlands and beyond. The African Female Theologians in Europe is a network of theologians collaborating to make African and African Diaspora Christian female theologians' contributions more visible in Europe's (Protestant) Christian theological discourse.

African Female Theologians in Europe (hereafter, AFTE) is the name we decided to use when in 2020, Tabitha Poline Moyo (Zambia), Shingirai Eunice Masunda (Zimbabwe) and Thandi Soko-de Jong (Malawi) were sharing our experiences in the field of theology. As an African woman studying theology alternately in Belgium (Flanders) and the Netherlands, Tabitha Moyo had long observed that many African women theologians she encountered shared similar experiences. Some of these experiences include an expectation to focus on topics that frame African societies negatively or scepticism over how "authentic, rigorous or African" our theories and approaches are. Other experiences include the expectation to contribute to knowledge production with little or no recognition and acknowledgement. There is also limited diversity, which lessens the likelihood of accessing qualified scholars in our field/s from a range of backgrounds. Tabitha Moyo had also observed that we have many things in common, but few networks exist that provide a platform for exchanging ideas and support unique to our opportunities and challenges in the diaspora while enabling our contributions. She felt compelled to help fill this gap and envisioned a platform that would invite African female theologians to share, collaborate, and support each other with like-minded women scholars from Europe and beyond. AFTE, therefore, seeks to be a platform where knowledge and collaboration that respond to these realities can be shared.

With this in mind, we note that although it is well recognised that most Christians today live in the Majority World (Latin America, Africa and Asia), these groups remain less represented within the academic theology of many European contexts, including those having significant Christian populations with a Majority World background. The Dutch and Flemish theological landscape, in which we three founding members are located, fall within this

Round Table
African Female Theologians Telling Stories: 'Connected but Disconnected'

category of theologians who are from a non-European/Western background but remain underrepresented, less visible, and whose influence on theological discourse remains marginal. There are a variety of reasons why this remains so, including limitations tied to language barriers, particularly for visiting scholars and new arrivals. Another reason is that there remains a tendency for institutions to adhere to specific canons of theological texts that may exclude the experiences, points of view and reflections of scholars of other cultural backgrounds. As founding members, we recognise that we share, in our own various ways, the experience of being outsiders-insiders. We regularly find ourselves having to negotiate *(dis)connections* as we participate in theological discourse in the Dutch/Flemish context. In our case, as African female theologians, the negotiations are intersectional and crosscut our embodied and positional engagement with theology in terms of perceptions of gender, race and ethnic background.

Against such a background, AFTE organised its first symposium in order to explore these realities under the theme "Connected but Disconnected". This theme sought to critically explore this notion through a conversation with Dutch scholars whose work engages with, and intersects with, the symposium's theme, aims and concerns. Panellists were invited to be creative and engage the topic from their preferred formats. Part of this encouragement was to reflect AFTE's goal of being a space whereby the diversity of contributors' ontological and epistemological aims is recognised. To this end, "essays" is the umbrella term used to describe this collection. In practice, it includes theoretical papers, narrative essays and spoken word poetry, all of which engage theologically and practically with the overall theme of "connected but disconnected" and its relation to the experiences of being an "insider-outsider". The essays are ordered so as to respond to one another in accordance with some sub-themes.

Thandi Soko-de Jong

Prologue

Words and Words

Spoken Word Poem by Thandi Soko-de Jong

Some will say:
Speak only as if to an audience of One,
But the truth is, the One gives us an audience of many.

You see, I fell asleep right here.
But I woke up in a future year.
You were there, greying.
And you could hear me saying...
Asking...
When did it all start?

You said,
It all started when I used words and they listened.
At first, they crowned me with many titles:
A word smith, a rare talent, a scholar, a theologian.
But that did not last.
Because soon, I used some more words and they refused to listen.
They told me, instead, what was wrong with my words.

They said,
"Your grammar is poor, your spelling is wrong,
Too many run-ons and what is up with the fonts?"
With concern they said to me, "Your meaning is unclear, darling,
with these many mistakes.
Fix them in time, and only then will we understand you.
You don't truly know the meaning of words, do you?"

How could I respond? Their words against mine,
So, I sat in my silence, waiting to fix my words with new words.
And in that time a new word came sweeping across the world,
We became **lockdown**-ed, unto ourselves, in a **quarantine** of soft silence.
That's when they came to me, one by one,
with words spoken by **she**.

First, the familiar voice that taught me to be.
Of my mother, her songs, her stories, an oral heritage,
Handed down to me as she added up the numbers and sums in her head,
To build and expand her business enterprise.
I remembered the voices of my teachers,
Who added a whole world,
Of images, drama, movies, experience, African philosophies,
To that curriculum made at Cambridge,
For Africa.
My mother, my teachers and a teeming number of sisters.
An ebb, and then a steady flow.
Many words they said to me:
"O' theologian! Do watch out for heresy and unwanted controversy!
But watch out too, and see,
Whose words you elevate and whose you don't see."
So, I opened up new books to see what I never saw.
Nansubuga Makumbi[1] squared up with Namwali Serpell:[2] Who will write the true postcolonial tale?
Adichie[3] and McCall Smith[4] prepared for battle: Who will give us a heroine against the decay?
Olanna?[5] with her passion for justice like Binti,[6] Shuri[7] or perhaps Joana Coelho?[8]

---

[1] Jennifer Nansubuga Makumbi (b.1967) is a Ugandan award-winning writer. This line is in reference to her novel *Kintu* (2014).

[2] Namwali Serpell (b.1980) is an American and Zambian writer and professor of English. This line is in reference to her novel *The Old Drift* (2019).

[3] Chimamanda Ngozi Adichie (b.1977) is a Nigerian writer, feminist and public figure. Her novels that feature strong female lead characters include *Purple Hibiscus* (2003), *Half of a Yellow Sun* (2006) and *Americanah* (2013).

[4] Alexander McCall Smith (b.1948) is a British writer. He is well-known for his fictional series *The No. 1 Ladies' Detective Agency,* to which I am referring in this line. The female lead in this series is the character Mma Ramotswe.

[5] Olanna Ozobia is a character in Chimamanda Ngozi Adichie's book *Half of a Yellow Sun* (2006). She is depicted as an attractive, intelligent and complex young woman living in the midst of the Biafran War in Nigeria (1967-1970).

[6] Binti is the main character in Nnedi Okorafor's science fiction, afro-futurist novella series titled *Binti* (2015), *Binti: Home* (2017) and *Binti: The Night Masquerade* (2018). She is a young woman and the first from her ethnic group on Earth to attend an intergalactic University.

[7] Shuri is a character in the Marvel comic book *Black Panther* (and films). She is the princess and sister of the titular character, T'Challa the Black Panther.

[8] Joana Coelho is an Afro-Brazilian character in the Brazilian series titled *3%*. She is involved in the struggle against the injustice of the "process", a system that offers a good quality of life to only a few members of society.

Or Mma Ramotswe?[9] with her charming, sweet innocence and wit?

I looked up from the books that taught me about *Earthseed*[10] to stories in real life,
as we called it in those days,
To the news, social media, stars and influencers, to see what they had to say.
Struggles were many but triumphs there were.
New heroines were emerging,
As fast as they fell.
There were words from those who rose only to fall.
And words from defenders of the system,
and from those raising a fist.
"Enemies of progress", depending on the plot twist.

There were fighters and changemakers and those in-between.
Blandina,[11] a champion for women's health who was also a beauty queen,
Pink balloons floating in her memory where she now rests.
Some had no dissertation, no thesis and no sermons to their name,
But the African women were rising.
But where were the female theologians in this mainstream to be seen?

Slowly, carefully, quietly, I saw.
That some theologians live to use their words a different way.
Some Christian, some not,
All with a religion of some sort.
Or none at all.
Some spoke about bringing the Bechdel test to life in words and words.
Others reminded me, "Don't leave the men and the children behind!"
Others still were there to say, "Gender is more than a binary, there are others more."
And some reminded me, "Don't just look here, the diaspora has more."

---

[9] Mma Ramotswe is the main character in Alexander McCall Smith's novel series titled *The No. 1 Ladies' Detective Agency* (see footnote 4). In my view, this character reinforces a stereotype of an African woman as overweight, nurturing/mothering, pleasant, gentle, wise, resilient and strong particularly in the face of adversity. Each of these traits is not bad on its own. However, when combined, Mma Ramotswe is a caricature and stereotype based on a false imagery of African women.

[10] *Earthseed* is a fictional religion based on the idea that God is "change". The religion serves as the centrepiece of Octavia Butlers' novels *The Parable of the Sower* (1993) and *The Parable of the Talents* (1998).

[11] Blandina Khondowe (née Mlenga) was a Malawian beauty queen (b.1980-2020) who later became a cancer awareness activist known for raising consciousness about the disease across the nation of Malawi. She succumbed to the disease in Lilongwe, Malawi, in 2020.

Thinkers and leaders in diverse spheres:
Wekker[12] and Hazel[13] here, Hudson-Wilkin[14] across the pond.

Some hushed tones and secrecy, a longing for a life of progress,
Loud, resolute protest, a longing for the past.
Anger at the abuse, the pain and the fear.
A chant for hope, for fullness of life to come near.
Spaces for custodians, and for those we have failed.
Words to beat into shape what gives life and a voice,
For the fragile, for the young and the "different".
For Eudy Simelane[15] and many others whose names we'll never know.

At last, you told me, about when your words began to flow.
The morning you got up and a new theologian was born.
Your audience was *many*, but God made your hand one.
To spin words that you had heard from those who had long began,
Words from sisters long asleep, Makeba[16], Maathai[17], Fassie[18], Simone[19] – the list went on.
In your own journey in theology,
many words spill over,
To lead, guide and to remind;

---

[12] Gloria Wekker (b.1950) is an Afro-Surinamese Dutch emeritus professor and author. Her work is influential in numerous discourses, including gender, sexuality and race. Of all her works, I have been most influenced by *White Innocence: Paradoxes of Colonialism and Race* (2016).

[13] Doreen Hazel († 2014) was an Afro-Surinamese Dutch Womanist theologian. Among her major works is the 1998 publication *Dochters van Cham* ("Daughters of Ham"), in which she examined the legacies of slavery and racism from a Womanist theologian perspective.

[14] Rose Hudson-Wilkin (b.1961) is a British Anglican bishop. She is the first black woman to serve as a Church of England bishop.

[15] Eudy Simelane (1977-2008) was a South African footballer and an LGBT rights activist. She was a victim of a hate crime when she was attacked and murdered in 2008 because of her sexual orientation and activism.

[16] Miriam Makeba (1932-2008) was an anti-Apartheid and civil rights activist, as well as a Grammy-award winner (1965) and nominee (2000).

[17] Wangarĩ Muta Maathai (1940-2011) was a Kenyan environmental, political and social activist. She was the first African woman to win the Nobel Peace Prize (2004).

[18] Brenda Fassie (1964-2004) was a South African singer-songwriter and anti-Apartheid political and queer activist.

[19] Nina Simone (1933-2003) (born Eunice Kathleen Waymon) was an African American musician, singer-songwriter and civil rights activist.

Oduyoye,[20] Dube,[21] Moyo,[22] Nadar,[23] Phiri,[24] Kamba Kasongo[25] and more.
From yet more sisters brimming with youth,
words still flowed, Nakate,[26] Koffee,[27] Kansiime[28] and Coel.[29]

I'm now awake in the present and I remember the words you gave:
Sponge all the words up and have your story to tell.
Hear Angelou[30] ask, "Will you rise?" And hear Chisala[31] respond,
"I have. And I have found that I don't always speak in honey,
and that I may not be the girl you dreamt me up to be."
Hear the rejoinder from Koffee who stands up to shout, "Girl, so, *tun* it up higher!
Keep the fire burning. Your words are a flame!"
Evaristo[32] reminds, "Never give up."

---

[20] Mercy Amba Oduyoye (b. 1934) is a Ghanaian theologian known for her pioneering work in African women's theology. Among her many notable accomplishments is her founding in 1989 of the Circle for Concerned African Christian Women Theologians, a continent-wide ecumenical body supporting African women theologians' scholarly research.

[21] Musa Dube (b. 1964) (born Musa Wenkosi Dube Shomanah) is from Botswana. She is a feminist theologian specialising in New Testament and postcolonial biblical scholarship.

[22] Fulata L. Moyo is a Malawian theologian specialising in systematic theology and feminist theology. She is an activist and an advocate for gender justice.

[23] Sarojini Nadar (b. 1976) is a South African theologian and biblical scholar. In this poem, I am inspired by her 2014 article, "'Stories are Data with Soul' – Lessons from Black Feminist Epistemology, in: *Agenda* 28:1 (March/2014), 18-28.

[24] Isabel Apawo Phiri is a Malawian theologian and the current Associate General Secretary of the World Council of Churches.

[25] Micheline Kamba Kasongo († 2020) was a Congolese (DRC) Presbyterian theologian and ecumenist. She was known for championing the rights of people living with disabilities.

[26] Vanessa Nakate (b. 1996) is a Ugandan climate justice activist. She is the author of *A Bigger Picture: My Fight to Bring a New African Voice to the Climate Crisis* (2021).

[27] Koffee (b. 2000) (born Mikayla Simpson) is a Jamaican singer-songwriter and musician. She is a Grammy award winner (2020).

[28] Anne Kansiime (b.1986) is a Ugandan actress, comedian and entertainer. She is popular across Africa, where she is described by some media outlets as "Africa's Queen of Comedy".

[29] Michaela Coel (b. 1987) (born Michaela Ewuraba Boakye-Collinson) is a British actress, director, screenwriter, singer and producer best known for creating and starring in *Chewing Gum* (2015–2017) and *I May Destroy You* (2020).

[30] Maya Angelou (1928-2014) (born Marguerite Annie Johnson) was an African American writer, poet and civil rights activist. Her poem "Still I rise" has been influential in developing some of my general viewpoints.

[31] Upile Chisala is a Malawian storyteller and poet. She is known for her short and powerful poems, including her three collections of poetry and prose *soft magic* and *nectar* (2019) and *a fire like you* (2020). She was among the 2019 Forbes Africa 30 under 30 list.

[32] Bernardine Evaristo (b. 1959) (also known as Bernardine Anne Mobolaji Evaristo, OBE FRSL FRSA) is a British author and academic. She is the first black woman, and the first black

Words are powerful, they are roots, they are branches, they are fruits.
However, you are a theologian like me so don't forget the words that make the greatest Story of all.
Words, were the greeting that made Elizabeth's belly leap for joy,
As the two women took their role.
In the story of Good News passed down by the matriarchs and the patriarchs.
Only then, will you like me choose the words over words,
To tell the story uninhibited by other words.
Words that grammar, tense, structure and font will ignore,
But words that content, context, praxis will bring to the fore.

May my hands be ready to form the words,
That will free my hands to be, and to let others be…
Free.

Thandi Soko-de Jong is a Malawian-Dutch activist-theologian. She is a PhD candidate at the Protestant Theological University in the Netherlands, where the focus of her studies lies within Intercultural theology. She has a background in African Studies (African Studies Centre Leiden, Leiden University, the Netherlands), Theology and Development (University of KwaZulu-Natal, South Africa), and Biblical Studies and Mass Communications (African Bible College, Malawi). She is a tutor at the Foundation Academy of Amsterdam and is involved in various networks and working groups, including the Werkgroep Heilzame Verwerking Slavernijverleden and the MissieNederland (formerly Evangelical Alliance). Thandi is married to Folkert, a reverend in the Protestant Church of the Netherlands. Together with their daughter, they live in Gelderland, the Netherlands.

British person, to win the Booker Prize (2019) for her book *Girl, Woman, Other* (2019). This line is in the poem is in reference to her memoir *Manifesto: On Never Giving Up* (2021).

Tabitha Poline Moyo

The Returning Insider: Tensions and Challenges of an African Female Researcher Conducting Research in her Own Country

The Insider Outsider Debate

> Whether the researcher is an insider, sharing the characteristic, role, or experience under study with the participants, or an outsider to the commonality shared by participants, the personhood of the researcher, including her or his membership status in relation to those participating in the research, is an essential and ever-present aspect of the investigation.[33]

The status of insider-outsider continues to be a heavily debated topic in qualitative research because when conducting research, the researcher's positionality should be highly considered.[34] The idea underlying the researcher's positionality is that how one is perceived is vital to what information one receives. This article debates how researchers are positioned as either 'insiders' or 'outsiders' when conducting research across cultures.

For the most part, scholars agree that the idea of being an insider involves one doing research within one's own organisation, culture or group and thus giving them natural access to participants. The outsider positionality is the opposite of this and has the researcher exploring aspects of a culture, organisation or group they have limited or no affiliation to.[35] The majority of these debates tend to gravitate towards which option is superior, and this creates a dichotomy where no overlap between the two is considered. Nonetheless,

---

[33] Sonya Dwyer and Jennifer Buckle, "The Space Between: On Being an Insider-Outsider in Qualitative Research", in: *Interanational Journal of Qualitative Methods* 8 (March/2009), 54-63, here 55.

[34] According to Holmes, "the term positionality both describes an individual's worldview and the position they adopt about a research task and its social and political context." Andrew Holmes, "Researcher Positionality – A Consideration of Its Influence and Place in Qualitative Research – A New Researcher Guide",' in: *Shanlax International Journal of Education* 8 (September/2020), 1-10, here 1.

[35] Teresa Brannick and David Coghlan, "In Defense of Being 'Native': The Case for Insider Academic Research", in: *Organizational Research Methods* 10 (January/2007), 59-74.

much of this earlier research favoured outsider research approaches because it is argued as being more objective, allowing for a more critical exploration of the participants by an expert on the research topic. However, in recent years insider research has gained more interest. According to Been, it is common for qualitative researchers to study familiar spaces such as a group, culture or organisation they belong to, thus beginning the research process from the position of an insider.[36] As an insider researcher, one is considered more intimately engaged with the subjects of the research study, thus offering a much richer understanding of the research group because they have a better ability to interact with their participants, which further creates a better rapport with them.

Navigating Western Academic Spaces
I was born and raised in Zambia. I did my bachelor's in theology at Justo Mwale Theological University in Lusaka. I later did two master's degrees, both in the Netherlands and in Belgium, after which I pursued a PhD with these two universities. Consequently, I have spent approximately six years in European academia.

During this time abroad at my various European universities, I have spent my years exploring and mastering issues pertaining to gender and religion, especially as it relates to African women's experiences of sexual and physical violence. This has positioned me as an outsider researcher because I have had to use European theories and constructs on an African topic, which requires bending and adapting the various concepts and constructs not native to African thought to suit Western academia and vice versa.

My decision to do my PhD in Europe always surprises people in my homeland. I think this has a lot to do with the fact that I am considered too young to do a PhD[37] or even that I am a woman. On the other hand, here in Europe, it is somewhat expected and not surprising for people to see students from the Global South coming to study in Europe. The presumption, I suppose, is that as a student from the Global South coming to study at a Western university, I am expected to "learn something" and then return to my country and improve or exert change. This is an aspect that I see locks us up as researchers in a continuous status of outsider because it inhibits our assimilation in the host

---

[36] Lauren Breen, "The Researcher 'in the Middle': Negotiating the Insider/Outsider Dichotomy", in: *The Australian Community Psychologist* 19 (May/2007), 163-74.
[37] The average age of PhD students in Zambia tends to be between 40-55 years, although this is slowly changing.

countries, especially when the question and statement that follows is always: "When are you returning to your country? Your country needs women like you", leading me to ask: "Does this country not need women like me?"

Additionally, the assumption that, as a student from the Global South, you must "learn something" and that you are not necessarily one who could "teach something" blocks possibilities for mutual learning in our host countries. However, I feel this is a problem related to gender, power and privilege structures within Western academic spaces, in which, for the most part, people from the Global South have been objects of research and seldom are they seen as researchers inside their own context. Presenting Western scholars as "natural insiders" in global research and African scholars as outsiders in their own research is an aspect also pointed out by Cobb, Rodríguez and Missbach when they reflect on hierarchies, privileges and positionalities in Western academic research.[38] Thus, my research topic and choice of research location were deliberately selected to contribute to the discussions in my home country from an insider's perspective.

Returning Home as an Insider Researcher
Between the years 2017 and 2019, I travelled several times to Zambia to conduct a case study on the roles of women in shaping masculinity in the Zambian Christian community, a topic that I knew would pull me out of my comfort zone because it bordered on explorations on Zambian men and dominant masculinities. Consequently, the data collection processes involved spending several months conducting focus groups, in-depth interviews and observations with various Chewa speaking men and women in the Eastern province of Zambia.

Conducting this research in this area felt like returning home. My tribe was from this area, so I felt a sense of kinship and familiarity with the way of life, culture, worldview, customs, norms and, more importantly, the language of my participants. In addition, because most of the Christians in the region belong to the Reformed Church in Zambia, a church I continue to be a member of and was ordained in, I felt a sense of shared faith and spiritual belonging, further solidifying my insider status as a returning researcher.

---

[38] Michael Cobb et al., "'Insiders' and Outsiders': Reflections on Hierarchies, Privileges and Positionalities in Academic Research", in: *ABI Working Papers* No 15 (Arnold Bergstraesser Institute: Freiburg 2020), 1-35, here 6.

Round Table
African Female Theologians Telling Stories: 'Connected but Disconnected'

Tales from my Experience: An Insider?

Most of my data collection went reasonably smooth, with participants eager to speak with me, inviting me to their homes and visiting me to share more things they felt would be useful for my research. I felt very much a welcomed part of the communities I visited, which gave me confidence in the feasibility of the entire project.

Although most of my field experience was positive, I did feel that my insider status presented me with some challenges. For instance, some participants saw me as a confidant with whom they could share their deepest problems. So, instead of answering the questions I had prepared, some wanted just to share their stories. However, when I think about this, I think the participants felt that way because I would leave and go back to a faraway land called the Netherlands. Their secrets were safe. Thus, while treating me as an insider, privy to their secrets, they simultaneously saw me as an outsider. I was the visitor who would eventually leave. At the same time, it was very common for participants to assume a shared experience with me, making statements such as, "You know us Zambian women and what we go through" or "You know since you are married as well." I realised I had to make it known to the participants that I needed them to explain in more detail. Thus, I constantly had to reiterate, "No, I do not know. Please, tell me."

I also encountered situations where I was excluded entirely and made an outsider because of my gender and age, especially when I conducted focus groups with men. Certain questions asked seemed to create much unease because I did not account for the strict gender roles within most cultures in Zambia and the fact that these strict gender roles also apply when accessing information. There is certain information only accessible to men and vice versa, thus making it too taboo to be spoken of in public, worse off in the presence of a woman. The male participants retorted, "We cannot speak about such things in front of a woman" or "You are too young to hear such things."

Similarly, with the women's fellowship group, the determining factor between my insider or outsider status was based not just on my being a woman but also on my marital status. Between 2017 and 2019, when I visited my case study locations and conducted initial focus groups and interviews, the women seemed reluctant to answer certain questions. Since I was a woman, I assumed that they would easily open up to me because the questions catered toward issues affecting us as women. But this was not the case. In 2019 I returned for further sessions. This was right after my wedding. In my visit that year, I expected the reluctance I received the previous year, but the women were more open to answering my questions, to my surprise. When I asked the women what had changed, they simply said, "You have now been taught", referring to the rite of passage called Chilangizo that all women in the Reformed Church must undergo before marriage. For the women, the fact that I had undergone the Chilangizo had made me a fully mature woman like them, now able to understand and grasp deeper meanings of womanhood.

Additionally, there was significant tension between my role as a pastor and a researcher as perceived by my participants. Pastors are highly respected within Chewa society, while a researcher is a foreign concept. This created an imbalance of power and status, with me being in the position of power. My position as pastor gave me access to participants because I was an insider in the religious body they belonged to. But it also made me an outsider because of the problematic relationship between the church and Chewa culture. Indeed, these tensions date back to the influence of Dutch missionaries, who frowned upon a lot of Chewa cultural practices and considered them pagan. Because of this, many Chewa beliefs, cultural practices and traditions consolidated into the private life of Chewa Christians. Participants were surprised that a pastor inquired about their cultural practices, believing that pastors are against these. Participants seemed fearful, uneasy, defensive and scared at times, saying things like, "Don't tell the church elders that I have done this before" and "I don't know if this is a sin."

To mitigate this tension, I drew on my role as a researcher and used this to assure participants that I was not there in my capacity as a pastor but solely as a researcher. I humbled myself to their expertise, taking on the role of a child eager to learn. Because ultimately, they were my teachers.[39] It made participants more at ease.

Finding Spaces Between

During this entire process, I kept a research diary, in which I documented and reflected on how participants responded to my role. This included documenting moments in which my positionality had either a positive or negative

---

[39] The metaphor of a child in field research refers to the idea that the researcher starts his/her research from an inferior position pertaining to the topic, allowing the researcher to ask questions from an appeared sense of uninformed, naïve perspective. Målfrid Råheim et al., "Researcher-Researched Relationship in Qualitative Research: Shifts in Positions and Researcher Vulnerability", in: *International Journal of Qualitative Studies on Health and Well-Being* 11 (June/2016), 1-12, here 10.

influence. I documented times when I felt excluded or included, which brought me to a realisation. When I started my research project, I began with the idea that, as a researcher, I am either an insider or an outsider, and therefore I must position myself as such. However, this ended up not being to the benefit of the research. As a researcher, I should rather occupy a fluid space in-between, where I would acknowledge the ways in which my role could be the best fit in the current environment – and would consequently influence the willingness of my participants to share information.[40] It required a continuous reflective approach in which I would identify which positionality was more acceptable for my participants so they would share sensitive information with me. Through this, I could also formulate my own story within this process and cultural context, some of which I have also shared in this paper.

I end by saying that as daunting and exciting as the process of conducting research in one's own country might be after spending so many years abroad, it must never be taken as a given that the returning researcher automatically is an insider. In fact, at times, this should not even be seen as a favourable role. Instead, the researcher could try to position themselves as an in-betweener and, as such, shift between these identities to create favourable encounters and connections. It is my hope that, by taking on such positionality, we as African women theologians in the diaspora can be a bridge between offering insights from both an insider and outsider perspective further, contributing to the growing body of research within our varied expertise.

Tabitha Poline Moyo is a Zambian feminist theologian pursuing a joint PhD candidate at Evangelische Theologische Faculteit (Leuven) and the Protestant Theological University (NL), focusing on Intercultural Theology and Religious Studies. Her research project explores women's roles in shaping masculinities in the Zambian Christian community in an attempt to expose women's agency. Her expertise is within the fields of Religion and Gender Studies. Tabitha Moyo is an ordained minister in the Reformed Church of Zambia. She currently resides in the Netherlands, where she lives with her husband, Tom de Greef.

---

[40] Dwyer and Buckle, "The Space Between", 56.

Heleen Joziasse

A *Muzungu* Woman Navigating Outsider-Insider Academic Research in Kenya

Introduction
Between 2009 and 2014, I had the opportunity to live and work in Limuru, Kenya. While teaching at St. Paul's University (SPU), I felt challenged to increase my engagement with and knowledge about women's faith. Yet, I hesitated to start a PhD-research, being deeply aware of my privileged and outsider position as a *muzungu* – a white, Dutch, ordained, well-educated woman. It is one thing to theoretically acknowledge the epistemological entanglements and contestations brought about by positionality, power, knowledge construction and representation. However, it is another thing to live out an appropriate response as a researcher and theologian in daily life.

My response to the question of how I negotiated the insider-outsider position in cross-cultural research in Kenya is a blend of narration and reflection, a method I learned from African Women's Theologies (AWT). Here, women's stories are important sources of knowledge.[41]

My story started with my observation as a student that theology in the Netherlands is Western – and male-centred. African women's voices are absent in theological discourse and are scarce in feminist theologies. Caught by an idealist intention to change the theological discourse, I decided to live and study at Trinity College in Legon, Ghana (1991/1992). Apart from attending lectures of Elisabeth Amoah and Rabbiatu Ammah and interacting with women students in Trinity College, I listened to and learned from the experiences with Jesus of women in the Circle of Concerned African Women Theologians, interviewed women pastors and laywomen and attended meetings of several women's fellowships of the Presbyterian Church in Ghana. This resulted in a thesis entitled: "You are My Everything: Christology from the Perspective of African Women Theologians".[42]

---

[41] Sarojini Nadar, "'Stories Are Data with Soul' – Lessons from Black Feminist Epistemology", in: *Agenda* 28, no. 1 (2014), 18-28, here 23.
[42] Heleen Joziasse, *You Are My Everything: Christology from the Perspective of African Women Theologians* (MA diss., Vrije Universiteit Amsterdam 1992), unpublished manuscript.

Theological Tourism

During a presentation of this research at the Free University (Amsterdam, 1993), I found myself in the middle of a heated debate between black/African and white/Dutch women theologians. By that time, dialogue about power and difference between women in the Netherlands had just started.[43] African theologians present termed my research an example of theological tourism and told the conference organisers: "White women, go home". I felt deeply misunderstood and not well equipped to immerse myself in the debate with those who had more experience and authority and who had their boundaries drawn: outsiders cannot write about insiders, white women cannot study ideas of black women, colonisers cannot engage with the colonised.

In retrospect, the complexities of power, positionality and representation made me withdraw from this debate and theoretical engagement with AWT altogether. Yet, these experiences motivated me, first as a pastor in Abcoude and later as a community worker in The Hague, to actively establish relationships with nearby Ghanaian church communities and women's groups. Moreover, I witnessed that marginal voices (from African communities) in Dutch society and church are not heard, while theological and social discourse is dominated by the agenda and the dominant themes in the Minority World in the interest of those in power.

A *Muzungu*, a Privileged Outsider

Fifteen years later, in 2009, I accompanied my husband to St Paul's University in Kenya. Some of our family members questioned our decision to be sent by our church[44] to Africa and asked whether we still had the intention to convert poor black people. Others argued they would never travel to an African country as this is politically incorrect in view of the colonial past. However, I perceived our migration as a unique opportunity to immerse myself in an African

---

[43] In the second *Oecumenische Vrouwensynode* in 1992, black women gathered in the focus group Womanist Theology, led by Doreen Hazel. The remembrance of 500 years of colonialism and slavery through a public silent march in front of white women deeply affected the women's movement. "From then on, racism was part of the agenda of our synods and gatherings." Denise J. J. Dijk, "Celebrating Women's Power. Oecumenische Vrouwensynoden in The Netherlands", in: Teresa Berger (ed.), *Dissident Daughters: Feminist Liturgies in Global Context* (Louisville: Westminster John Knox Press 2001), 69-86, here 76.

[44] Kerk in Actie, the missionary organization of the Protestant Church in the Netherlands.

society and re-engage with my "old" passion for AWT. During our five-year stay in Kenya, I tried to navigate missionary histories and relations, ideas, power and money.

Moreover, I lived the outsider position day and night in a space of tension. I was a *muzungu*, the common Swahili word for people with white skin. A *muzungu* is "one who is wandering around", a "passerby", someone who does not stay in one place – an outsider. I struggled to express myself in various languages and to find an identity. As a Dutch couple, we were perceived – and often reminded – of our outsider's identity, representing the Minority World, the liberal Dutch society, where gender issues are blurred and euthanasia and homosexuality are promoted.

My position as an outsider was yet more pronounced in the ways the students responded to me in class, especially when co-teaching courses on Gender and Theology and AWT. Students (often male) challenged me with phrases such as: "Don't come with this AWT, this feminist crap from the West, which breaks our marriages", and "Our mothers in the village are fine." When I asked women in class to share their gendered experiences, they became more vulnerable and target of insinuations.

Yet, my outsider's position was tied to a position of privilege in terms of race, nationality, class and education: owning a Dutch passport, a master's degree in theology from a Minority World university, a guaranteed salary and a sponsorship for our children to attend a high-standard international school. Socially/culturally, I was married with children. With regard to gender and race, as a white woman, I was granted a position of an honorary man – something that is often not understood but is the reality from the colonial past. My status as an ordained pastor should have come with privileges and power too. However, as a white woman, I was never invited to preach in the chapel of SPU, nor was I allowed to preach from the pulpit in the Reformed Church of East Africa (RCEA).[45]

---

[45] It was only in December 2018 that the synod of the RCEA opened up the ordained ministry to women.

Relations across Boundaries

In SPU, Prof Esther Mombo[46] and Dr Nyokabi Kamau[47] received me as their sister-guest, thus opening a shared space. As insiders, they narrated their stories and experiences and asked to share mine. They invited me to classes and meetings and to participate in the meetings of the Circle of Concerned African Women theologians, SPU-chapter. They also challenged me to co-teach various courses in the Faculty of Theology. They opened the way to interact with and teach students.

Mercy Amba Oduyoye commented critically on the value of research on the position of African women done by American or European women: "Only when such research is thorough and empathic does it become valuable as an expression of solidarity with the oppressed."[48] Various (feminist) liberation theologians have emphasised that true solidarity does not take place in the abstract but in relationships and everyday engagement as prerequisites for dialogue.[49] The postcolonial and feminist Indian scholar Chandra Mohanty, for instance, defines transnational feminist solidarity as follows:

> I define solidarity in terms of mutuality, accountability, and the recognition of common interest as the basis for relationships among diverse communities. Rather than assuming an enforced commonality of oppression, the practice of solidarity foregrounds communities of people who have chosen to work and fight together. Diversity and difference are central values here – to be acknowledged and respected, not erased in the building of alliances.[50]

---

[46] Esther Mombo (PhD, Edinburgh University) is Professor of African Church History, Gender and Theology at St. Paul's University (SPU) in Limuru, Kenya. Between 2007 and 2013, she was Deputy Vice-Chancellor of Academic Affairs at SPU. In 2007 she received an honorary doctorate from Virginia Theological Seminary for her work in bringing to the fore issues of gender disparities and gender justice in church and society. A recent publication from her is "Pray! Pray! Pray! Women and the Prayer of Persistence and Resistance" in: Muthuraj Swamy and Stephen Spencer (eds.), *Listening Together: Global Anglican Perspectives on Renewal of Prayer and Religious Life* (London: Forward Movement 2020), 15-28.

[47] Professor Nyokabi Kamau (PhD, University of London) is a sociologist who specialized in gender studies. She is the director of the Centre for Parliamentary Studies and Training (CPST), Kenya.

[48] Mercy Amba Oduyoye, *Daughters of Anowa: African Women and Patriarchy* (Orbis Books: Maryknoll, NY 1995), 82.

[49] James Cone as well underlines the importance of personal relations if a white person is to grasp race. See: James Cone, *The Cross and the Lynching Tree* (Orbis Books: Maryknoll 2013), 52.

[50] Chandra Talpade Mohanty, *Feminism Without Borders: Decolonizing Theory, Practicing Solidarity* (Duke University Press: Durham and London 2003), 7.

In doing cross-cultural research and navigating the insider/outsider positions of race, class and gender, it is vital to find companions, sisters-insiders, who affirm and confront, who help to navigate critically, with love and humour. It is from these relationships and engagements that my research became research with and for Kenyan women.[51]

Positionality Is Multi-dimensional
Gradually, I discovered that the outsider/insider position in cross-cultural encounters is complex and multi-dimensional.[52] I observed that my Kenyan women colleagues, too, were navigating issues of gender and class, ethnicity, marital status and clericalism. We had shared experiences, and I observed that part of their struggles was also my struggle: How to navigate patriarchy in the university, in theology and in daily life? How to deal with economic and class issues resulting, for instance, in unsafety? Nearly all our colleagues were car-hijacked, irrespective of skin colour. How to navigate the never-ending appeal for financial support?

Whilst difference is part of the human condition and connected to systems of power, we are all part of these various systems of power. Hence, the insider-outsider position, like the oppressor-oppressed dichotomy, is fluid and shifting, depending on different contexts and situations – one's age, gender, social class, education and religious affiliation.[53]

Knowledge Construction and Decolonialism
In doing research, the insider-outsider or the exclusion-inclusion dichotomies are tied to questions of epistemology or knowledge finding. Who has knowledge about life, about God, and who is allowed to produce this knowledge? Whose experiences are underlying this knowledge? I learned from AWT that theological knowledge production is not the preserve of the academy; theology is always contextual and, in order to be relevant, must be rooted in the lived experiences of women and men. This implies the valuation of multiple forms of knowledge, for example, oral, verbal, embodied and practised knowledge.

---

[51] Instead of research about women, this was a collaborative research in which the co-researchers and participants had an interest and were actively involved in terms of method, content and product.
[52] See also Sharan Merriam et al., "Power and Positionality: Negotiating Insider/ Outsider Status within and across Cultures", in: *International Journal of Lifelong Education* 20 (October/2001), 405-416, here 408.
[53] Merriam et al., 411.

I, therefore, deliberately designed a qualitative research in which churchwomen[54] voiced their experiences, if desired, in the local languages.

Apart from the subject question in research, there is the issue about the object of knowledge construction: Who decides which knowledge is researched? Who sets the research theme and questions? In retrospect, in Kenya and back in the Netherlands, I experienced the challenge of theologising in the "margins of the world" or the "global periphery". The Benin philosopher Paulin Hountondji talks about the "extraversion of knowledge production".[55] I think I experienced it: the prioritising of themes and discussions, the new approaches and discourses, the terminologies, the methodological developments, and the resources and facilities are located or originating in the West.[56] Therefore, in my research, I deliberately choose to engage and dialogue with the "outsiders" discourses and epistemologies of the Majority World, e.g. of African women theologians.

Researching in a Team

Triangulation involves the application of different methods and sources for data collection, multiple theories and perspectives, and the cooperation of multiple researchers. I used triangulation to acknowledge the African postcolonial critique of hegemonic epistemology and power relations and come to terms with my outsider's position. Particularly, researching in a team enabled me to mirror my outsider's perspective with the insider's perspectives of groups of trained theological students and St. Paul's University graduates. These co-researchers were members of the particular churches cooperating in the research. As insiders, the co-researchers conducted (group-)interviews and recorded life stories of churchwomen in the local languages. They also translated and guided me with the interpretation of idioms and phrases.

Researching in teams of researchers enhanced critical reflection and analysis. Moreover, through cooperation in teams of researchers, insights and

---

[54] I use the created term "churchwomen" in order to avoid the more derogatory expressions "grassroots women" or "ordinary women". "Churchwomen" does imply all female members of a church, irrespective of class or level of education.

[55] Paulin J. Hountondji, "Introduction: Recentring Africa", in: Paulin J. Hountondji (ed.), *Endogenous Knowledge: Research Trails* (CODESEIA: Dakar 1997), 1-39, here 4-5.

[56] Most terminologies, discourses and thought frames to theorise power and difference are invented and produced in the Minority World: intersectionality, identity, agency, resistance, navigation, positionality.

knowledge were shared about methodologies and findings.[57] Prof Esther Mombo's participation in the research teams was crucial. She acted as gate-opener[58] and was my main interlocutor during the different phases of the research. She critically interrogated the process of positioning the research and the interpretation of the findings.

Researching in teams advanced reflectivity on my methodological, theoretical and ideological predispositions and helped me recognise my taken-for-granted positions.[59] However, my viewpoints and "strange questions" as an engaged outsider also provided some sort of "advantage" in signalling trends and linking this to global feminist debates.[60]

Conclusion

Relationality, solidarity and mutual cooperation are of crucial importance in feminist cross-cultural theological research. It is my experience that in a collective process of discussing, singing, praying, eating and travelling together, boundaries and differences in positions of power, of being outsider and insider, blurred. Together, and gradually, we discovered and uncovered embedded collective knowledge.

The postcolonial feminist theologian Musa Dube from Botswana proposes a theory of liberating interdependence and argues that the interconnectedness of differences and the relatedness within specific and global contexts must be

---

[57] I did not intend to become the "single expert" or gain "unique knowledge". To participants, it was clear that the research had two aims: the compilation of two books about the faith and life of women in particular churches and my PhD project.

[58] See for the technical term Johnny Andoh-Arthur, "Gatekeepers in Qualitative Research", in: Paul Atkinson, Sara Delamont, Alexandru Cernat, Joseph W. Sakshaug and Richard A. Williams (eds.), *SAGE Research Methods Foundations* (SAGE Publications Ltd.: London 2019) (https://dx.doi.org/9781529748543, 6 May 2022).

[59] It is stated that ideally, researching in a team can produce "perspective-transcending knowledge". See Flora Cornish, Alex Gillespie and Tania Zittoun, "Collaborative Analysis of Qualitative Data", in: Uwe Flick (ed.), *The SAGE Handbook of Qualitative Data Analysis* (SAGE: London 2013), 77-93, here 83. One example of the influence of working in a team was that, different from our initial research design, we decided to conduct more life stories and fewer individual interviews in each case study because the research assistants viewed the life stories as of more importance and more insightful.

[60] "The outsider's advantage lies in curiosity with the unfamiliar, the ability to ask taboo questions, and being seen as non-aligned with subgroups thus often getting more information." In: Merriam *et al.*, "Power and Positionality", 411.

described and emphasised – underlining the dignity of all things and beings.[61] It is my hope that through relationality and solidarity in research, the dignity of all women in and outside Kenya is affirmed.

Dr Heleen Joziasse studied Theology at the Free University, Amsterdam (Masters in 1992), and holds a PhD from the University of Utrecht (2020) with the research titled: *Women's Faith Seeking Life. Lived Christologies and the Transformation of Gender Relations in Two Kenyan Churches* (Utrecht, 2020). She taught between 2009 and 2014 at St Paul's University Limuru in the Faculty of Theology in the areas of Systematic Theology and African Women's Theologies. She is currently a diaconal worker with Stek (Voor Stad en Kerk) in The Hague Southwest, the Netherlands.

---

[61] Musa W. Dube, *Postcolonial Feminist Interpretation of the Bible* (Chalice Press: St. Louis 2000), 186.

Shingirai Eunice Masunda

Running the Metaphor Blend with Jesus: How the Canaanite Woman Transformed Jesus' Metaphor

Introduction
I am a biblical scholar whose research interests converge on the intersection of New Testament studies (particularly the Gospel of Matthew), metaphor theory and leadership studies. For the inaugural symposium of the AFTE, whose theme was 'Connected But Disconnected', I chose to explore the outsider voice of the Canaanite woman in Matt 15:21-28.[62] The Canaanite woman is an outsider in relation to the disciples of Jesus. She is also an outsider in relation to the crowds that gather around Jesus. The author of the Gospel of Matthew designates her as a "Canaanite woman" to emphasise her outsider status.

Generally, interpretations and analyses of this text ignore the voice/agency of the Canaanite woman. Traditional interpretations focus on her subservience as a virtue, while contemporary ones portray her as a victimised woman. In this paper, I will explore an approach to New Testament texts that can be employed to let the outsider voice of the Canaanite woman be more audible. I argue for the probability that the way the Canaanite woman processes Jesus' response to her request for help is different from how the others around her process it. A theory that can be helpful in depicting my hypothesis is the Conceptual Blending Theory (CBT) of Gilles Fauconnier and Mark Turner. Applying this theory to Matt 15:21-28 offers us further possibilities for understanding the Canaanite woman's response to Jesus. For this paper, I am particularly interested in verses 26-27. My interest is in the imagery or metaphor used here by Jesus and further extended by the Canaanite woman in her response.

The text of Matt 15:21-28 (ESV) reads as follows:

> 15:21 And Jesus went away from there and withdrew to the district of Tyre and Sidon. ²² And behold, a Canaanite woman from that region came out and was

---
[62] See for example Anders Runesson's discussion on how ethnic outsiders are used as a theological tool in the Gospel of Matthew. Anders Runesson and Daniel M. Gurtner (eds.), *Matthew Within Judaism: Israel and the Nations in the First Gospel* (Atlanta: Society of Biblical Literature 2020), 114.

crying, "Have mercy on me, O Lord, Son of David; my daughter is severely oppressed by a demon." [23] But he did not answer her a word. And his disciples came and begged him, saying, "Send her away, for she is crying out after us." [24] He answered, "I was sent only to the lost sheep of the house of Israel." [25] But she came and knelt before him, saying, "Lord, help me." [26] And he answered, "It is not right to take the children's bread and throw it to the dogs." [27] She said, "Yes, Lord, yet even the dogs eat the crumbs that fall from their masters' table." [28] Then Jesus answered her, "O woman, great is your faith! Be it done for you as you desire." And her daughter was healed instantly.

Brief History of Interpretation/Reception

The history of interpretation of this text has focused on humility as a virtue in the past. Thus the Canaanite woman has been presented as humbling herself before Jesus. In present times humility (particularly in submission) is viewed differently. Ulrich Luz, for example, observes that "[t]he saying about the children and the dogs is regarded as an 'atrocious saying' and the 'worst kind of chauvinism', and it is inconceivable for many that Jesus could have demanded such submissiveness."[63] Luz argues, however, that the term κυνάριον does not refer to a small dog but rather to a dog that is a household pet.[64] House dogs were apparently a common motif in ancient literature. For instance, according to Aristotle, the choicest food in a household is set aside for the free persons. The inferior food and scraps are given to servants, while the worst food is given to the domestic animals.[65]

There is obvious discomfort and helplessness on how to interpret Jesus' use of the children and dogs imagery in response to the Canaanite woman. In his struggle to understand Jesus' choice of imagery, Joe M. Kapolyo, writing in the Africa Bible Commentary, comments that "[t]he use of this term on Jesus' lips is surprising, and perhaps it was spoken in humour."[66]

Musa Dube offers yet another approach. Her article on the interpretation of this text by Setswana women from African Independent Churches in Botswana presents interesting insights on how the imagery of children and dogs as used

---

[63] Ulrich Luz, *Matthew 8-20: A Commentary,* trans. James E. Crouch (Fortress: Minneapolis 2001), 337.

[64] Luz, *Matthew 8-20,* 340.

[65] Aristotle, *Generation of Animals,* translated by A. L. Peck. Loeb Classical Library 366 (Harvard University Press: Cambridge 1942), 2.6-744b.

[66] Tokunboh Adeyemo (ed.), *Africa Bible Commentary* (Word Alive Publishers: Nairobi 2006), 1142.

by Jesus in the Matthean text can be understood.[67] When questioned about the identity of the 'dogs', the women emphasise that Jesus often spoke in parables. According to Dube, "[t]his emphasis was a warning that the meaning of his words was not always apparent nor to be taken literally."[68]

It cannot be disputed that the text of Matt 15:21-28 is replete with imagery and metaphor, which is why applying metaphor theory to its controversial imagery is particularly suitable.

The Conceptual Blending Theory

Since the 1980 work of George Lakoff and Mark Johnson, the use of metaphors has largely been understood to be part of our thought processes.[69] The initial work of Lakoff and Johnson was referred to as Conceptual Metaphor Theory. A conceptual understanding of metaphor argues that we generally use more concrete terms to expound abstract ones. A common example from the synoptic gospels is the SHEPHERD/SHEEP[70] metaphor. The relatively abstract concept of LEADING/FOLLOWING is understood from the concrete SHEPHERD/SHEEP domain. There have been further developments in the understanding of metaphor used as a conceptual process, and for this paper, I focus on the Conceptual Blending Theory (CBT) of Gilles Fauconnier and Mark Turner.[71]

CBT argues that our construction of meaning involves the integration and blending of concepts. This includes our use of metaphors, and the process occurs on the cognitive level and at lightning speed. The following diagram is a depiction of the conceptual blending process.

In the diagram, all the circles depict the mental spaces, with two minimum circles for the input fields. For the purposes of the present analysis, three components of the conceptual blending theory are of relevance. These are blending, emergent structure and selective projection. In the blending process, structure from the two (or more) input spaces and from the generic space is projected to a new mental space, called the blend. It is in the blend

---

[67] Musa W. Dube, "Readings of Semoya: Batswana Women's Interpretations of Matt 15:21-28", in: *Semeia* 73 (1996): 111-130.
[68] Dube, "Readings," 117.
[69] George Lakoff and Mark Johnson, *Metaphors We Live By* (University of Chicago Press: Chicago 1980).
[70] Small caps are used for conceptual domains and also for the input fields in this paper.
[71] Gilles Fauconnier and Mark Turner, *The Way We Think: Conceptual Blending and the Mind's Hidden Complexities* (Basic Books: New York 2002).

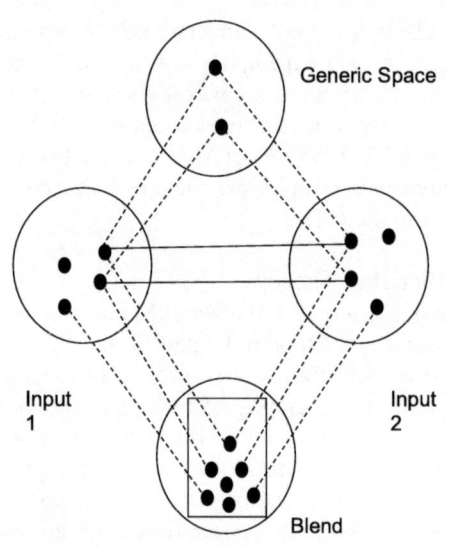

Figure: The Basic Diagram for Conceptual Blending Theory
(Source: Gilles Fauconnier and Mark Turner, *The Way We Think: Conceptual Blending and the Mind's Hidden Complexities*, 46)

that structures that are not possible for the inputs may be found. Due to selective projection, some elements and relations from the input spaces are not projected to the blend. Emergent structure (depicted by the square in the diagram above) is generated in the blend through composition, completion and elaboration.[72]

Fantastic or seemingly impossible scenarios can be generated when a blend is run. Fauconnier and Turner observe that "[m]any blends are not only possible but also so compelling that they come to represent, mentally, a new reality, in culture, action, and science."[73] From its intratextual context, one can imagine how Matt 15:21-28 represented a new reality where, for example, outsiders were viewed more favourably than insiders. In the following section, I will elaborate on this.

---

[72] Fauconnier and Turner, *The Way*, 45-48.
[73] Fauconnier and Turner, *The Way*, 21.

Applying CBT to Matt 15:21-28

From the exchange between Jesus and the Canaanite woman, we can envisage the following input fields: THE HOUSEHOLD, MEAL, TABLE, RELATIONSHIPS, ETHNICITY/NATIONALITY and the CHARACTERS/ACTORS input fields. The following are some of the elements and relations in these input fields: the household (patriarch/master, children, women, servants/slaves, pets/dogs), meal table (table, floor, bread, food, crumbs, scraps), relationships (dog and master, father and children, master and slaves/servants), ethnicity/nationality (Israel, Canaan), characters/actors (Canaanite woman, demon-possessed daughter, Jesus, disciples). There is an overlap in these input fields. This is particularly the case with the HOUSEHOLD and RELATIONSHIPS input fields. While the elements in these two input fields are the same, the difference is that in the RELATIONSHIPS field relations are generally between two personalities. Hence, in the RELATIONSHIPS input field we consider the interaction dynamics between master and slaves/servants.

My interest in applying CBT to Matt 15:26-27 is to explore how it is conceivable that the Canaanite woman is able to respond to Jesus' rebuttal and actually transform it to her advantage. In 15:26, Jesus refuses the woman's request by stating that what he has (the bread) is only for the children. In the immediate context of the story, we understand that the children are 'the lost sheep of the house of Israel'. Jesus states that the food is not for the "dogs". Jesus' rebuttal is taken from the MEAL TABLE input field with the elements of table, floor, children, dogs, bread and crumbs. Interestingly, this input field from Jesus is one where lack or shortage seems to be highlighted. There is enough food for the children but not for the dogs.

By asserting that "even the dogs eat the crumbs that fall off the masters' table", the woman expands Jesus' imagery. In laying claim to the food that Jesus has to offer, the Canaanite woman seems to employ elements from the HOUSEHOLD domain. She speaks from an image of abundance where the master/s have enough food for every household member. As an outsider, she claims what is on the table. Now we can imagine a household in antiquity with its pecking order even at the meal table. With this imagery or metaphor, the woman argues that dogs, just as children, are insiders; they belong in the same household. The masters are therefore obliged to feed all that are within the household. By selective projection, the Canaanite woman ignores/discards the negative connotations in the dog imagery and includes herself in the household.

In their exchange, Jesus and the Canaanite woman are running the metaphorical blend together. Two social worlds are portrayed, one of exclusion, shortage and boundaries, and another of inclusion, abundance and community.

The bread that Jesus has is, in light of the woman's plea, healing for her demon-possessed daughter. Jesus' capitulation in verse 28 is evidence of how the Canaanite woman transforms Jesus' mission from one of shortage and boundaries into one of inclusion and community.[74]

Way Forward and Conclusions

As already observed, this text has problematic aspects in terms of the choice of imagery used, particularly the "dogs" imagery. While various biblical scholars and commentators have explained the problematic aspects in varied ways (for example, as irony or humour on the part of Jesus), CBT offers us a way of understanding how it is possible to take some elements from a concept/image while discarding others. This interpretation is made from the positionality of the Canaanite woman who, as an outsider, negotiates the insider/outsider binary so as to get what she requires. By a seeming process of "selective projection", the Canaanite woman ignores the possibly derogatory aspects of the "dogs" imagery. Instead, she chooses to focus on an imagery of inclusivity and abundance as she lays claim to the bread that Jesus has to offer. Admittedly this says nothing about how Jesus' disciples viewed her, for example. As insiders, they probably still look at her as an outsider. But analysing the text using CBT offers possibilities for recognising the outsider's voice/agency.

Shingirai Eunice Masunda is a PhD candidate at the Protestant Theological University in the Netherlands. Her research focuses on the metaphors of leadership in the New Testament, particularly in the Gospel of Matthew. She is a tutor of the New Testament at the Foundation Academy of Amsterdam. Shingirai is an ordained minister in the Uniting Presbyterian Church in Southern Africa (UPCSA).

---

[74] See here for example Craig A. Evans, *Matthew* (Cambridge University Press: Cambridge 2012), 303-304.

Anne-Claire Mulder

Intersectionality. In-Between Spaces. Authority. Some Concepts to Reflect on the Relations between Insider and Outsider

Introduction
When the members of the Dutch-based Network of African Female Theologians in Europe invited me to contribute to their reflections on the tension between insider and outsider, I felt both honoured and challenged. Honoured to be asked to contribute, although I am in so many ways an outsider to their network. For although I have learned a lot from the international students whose theses I supervised through the years, I do not have the experience of living and working in Africa, nor am I familiar with African Theology;[75] and challenged to think through my position as an insider – being a native Dutch theologian with a permanent position as Associate Professor.

On the other hand, being a committed feminist theologian at a theological university often brings me in an outsider position, or in the more ambivalent position of being recognised as part of the group as long as I participate on the group's terms.

In the following, I will reflect upon these experiences of being both an insider and an outsider, using three concepts from the feminist discourse developed in my world – the Minority World – notably location and intersectionality, boundaries and in-between spaces and authority.

Location and Intersectionality
I will start my reflections with the text "Notes towards a politics of location" by Adrienne Rich.[76] In that text, she suggests to "Begin with the body" when thinking about differences between women: with a concrete body and not with

---

[75] For example, reading Heleen Joziasse's PhD *Women's Faith Seeking Life. Lived Christologies and the Transformation of Gender Relations in Two Kenyan Churches*. Questiones Infinitae Vol. 127 (Publications of the Department of Philosophy and Religious Studies: Utrecht 2020), made me very aware of the extent of my ignorance of African (Feminist) Theology.

[76] Adrienne Rich, "Notes towards a Politics of Location", in: Myriam Díaz-Diocraretz and Iris M. Zavala (eds.), *Women, Feminist Identity and Society in the 1980's: Selected Papers* (John Benjamins Publishing Company: Amsterdam and Philadelphia 1985), 7-22.

an abstract, indeterminate, non-gendered, non-coloured, ageless or asexual body: my body, your body; a sensible body through which a subject gathers knowledge of the world through smelling, tasting, touching, seeing and hearing.[77] According to her, this emphasis on the embodied-ness of the knowing subject would make it impossible to lump women together into an indeterminate collective or category 'woman'. For that would deny the constraints of time and place and, therefore, the differences that come with their embodiedness. Rich points out that "location" is a thoroughly political category, a category in which power differences, of privilege and disenfranchisement are played out. The following observation about her location illustrates this:

> This body. White, female, or female, white. The first obvious lifelong facts. I was born in the white section of a hospital which separated Black and white women in labor and white babies in the nursery, just as it separated Black and white bodies in its morgue. I was defined as white before I was defined as female. The politics of location.[78]

Taken together, these ideas illuminate that knowing subjects cannot claim that their points of view are universal because their knowledge is limited by their location and the symbolic order in which they are raised.

The discourse of intersectionality further develops the importance of one's standpoint for one's knowledge formation. Intersectionality understands personal and social identity as constituted by multiple, overlapping or intersecting social categories such as gender, class, education, age, sexuality, religion and more.[79] Thus, personal and social identity are understood as constituted by the intersection of these categories in one's lifetime. Each of the categories I mentioned is made up by an axe of difference or basic opposition, and all categories come with their concomitant system of privilege and disenfranchisement. To give an example: the axe of difference of the category "education" spans the opposition between "highly educated" and "poorly educated" or "(functionally) illiterate" and influences the options in one's professional life.

---

[77] See also "Body", in: *ABC of Good Life. A Postpatriarchal Ethics in 56 Keywords* (https://abcofgoodlife.wordpress.com/category/body/, 30 March 2022).

[78] Rich, "Notes", 10-11

[79] To visualize the kaleidoscopic nature of intersectionality Herma Tigchelaar developed 'the circle of diversity'. See Toinette Loeffen and Herma Tigchelaar, *Retourtje Inzicht. Creatief met diversiteit voor sociale professionals* (*Return-ticket Insight. Creative with Diversity for Social Professionals*) (Coutinho: Bussum ²2013).

When I look from an intersectional perspective at the manner in which the categories colour, class and education have influenced each other in my identity formation and social position, I see that my position is one of privilege, constituted by the fact that the privileges which come with being white, middle class and highly educated have reinforced each other in my course of life.

However, someone's position is constituted by many axes of difference. It is therefore important to ask "the other question"[80] because that might illuminate hidden dynamics of privilege and disenfranchisement. The question "what if I were an educated, female migrant from Poland in the Netherlands" would illuminate that my insider position is also due to my being a native Dutch inhabitant and even reinforced by it.

This position of privilege makes me an insider in many different ways – I know the customs and the rules, have learned "how to behave myself", I can understand the mechanisms of the bureaucracy and read its letters or emails. However, when I throw the category of gender into the mix, this insider position becomes relativised, for being a woman makes me "other", different from the other insiders. The most obvious example of this being "other" is the fact that the street or another public space is not very safe for me and other women; a position of privilege does not safeguard me from (verbal) harassment or the threat of sexual violence. The dynamics of insider-outsider manifest themselves also in more subtle ways, for instance, in the (customary) practice at Dutch universities to put women in a lower salary scale than men, indicating that they are still seen as a bit of an outsiders.[81]

In short, making an intersectional analysis of one's own location and the location of the other illuminates the differences between two subjects that come with different locations. This is especially relevant in the encounter with the other because, in meeting the other, the differences and the boundaries that come with these differences become apparent.

Boundaries and In-Between Spaces
This brings me to in-between spaces and boundaries. In the encounter of the other, an in-between space becomes manifest. This space connects *and* separates the one and the other. It is a site of co-creation and a site of struggle.

---

[80] This analytical instrument is coined by Mari Matsuda. See, Loeffen and Tigchelaar, *Retourtje Inzicht*, 112.
[81] I use the conditional "a bit" to indicate the often unacknowledged and unconscious prejudices, expressed in this practice, which turn women into outsiders.

Mary Louise Pratt has called these in-between spaces "contact zones". She describes them as

> social spaces where cultures meet, clash and grapple with each other, often in contexts of highly asymmetrical relations of power, such as colonialism, slavery, or their aftermaths as they are lived out in many parts of the world today.[82]

I discovered the notion "contact zone" last year. It made me reflect critically upon my own writing on the encounter of the other and the in-between space that opens up in this encounter.[83] Inspired by Luce Irigaray's text on the passion of wonder in encountering (the otherness of) the other,[84] I presented this encounter in my texts as governed by wonder. I wrote that amazement about the alterity of the other would have the effect of stopping the subject in her forward movement towards the other. The subject would be propelled to ask this other: "Who are you?" thereby creating a space between them. And lastly, I argued that the passion of wonder would bring the subject also to ask the self-reflective question "Who am I". These two questions would open both subjects for an exchange in the in-between space.

I realised, however, that my description of the encounter of the other covers only the first step of the interaction of subjects from different locations. I had neglected the fact that after the initial amazement about the otherness of the other, one is confronted with boundaries created by the systemic asymmetries between the participants, by their different position and worldview. I attribute this omission to the yearning for co-creative encounters, on the one hand, a romantic yearning that effaces the reality of the often-painful struggles and experiences in encounters with others. On the other hand, this neglect can also be interpreted as a form of trivialising the extent of the divide between insider and outsider and the struggle between them.

Insiders often experience this struggle as a challenge to their worldview and position. It can make them uneasy, embarrassed or emotional when treasured insights are critiqued. The reaction of a pastor to the story of a female parishioner, saying "but you should not see it like that …", is a fine example of the

---

[82] Mary Louise Pratt, "Arts of the Contact Zone", in: *Profession* (1991), 33-40, here 34.

[83] See, among others, Anne-Claire Mulder, Sigríður Guðmarsdóttir and Erla Karlsdóttir, "In-Between", in: *Journal of the European Society for Women in Theological Research* 21 (2013), 7-12.

[84] Luce Irigaray, *An Ethics of Sexual Difference*, translated by Carolyn Burke and Gillian C. Gill (Cornell University Press, Ithaca and New York 1993), 73-75.

resistance to a challenge of one's worldview. He universalises his own worldview and undermines the parishioner as a knowing subject. I know from experience how easily I blurt out such a sentence when someone else challenges my worldview; how I forget to count to ten or to step back and reflect before responding, let alone omitting to ask in wonder, "Who are you". The same goes for admitting to my ignorance when confronted with a different body of knowledge. It is a confrontation with the tendency to take one's own point of view as the common point of view, thus universalising this viewpoint. This is extra painful when one realises how much this tendency is bound up with a position of privilege.

However, I experience the struggles in the contact-zone differently when I am in the position of outsider. Then I have to deal with the experience of being discounted as a subject with knowledge and wisdom; of finding the corpus of knowledge produced within my social group – feminist theologians – ignored, trivialised or appropriated without acknowledgement. It also presents me with the question of how to respond to these humiliations – with anger, silence, withdrawal? With swallowing my anger and pain and choosing non-confrontational modes of encountering the other, trying to discover what I and the other in the encounter hold in common and what dreams we share? Research suggests that the latter response seems to be more effective in getting one's authority recognised,[85] but these modes of interaction also run the risk of co-optation.

Authority

The last notion I want to discuss is "authority" because it plays an important role in the insider-outsider dynamics. At the core, authority characterises an asymmetrical relation in which someone places her/himself freely within the "jurisdiction" of another by granting this other authority. However, this voluntary element of granting authority to another is often forgotten in favour of an understanding of authority as "power over" the other or as the power of custom or the self-evident. These forms of authority relations are intimately connected with patriarchal and colonial power structures.

As "power over", authority is one of the instruments wherewith the insider-outsider dynamics are upheld. These insiders – both men and women – hold a position in which they can regulate the processes of attribution of authority

---

[85] Naomi Ellemers, *Morality and the Regulation of Social Behavior. Groups as Moral Anchors* (Routledge: Abingdon and New York 2017), 243.

to knowledge and wisdom by barring the (knowledge of the) outsiders from becoming part of the discourse, for instance, through the practice of never referring to their work, texts, art.[86] This explains why the struggles in the contact-zone often take the form of the contestation of the speaker's authority.

But contestation is not the only form of interaction in the contact-zone, although it might occur the most often. An encounter of the insider with the outsider might also be marked by the passion of wonder for the alterity of the other, creating an in-between space between them in which a shift in the authority-relation of the insider to the outsider might occur.

Underlying the idea that an encounter with the other could bring about such a shift is the idea that authority is a quality that circulates within relations and is therefore not bound to fixed relations or existing authorities; it is rather attributed or "given" to (the words and practices of) another.[87]

That happens when the desire of the subject is put in motion through the touch of the words of the other; when s/he inspires the subject, for instance, generating new ideas, challenging, encouraging or showing hitherto unknown possibilities and so forth. In all these situations, the subject "takes the other's word for it" and places her/himself in this asymmetrical relation by attributing authority to (the words and practices of) this other, even when s/he comes to the conclusion that s/he disagrees with or decides not to heed the words of this authority-figure. Attributing authority to the other therefore does not diminish the agency or freedom of the subject. Rather the person to whom she has attributed authority becomes a kind of touchstone, someone who offers orientation in navigating through life.

However, "taking the other's word for it" implies that the subject trusts the interpretation or the judgement of this person to whom she has attributed authority and that s/he deems the opinion of the other to be trustworthy. This implies that s/he trusts that this "authority" is prepared to be held accountable for the points of view s/he holds. That asks from this "authority" that she will not shy away when points of view are contested but rather engage her/himself with the words, viewpoints and criticisms of the subject in search of (some) common ground.

However, as I already indicated in the above, the encounters in the contact zone are often marked by contestation and distrust. In such a context, it is not

---

[86] Rhiannon Graybill, "Where Are All the Women?", in: *Journal of Biblical Literature* 140 (2021), 826-830.

[87] "Authority", in https://abcofgoodlife.wordpress.com/category/authority/ (30 March 2022).

easy to arrive at the assessment that the other's viewpoints, ideas, or knowledge are trustworthy. It requires a gesture of opening oneself to (the viewpoints of) the other, of letting oneself be challenged by them and of engaging with them, perhaps of taking them to heart; in short, acknowledging the truth in and of the words of the other, thus giving authority to her/his words.

I discovered that this process is easier in the life-encounter and engagement with the other, even when this encounter was characterised by the struggle to understand one another and find some common ground or shared ideal. I have also learned that this engagement is rooted in my desire to build mutual relation, or better, to "translate" this desire into a practice of listening and exchanging ideas with others and being corrected or challenged by them.

This is a desire that the different presenters at the African Female Theologians in Europe Symposium share(d). It can be traced in the texts of this round-table discussion. They witness, each in their own way, the importance of exchange, of interlocutors and of sisters and sister-outsiders to turn the in-between space into a co-creative space of mutual relations.

Dr Anne Claire Mulder is Associate Professor of Women's and Gender Studies Theology at the Protestant Theological University in the Netherlands.

REVIEWS

Irmtraud Fischer, Angela Berlis, Christiana de Groot (Hg.), *Frauenbewegungen des 19. Jahrhunderts*. Stuttgart 2021 (Die Bibel und die Frauen. Eine exegetisch-kulturgeschichtliche Enzyklopädie Band 8.1); und Irmtraud Fischer, Edith Petschnigg, Nicole Navratil, Angela Berlis, Christiana de Groot (Hg.), *Die Bibel war für sie ein politisches Buch. Bibelinterpretationen der Frauenemanzipationsbewegungen im langen 19. Jahrhundert*. Wien 2020 (Theologische Frauenforschung in Europa Band 29).

Beide Sammelbände stellen eine Bereicherung dar, da sie Forschungslücken füllen und gleichzeitig darauf aufmerksam machen, dass vieles im Bereich der von Frauen geleisteten Beiträge zur Bibelrezeption sowie neuen Interpretationsansätzen unter emanzipatorischen Gesichtspunkten immer noch nicht in ausreichendem Maß erforscht ist – trotz aller Fortschritte in den letzten Jahrzehnten. Das breite Themenspektrum dieser zwei Bücher kann im Folgenden nur exemplarisch vorgestellt werden. Diese Rezension beginnt mit dem zuletzt erschienenen Band *Frauenbewegungen des 19. Jahrhunderts* der auf 21 Bände angelegten Reihe *Die Bibel und die Frauen*. Mit diesem Band 8.1 liegt nun der zweite zum 19. Jahrhundert vor, nachdem Bd. 8.2 in der deutschen Ausgabe bereits 2014 erschienen war (Michaela Sohn-Kronthaler / Ruth Albrecht (Hg.): *Fromme Lektüre und kritische Exegese im langen 19. Jahrhundert*. Stuttgart 2014) und inzwischen auch ins Englische, Italienische und Spanische übersetzt wurde. Obwohl zwischen den Schwerpunkten beider Werke zahlreiche Verbindungslinien bestehen, liegt der Akzent dieser Aufsatzsammlung jedoch deutlich auf den sozialen und politischen Bewegungen. Allerdings stehen im Fokus der Beiträge nicht die Bewegungen als solche – wie der Titel nahelegt –, sondern diese werden charakterisiert anhand der einzelnen Vertreterinnen, die sich in diesen Bewegungen organisierten.

Der größere Teil dieser zwölf Beiträge richtet das Augenmerk auf die Bibelinterpretationen von Autorinnen des 19. Jahrhunderts und verortet diese in ihren jeweiligen nationalen Kontexten. Eine Inderin, eine Schweizerin, eine Isländerin, zwei Norwegerinnen sowie mehrere Engländerinnen und Amerikanerinnen werden porträtiert; daneben richtet sich der Blick auf eine Reihe von Italienerinnen sowie auf reisende und forschende Frauen aus den Niederlanden, Österreich, England und den USA. Das religiöse bzw. konfessionelle Spektrum der dargestellten Frauen umfasst neben einer Jüdin und mehreren Katholikinnen vor allem Mitglieder der unterschiedlichen Ausprägungen von protestantischen Kirchen und Bewegungen. Darüber hinaus kommt jedoch auch zur Sprache, dass einzelne Frauen ihre Anliegen in keiner der vorhandenen religiösen Gruppen repräsentiert sahen und sich einem überkonfessionellen Christentum zuwandten, um dann wie Pandita Ramabai eine eigene Kirche zu gründen.

Während nur ganz wenige der in diesem Sammelband vorgestellten Akteurinnen einer größeren Öffentlichkeit bekannt sein dürften, gilt für die allermeisten, dass sie erstmals mit dieser Veröffentlichung der internationalen wissenschaftlichen Erforschung zugänglich gemacht worden sind – ein großes Verdienst! Über den größten Bekanntheitsgrad verfügt zweifelsohne Josephine Butler, die unerschrockene englische Aktivistin und Vorkämpferin gegen die Ausbeutung von Frauen durch Prostitution; aber im Kontext dieser Beiträge, die jeweils die theologischen Beweggründe für das Handeln der Einzelnen herausarbeiten, erhält ihr Profil eine ganz spezifische Aussagekraft.

Der Band beginnt mit einer von Angela Berlis, einer der Herausgeberinnen, verfassten Einleitung, in der es ihr gelingt, kurz und präzise den geistes- und sozialgeschichtlichen Kontext der Beiträge zu skizzieren. Der umfangreiche rechtsgeschichtliche Text von Ute Gerhard, die Berlis als eine „Ikone der Frauenforschung" (22) bezeichnet, zum „Partikularismus der Frauenrechte" berücksichtigt die wichtigsten europäischen und amerikanischen Traditionen, die insbesondere die privatrechtliche Lage der Frauen bestimmten. Einschlägig für das Thema von Band 8.1 der Reihe sind vor allem das vierte und das fünfte Kapitel: „Aufbruch und Rechtskämpfe der Frauenbewegungen seit 1848" (76–85) sowie „Unterschiedliche Rechtsentwicklungen und die Strategien der Frauenbewegungen im Ausblick auf das 20. Jh." (85–104). Als etwas bedauerlich kann festgehalten werden, dass in den einzelnen Beiträgen kaum Bezug genommen wird auf diese detaillierten Darlegungen Gerhards.

Drei Beispiele müssen hier genügen, um die faszinierende Breite der dargelegten Materialien anzudeuten: Während mit Pandita Ramabai eine „frühe postkoloniale feministische Exegetin und Sozialreformerin Indiens" charakterisiert wird, unternimmt Christine Lienemann-Perrin es, diese in eine vergleichende Beziehung zur Amerikanerin Helen Barrett Montgomery zu setzen, „eine führende Figur in der amerikanischen Demokratie- und Frauen(missions) bewegung" (187). „Die Bibelforscherinnen Montgomery und Ramabai hinterlassen ... den Eindruck, dass nicht alles erstmalig und neu ist, was ein

Jahrhundert nach ihnen erforscht und wissenschaftlich vertreten wird" (208). Maria Stewart steht für die frühe afroamerikanische Frauenbewegung; sie bezog ihren Auftrag aus der prophetischen Tradition, besonders aus der Gestalt Jeremias. Die Isländerin Bríet Bjarnhéðinsdóttir trat 1887 als erste Frau ihres Landes mit einem öffentlichen Vortrag zu Frauenrechten auf. Dabei wies sie die diskriminierenden Auslegungen, die sich auf Gen 2 bezogen, entschieden zurück. Zu ihren Leistungen gehören ferner die Gründung einer Frauenzeitschrift sowie die der Isländischen Frauenrechtsbewegung.

Die sieben Beiträge des 2020 erschienenen Sammelbandes weiten den Blick auf Regionen und Personen, die zum großen Teil als noch weniger beachtet gelten können im Vergleich zu den Frauen des oben besprochenen Bandes. Zwei der Aufsätze sind auf Englisch verfasst, die übrigen in deutscher Sprache. Hier werden Autorinnen aus Finnland, Schweden, Lettland, Armenien sowie den USA in den Mittelpunkt gerückt. Auch dem Verfasser Izaak J. de Hulster, der mit Aufsätzen in beiden Büchern vertreten ist, gelingt es, trotz einer ähnlichen Thematisierung der in die sogenannten Länder der Bibel reisenden Frauen, jeweils andere Aspekte in den Vordergrund zu rücken. Der einleitende Beitrag zu diesem Werk stammt aus der Feder der Grazer Exegetin Irmtraud Fischer. Ähnlich wie das oben besprochene Sammelwerk trägt auch dieses dazu bei, eine bisher viel zu wenig bekannte Vielfalt der Bibelrezeption durch Frauen zu beleuchten. Die amerikanische Schriftstellerin Emily Dickinson etwa, die sowohl von einer konservativen puritanisch-calvinistischen Tradition geprägt war als auch von liberalen theologischen Strömungen, setzt sich mit traditionellen Theologumena über die Geschlechterordnung oder Auferstehung und Unsterblichkeit auseinander, um explizit gegen die paulinischen Aussagen eine eigene Position zu formulieren. Die armenische Schriftstellerin Sipil, die die Massaker an ihrem Volk im Osmanischen Reich miterlebte, entfaltet das Bild Gottes als einer „Mutter-Schöpferin" (99). Dabei knüpft sie an biblische Texte an, erweitert jedoch die Motivik eines mütterlichen Gottes in ihren Gedichten. Ausdrücklich geht sie in ihrem literarischen Werk auf die Notwendigkeit der Frauenemanzipation ein. Mariam Kartashyan fasst ihren Einfluss folgendermaßen zusammen: „Sipils Beiträge waren von großer Bedeutung für den Wandel des sozialen Lebens der Armenier. Die Dichterin erzog durch ihre Moralvorstellungen und Ideen nicht nur Frauen ihrer Zeit. Die Auswirkungen dieser Erziehung lebten auch danach weiter und trugen wesentlich zur Stärkung der Rolle der armenischen Frauen in der Gesellschaft bei." (105) Das für diesen Sammelband gewählte Motto der Bibel als politisches Buch trifft allerdings nicht für alle hier behandelten Aspekte in vollem Umfang zu. Die finnische Trancepredigerin Helena Konttinen zum

Beispiel wurde von ihren ZeitgenossInnen als Prophetin wahrgenommen und nicht als politische Aktivistin. Das entsprach auch ihrem Selbstverständnis und ihrem Auftreten. Auch die in den Nahen Osten reisenden Frauen verfolgten keine politischen Ziele. Insgesamt jedoch illustriert dieses Buch eindrücklich, wie weit die internationale Vernetzung der Frauenbewegung reichte. Diesen Verbindungen sollte unbedingt in Forschungsprojekten weiter nachgegangen werden, denn es steht nach der Lektüre dieser Arbeiten zu vermuten, dass in etlichen bisher kaum beachteten Regionen Netzwerke der feministischen Aktivistinnen präsent waren.

Diese beiden Sammelbände werden den Diskurs um den Beitrag von Frauen zur Bibelauslegung mitsamt den daraus von Frauen und Männern gezogenen sozialen und politischen Konsequenzen auf entscheidende Weise prägen, da sie eine solche Fülle von bisher nicht beachtetem Material vorlegen. Ein Desiderat, das in diesen Beiträgen erkennbar wird, scheint mir in einer näheren Analyse der Verwendung des Feminismus-Begriffs zu liegen. Sowohl das Quellenmaterial als auch die Kommentierung lassen unterschiedliche Zugänge erkennen, die gerade im Hinblick auf die Frage nach der Definition einer feministischen Exegese von Bedeutung sind.

Prof. Dr. Ruth Albrecht

Silvia Martínez Cano, *Teología feminista para principiantes. Voces de mujeres en la teología actual* (Editorial San Pablo: Madrid 2021).

Several works produced by Spanish feminist theologians and targeting lay dissemination have found their way into the Spanish market in the last two years. That feminist theology is gaining traction amongst lay audiences is excellent news and speaks of the work of pioneering and contemporary feminist scholars in the country. It also echoes Pope Francis's current – if ambiguous – openness towards women in the Catholic Church. The publication of *Teología feminista para principiantes. Voces de mujeres en la teología actual* ("Feminist Theology for Beginners. Voices of Women in Current Theology") – a book engaging with the bases, method and character of feminist theology – by Silvia Martínez Cano can be seen as a further result of this kinder rapport towards feminist theology.

A welcome addition to feminist theology literature written and produced in Spain, *Teología feminista para principiantes* aims to provide an introductory presentation of the tenets of feminist theology. The wish to speak about theology in a way that "fosters harmonious relations between men and women, that is, feminist theology" and to seek "an understanding of God that makes out of us brothers and sisters as members of the same community, regardless of sex" (p. 9) lie at its core. The work results as much from concern as from experience: Martínez Cano's as a reader in feminist theology. Indeed, her lecturing notes provide the raw material for the book – its classroom genesis percolating from time to time into the writing style, which is otherwise engaging. Overall, the work strives for confluence as an expression of the incarnational Mystery in day-to-day life: "My life and other women's lives are rooted in this modest attempt to communicate our intimacy in God's bosom" (p. 12). Finally, it is also worth noticing that the book strings together Martínez Cano's main interests: she holds a doctorate in Education and is currently a PhD candidate focusing on theological aesthetics. She is also a multidisciplinary artist. Whereas the former account for the topic and mood of the book (a beginners' guide), the latter is to be found in the book's covers, which display one of her own paintings.

The book is organised into four chapters, introduced by a brief section entitled "By Way of a Proposal" and a prologue. The former exudes an apologetic instance and invites the reader to shed his/her prejudices toward gender and engage in an ethical and honest reading ("This book does not intend to remove some to promote others, but rather to enter into a synodal dynamic in which everyone counts, decides and has something to say", p. 10). Chapter one introduces feminist theologies and engages with some of its basic concepts: sex and gender, the overlapping between some feminist and Christian theology concepts, gender ideology and the impact and flourishing of the #8M and #MeToo movements in the Catholic Church. The second chapter presents a historical survey of feminist theology, from the earliest communities in the Gospels to medieval mysticism and the Second Vatican Council. Readers unfamiliar with the development of feminist theology in Spain, its focal groups and its connections with North American and Latin American theologies may find the subsection "Basis of feminist theology" of particular interest. A subsection dealing with basic tenets of feminist theology, "Character of Feminist Theology", sits somewhat awkwardly in this historical chapter as it engages with *loci* developed later more thoroughly in the book's plan: women's experience, particularly of those living in exclusion; patriarchy; ethical commitment in that feminist theology is a liberation theology; critical hermeneutics; the androcentric character of current theological systems in place in Church and society; and need for contextual approaches. The chapter then circles back to the historical overview, culminating with a section devoted to contemporary postcolonial feminist theology. Mujerista, Womanist, African and Asian feminist theologies have their due here. "Theological Issues of Interest to Feminist Theologies" is the third chapter, which brings to the fore methodologies and issues frequently addressed by feminist theologies: anthropological theology rooted in the female body; the urgent need for reform in the Catholic Church; and the development of female and feminist spirituality in the Church, among others. Feminist hermeneutics of suspicion, memory, imagination and proclamation are presented according to the model developed by Elisabeth Schüssler-Fiorenza, which is hugely influential in Spanish feminist theology even beyond biblical exegesis. As Martínez Cano is concerned with theological aesthetics, the chapter also includes a section dealing with metaphors of God. Sally McFague's and Elizabeth Johnson's classical works on the topic are explored side by side with other images stemming from experience, like "closeness" and "vulnerability". Those connected to Sophia-Wisdom are also under consideration.

The following sections deal with systematic/constructive theology. The historical Jesus/Christology section capitalises on the kenotic model, while the ecclesiological one revolves around the discipleship of equals and communion ecclesiology. An argument for women's ordination in the Catholic Church is also put forward. The section dealing with moral theology deepens in embodiedness (women's bodies, ecology) and the ethics of care. Lastly, Martínez-Cano deals with Mariology, rejecting the glorification of traditional female virtues and making way for Mary's emergence as a flesh-and-blood woman who was a Jesus' follower. The fourth and conclusive chapter is entitled "Dreaming While Awake. Challenges the Gender Perspective Poses to the Church". It is considerably shorter than the preceding ones and serves as a coda for the main concerns surveyed in the book. These are now summarised as pending challenges in need of addressing: disparaging of the female body in traditional theology, the underlying symbolical and practical violence against women and the need for a flourishing inner dialogue hand in hand with practical reforms in the Catholic Church, which should allow for equal participation of women in services and ministries. "If we are all children of God and share in the same dignity, then equality is just an expression of our Christified identity. We are called to be prophets for this world" (p. 199), Martínez Cano concludes.

Outlining the tenets of feminist theology in 200 pages is a challenging endeavour, but Martínez Cano succeeds in doing so. The book maps out a careful journey and displays resources for the lay reader not to get lost – comprehensible and direct language that uses the minimum amount of technical words and highlights key sentences with speech bubbles plus key references in footnotes. A comprehensive bibliography at the end is missing, though, which hinders the easy identification of works quoted in abbreviated form. Martínez Cano makes a conscious effort to present the diversity of feminist theologies, and her discussion of postcolonial and Asian authors, brief as it is, is especially welcome. She displays a more critical instance towards "radical feminisms", i.e., queer, since they "think that there is no difference between sex and gender, but rather that identity can be built out of total individuality" (p. 38). This early positioning eases up as the argument moves forward, and queer theology appears as a contributor to feminist theological anthropology (p. 105, 171), which is one of Martínez Cano's main concerns. It is also worth noticing that in a country where ecumenism is not particularly promoted, Martínez Cano takes the time to point out its impact on the rise of feminist theology in Spain. On the other hand, as a beginner's guide, some degree of generalisation is to be expected. For instance, the "resistance of Judaizers to free women of the sole role for which they gained recognition in Jewish culture, that is, being a mother" (p. 46-7) illustrates the tension between Jesus's message and the patriarchal impulses in the nascent church, which begs the question whether Greco-Roman culture was any different. Furthermore, the discipleship of equals is cast in an unadulterated positive light: "[the] expression … defines the community models during the first two centuries, where men and women shared in equality and authority" (p. 143).

These comments notwithstanding, the book is a remarkable contribution to Spanish feminist theology. Whether the timid reception that feminist theology is having at the moment will go on is yet to be seen. But be that as it may, *Teología feminista para principiantes* will remain one of its benchmarks for teaching introductory courses and lay dissemination.

Mireia Vidal i Quintero, PhD candidate

Andrea Günter, *Philosophie und Geschlechterdifferenz. Auf dem Weg eines genealogischen Geschlechterdiskurses* (Verlag Barbara Butrich: Opladen / Berlin / Toronto 2022).

Im neuesten Buch von Andrea Günter geht es nicht einfach nur um die Geschlechterdifferenz (wobei ja auch das nicht einfach wäre), sondern um die Verknüpfung grundlegender Kategorien der Philosophie(geschichte) mit dem Geschlechterdiskurs sowie um die Probleme und Erkenntnismöglichkeiten, die dieses Wechselverhältnis impliziert: „Geschlechtertheorien werden nicht nur entlang von etablierten Kategoriensystemen profiliert, Geschlechterbegriffe bringen selbst ein eigenständiges Kategorisierungsfeld hervor. Sie werden systematisch dazu herangezogen, vom Planeten Erde über den Geschlechts-Charakter von Automarken, Käsesorten und Kaffeetassen bis zu Gott sehr unterschiedliche Gegenstände zu charakterisieren" (147). Ein grundlegendes Problem ist dabei, dass es sich um genau zwei Kategorien handelt, nämlich „weiblich" und „männlich", durch die die Systeme strukturiert und immer von Neuem Oppositionen erzeugt werden. Denkt man jedoch (mit Hannah Arendt) von „Pluralität" ausgehend, wird das binäre System unterwandert; nunmehr legt sich eine Ordnung in Reihungen eher nahe als eine in Oppositionen – und zugleich werden politische Handlungsmöglichkeiten eröffnet.

Eine solche notwendige Ent-Dualisierung betrifft auch die Natur-Kultur-Opposition, die üblicherweise in der Diskussion über die Geschlechterdifferenz auftaucht. Ganz grundlegend gilt: „Wie sehr die falsche Identifikation von Ontologie und Natur eingeübt ist, zeigt die Geschichte der Bewertungen von nicht eindeutig zusammengesetzten geschlechtlichen Wesen an. Sie gelten als ‚unnatürlich', ‚widernatürlich' und beschädigt. Und dies obgleich es die Natur selbst ist, die genau sie hervorbringt. Hierzu das Semem ‚natürlich' zu benutzen, dient dazu zu verschleiern, dass diese Bewertungen nicht aus der Natur, sondern aus ontologischen Wahrheitskonzeptionen erwachsen" (23). Der Naturbegriff ist mithin aus der Dualisierung zu befreien und auf seine unterschiedlichen Bedeutungsebenen zu analysieren – was Günter auch vornimmt (vgl. besonders 148-153).

Die Bevorzugung von Reihungen statt der üblichen Dualität im Reden über die Geschlechterdifferenz lässt sich an einem Beispiel veranschaulichen: Das „andere" Geschlecht aus der deutschen Übersetzung von Simone de Beauvoirs Buch heißt tatsächlich: Das „zweite" Geschlecht (Le Deuxième Sexe) und dies macht einen Unterschied – ebenso wie die falsche Übersetzung des Begriffs der sexuellen Differenzierung im Ausgangstext durch „Geschlechterunterschied", bei der eine offene Begrifflichkeit durch eine statische ersetzt wird (60-61). Günter betont hierbei, dass Beauvoir gerade nicht von einem festgesetzten Unterschied, „sondern vielmehr von der Möglichkeit eines fortscheitenden Differenzierens innerhalb des menschlichen Geschlechtlichen ausgeht" (61), womit die Zeitlichkeit in das Denken eingeht. Das Konzept des „Genealogischen" aus dem Titel des Buches verweist darüber hinaus auch darauf, dass die Generationsbeziehungen sowie politische Aushandlungsprozesse im Hinblick auf die Gerechtigkeit eine Schlüsselrolle spielen (sollten).

Die sogenannten „Identitätspolitiken" sind in einem solchen Zusammenhang eher nicht förderlich, da aus Identität und Diskriminierung gerade nicht abgeleitet werden kann, was besser und gerechter wäre: „Ein Besseres und Gerechteres muss eigenen Überlegungen und Urteilen folgen und in Pluralität beraten werden" (261).

Günter bewegt sich auf hohem Niveau kreuz und quer durch die Philosophiegeschichte. Eine größere Rolle spielen Anknüpfungen an den Existenzbegriff Simone de Beauvoirs und Hannah Arendts Denken von Pluralität, Gebürtigkeit und möglichen Neuanfängen. Ebenso finden sich Verbindungen zu Luce Irigaray sowie den Italienischen Denkerinnen der Differenz wie Luisa Muraro und der Philosophinnengruppe Diotima. Kurze und längere Auftritte haben im Verlaufe des Buches aber auch Hegel, Kant, Fichte, Feuerbach, Freud, Fourier, Derrida und etliche weitere. Eröffnet wird die Darstellung mit der Diskussion der konzeptuellen Unterschiede dreier griechischer Philosophen: Parmenides, Aristoteles und Plato. Den beiden letzteren sind auch noch jeweils längere zusätzliche Passagen sowie je ein Kapitel gewidmet, in dem Platos Argumentationsgang im Gastmahl bzw. die Aporien der Klassifikationen in Aristoteles Nikomachischer Ethik durchleuchtet werden. Erwartungsgemäß hat Plato wesentlich mehr zu bieten für heutiges Nachdenken über die Geschlechterdifferenz, während die starren Konzeptionen, in denen Aristoteles Männliches und Weibliches in einem Überordnungs-/ Unterordnungszusammenhang als Besseres und Schlechteres hierarchisiert, eher fatale Auswirkungen für die europäische Geistesgeschichte gezeitigt haben. Neben den extra Kapiteln zu Plato und Aristoteles wird noch in zwei weiteren Kapiteln – mit Hildegard von Bingen einerseits und Jane Austens Roman Überredung andererseits – über zentrale Konfigurationen im Geschlechterverhältnis reflektiert, wobei in beiden Fällen die Differenz von Frauen untereinander und deren Bezugnahmen aufeinander eine Schlüsselrolle spielen und damit noch zusätzlich ein Thema in den Fokus rückt, das in der männlichen Philosophietradition weitestgehend ausgeblendet ist.

Der Text ist sehr dicht geschrieben und erfordert einige Vorkenntnisse. An einigen Stellen bin ich aus meiner Perspektive als Exegetin über den differierenden Zugang gestolpert (dies betrifft allerdings nicht allein dieses Buch, die Unterschiede zwischen systematischen und exegetischen Schreibweisen sind häufig beträchtlich). So fehlten mir gelegentlich etwas genauere historische Kontextualisierungen der jeweiligen Denker*innen; bei den Rückgriffen auf die Kategorienlehre des Aristoteles wäre ich über die Analyse der griechischen Begrifflichkeiten glücklich gewesen, und bei den Ausführungen über Parmenides stellte sich insgesamt eine leichte Verwirrung ein. Letzterer spielt insbesondere im ersten Kapitel des Buches eine nicht unwichtige Rolle, wobei er etwas abrupt und ohne jede Einführung auftaucht. Zudem sind die beiden entscheidenden Texte zur Geschlechterdifferenz hinsichtlich der Überlieferungssituation eher problematisch – was die geneigte Leserin aber erst merkt, wenn sie, leicht ratlos ob der fehlenden Kontextualisierung und glücklich über ein Exemplar der Fragmente der Vorsokratiker im Bücherschrank, eine Durchsicht der Überlieferungslage vornimmt und feststellt, dass in einem Falle der Wortlaut problematisch ist und im anderen Falle nur eine lateinische Übersetzung erhalten. Ob also Parmenides tatsächlich annahm, dass der Same auf der rechten Seite der Gebärmutter Knaben, auf der linken Mädchen entstehen lässt, scheint mir angesichts der nur noch vorhandenen Sekundärüberlieferungen ebenso diskutierbar zu sein wie die Frage nach seiner (negativen) Bewertung der Doppelgeschlechtlichkeit (vgl. dazu Diehls / Kranz, Die Fragmente der Vorsokratiker, 244-245 / Fragment Nr. 17 und 18).

Trotz dieser kleinen Unausgeglichenheiten: Ein sehr lesenswertes Buch für alle, die daran interessiert sind, das Denken der Geschlechterdifferenz im Kontext der Philosophiegeschichte zu verstehen und jenseits der üblichen Dualisierungen voranzubewegen.

Prof. Dr. Silke Petersen

EUROPEAN SOCIETY OF WOMEN IN THEOLOGICAL RESEARCH

EUROPÄISCHE GESELLSCHAFT FÜR THEOLOGISCHE FORSCHUNG VON FRAUEN

ASOCIACIÓN EUROPEA DE MUJERES EN LA INVESTIGACIÓN TEOLÓGICA

President – Präsidentin – Presidenta
Dr.[in] Gertraud Ladner, Innsbruck, Austria

Vice-Presidents – Vize-Präsidentinnen – Vicepresidentas
Doc. Halyna Teslyuk, Lviv, Ukraine
Prof. Dr Jone Solomonsen, Oslo, Norway

Secretary – Sekretärin – Secretaria
Judith König, Regensburg, Germany

Vice-Secretary – Vize-Sekretärin – Vicesecretaria
Sofia Nikitaki, Leuven, Belgium

Treasurer – Schatzmeisterin – Tesorera
Rebecca Gross, Tübingen, Germany

Vice-Treasurer – Vize-Schatzmeisterin – Vicetesorera
Prof. Dr Malgorzata Grzywacz, Poznań, Poland

Networking
Dra. Antonina Wozna, Valencia, Spain

Journal – Jahrbuch – Revista
Prof. Dr.[in] Martina Bär, Graz, Austria
Dr Anne-Claire Mulder, Utrecht, The Netherlands
Prof.[in] Dr.[in] Agnethe Siquans, Vienna, Austria
Lic. Mireia Vidal i Quintero, Barcelona, Spain

Website of the ESWTR
http://www.eswtr.org

ESWTR Journal – Advisory Board

- Prof.^{in} Dr.^{in} Elzbieta Adamiak, Univ. Koblenz/Landau, GER
- Sr Dr.^{in} Jadranka Rebeka Anić, Inst. für Sozialwissenschaften Ivo Pilar, Split, KRO
- Prof.^{in} Dr.^{in} Kristin De Troyer, Univ. Salzburg, AUT
- Prof. Dr Annemie Dillen, Kath. University Leuven, BE
- Dra. Montserrat Escribano Cárcel, Universitat de València, ESP
- Dra. Teresa Forcades i Vila, OSB, Barcelona, ESP
- Prof. Dr Judith Gruber, Kath. University Leuven, BE
- Emer. Prof. Dr Maaike de Haardt, Radboud Universiteit Nijmegen, NL
- Prof.^{in} Dr.^{in} Judith Hartenstein, Univ. Koblenz/Landau, GER
- Prof.^{in} Dr.^{in} Maria Häusl, TU-Dresden, GER
- Prof. Dr Susanne Scholz, Southern Methodist University, Texas, USA
- Prof. Dr Nicola Slee, The Queens Foundation Birmingham, UK/VU Amsterdam, NL
- Profa. Dra Teresa Maria Leal de Assunção Martinho Toldy, Univ. Fernando Pessoa, Porto, PT
- Prof.^{in} Dr.^{in} Angelika Walser, Univ. Salzburg, AUT
- Prof. Dr Heleen Zorgdrager, Protestant Theological University, NL